BEYOND INTEGRATION

Beyond Integration

Challenges of belonging
in diaspora and exile

Edited by
Maja Povrzanović Frykman

NORDIC ACADEMIC PRESS

Nordic Academic Press
Box 1206
S-221 05 Lund
Sweden
infonap@pophist.se

© Nordic Academic Press and the authors 2001
Coverdesign: Svante Ström
Printed in Sweden
AiT Falun AB 2001
ISBN 91-89116-17-8

Contents

Preface

The social and cultural complexity of Western European countries has been deeply affected by the numbers of people from other countries needed for industrial expansion, and those seeking political refuge. This certainly reaches beyond the stereotypes of poorly educated refugees exploiting the taxpayers' money and beyond the stereotypes of homesick diaspora groups indulging in nationalist rhetoric. If this complexity is to be addressed – by individuals and institutions – in a manner which will help the interaction of people with radically different experiential frames of reference, research insights into the processes of their identity formation are needed.

This standpoint was shared by the scholars who participated in the conference "Identity Formations in Diaspora and Exile" (Lund, 4–5 December 1998), organized by the Department of European Ethnology, Lund University, and supported by *Erik Philip Sörensens stiftelse*. The chapters in this volume, published thanks to generous funding by *Ebbe Kocks stiftelse*, are based on the papers presented at the conference. They reveal current research on topics ranging from torture and traumas of people who later become refugees, to their individual experiences of refugee policies, from the ambivalent political loyalties within transnational networks, to the manifold strategies of defining belonging within or against ethnic or religious groups. Zoran Slavnić, who also participated in the conference, has in the meantime published his insights into these issues in the dissertation *Existens och temporalitet: Om det samtida flyktingskapets komplexitet* (Umeå 2000).

Social scientists have shown that inter-ethnic contacts and transnational networks do not point to a single historical direction; some are individually chosen and some are imposed on entire ethnic groups. When intra-ethnic contacts are highlighted, it is also obvious that new and hardly predictable social and cultural differentiations are occurring in local settings. They are related to political mobilization projects that presuppose the globally changed possibilities of communication, but also to the local, everyday experiences of "living in a foreign country", or "having two homelands".

This volume is an effort to historicize, describe and analyse some examples of identity dynamics among people living out of their national states, from ethnological, anthropological and sociological perspectives. Several contributions offer insights based on research in Sweden in the 1990s. The ones concerning Denmark, Germany and Croatia analyse situations and practices that have parallels in the Swedish socio-cultural context. After all, doing research on migration, transnational political concerns or syncretic identities implies crossing borders in order to understand the interplay of places, practices and meanings. Thus, several contributors have been engaging in multi-sited ethnographic research – the sites being not only geographical, but also virtual.

The themes discussed in this book reflect the long-lasting scholarly interests of the authors. A number of them also share the experience of "living away from homeland" with the people they are writing about – a distinctive and scarcely surprising feature of the existing literature on transnational issues worldwide.

The terms *diaspora* and *exile* in the subtitle should remind the reader of the basic difference between identities which may be individually chosen or belong to a culturally elaborated tradition of migration, and those which are violently forced upon people.

Maja Povrzanović Frykman

Notes on contributors

Dr. **Gunnar Alsmark** is Associate Professor at the Department of European Ethnology, Lund University, writing on integration issues, media policy regarding immigrants, as well as on conflicts and violence in multicultural contexts.

Dr. **Magnus Berg** is Assistant Professor at the Department of Work, Economy and Health at the University of Trollhättan-Uddevalla, focusing on questions of modern migration, postcolonial issues, Orientalism, and the presence of the Orient in Sweden.

Dr. **Mehmet Ümit Necef** is Senior Lecturer at the Centre for Contemporary Middle Eastern Studies, University of Southern Denmark, Odense, publishing works on multiculturalism, the welfare state, labour market and citizenship, with emphasis on immigrants.

Eva Norström is an independent consultant and President of the Swedish Refugee Council and doctoral candidate at the Department of European Ethnology, Lund University. She is interested in processes related to integration and in the concepts about refugees held by the majority population.

Dr. **Maja Povrzanović Frykman** is Assistant Professor, Department of European Ethnology, Lund University, and an external associate of the Institute of Ethnology and Folklore Research in Zagreb. She is interested in experiences and representations of war and exile, as well as in concepts and practices within the semantic domains of diaspora and transnationalism.

Dr. **Jonathan Schwartz** is Associate Professor, Institute of Anthropology, University of Copenhagen. He is interested in the theory and practice of tropes in representing experience, and doing research on migration and ethnicity in the Balkan region and in North America.

Dr. **Paul Stubbs** is based in Zagreb and is an Associate Senior Research Fellow of GASPP (Globalism and Social Policy Programme), University of Sheffield, and STAKES, Helsinki. His main fields of interest include: social policy and social movements in post-Yugoslav countries; theories and practices of peace building and civil society; and virtual states, spaces and networks.

Prof. **Charles Westin** is director of CEIFO (The Centre for Research in International Migration and Ethnic Relations) at Stockholm University. He publishes on international migration and ethnic relations, transnational minorities, multiculturalism, identity, traumatization and political violence.

Challenges of belonging in diaspora and exile
An introduction

Maja Povrzanović Frykman

The number of refugees from the former Yugoslavia, the visibility of Kurdish problems and the plight of Kosovo Albanians have marked Europe in the 1990s, and will for decades ahead have consequences for political decisions and for migration within Europe. Existential and political problems related to migration processes that are far from being settled bring about the need for scientific investigation into their cultural aspects. From a Swedish perspective, the scientific relevance and social importance of such research has been confirmed in spring 1999: the Serbs living in Sweden wrote letters to Swedish newspapers and organized public demonstrations against the NATO bombing of Serbia, while many Albanians born in Sweden went to fight in Kosovo. Some Serbian teenagers born in Sweden complained in the local media about being bullied by their Albanian school-mates. At the same time, they claimed not to believe the Swedish television news on the Albanian exodus from Kosovo, since the Serbian television they watch at home denied it. Kosovo Albanians, old and young, were coming to Sweden frightened, frustrated and traumatized. Those who happen to stay for good will have to deal not only with their personal experiences of violence and losses, but also with social demands made on them in the course of becoming immigrants. They are involved in the adaptation to a life in an unfamiliar setting, as well as in contacts with the Albanian diaspora in Sweden. In such a context, the importance of ethnological, anthropological and sociological understanding of identity-formation processes in diaspora and exile is hard to overestimate.

Since the 1970s, there have been dramatic changes in the numbers of people spatially and socially displaced. The patterns of international migration, including people legally classified as refugees, have been changing, too. The economic context is clear: less than 25 percent of the population was appropriating 85 percent of world income at the beginning of the 1990s (Anderson 1994: 321). Labour migration is thus the result of global economic assymetries within which immigrant labour is an important component of economic growth in the developed parts of the world. Labour migrants might have been arriving in the industrialized countries in search of the so-called "better life", meaning a more affluent situation for themselves and their families. But that should not obscure the fact that they have been encouraged to come because they were needed – until they were needed. In a similar way, the involuntary or forced movements of people cannot be seen as results of the historical "spell" of some regions. They are results of human rights denial, terror and violence on different scales. At the beginning of the 1990s, around 20 million people were refugees (see Jayawardena 1995 and Nuscheler 1995 for more detailed data).

We live in a world where some states are bombarded for their state-sponsored ethnic violence, but many more are allowed to proceed in terrorizing their ethnic minorities since it is their "internal affair". For the people who manage to escape terror, exile does not necessarily become "the nursery of nationality" (cf. Anderson 1994). It may unburden people from ethnic or national belonging as a category defining one's entire life, as a supreme context of all personal efforts, and eventually the reason for victimization.

Yet, in Sweden, for example, qualitative research among immigrants and their children, reveals forms of identification that often decisively rely on ethnic and national references reaching beyond Swedish borders. Especially people who came as refugees tend to continue relating to their old social settings, and their political allegiances in the countries of origin retain a special significance.

In the traditional immigration countries like Australia, Canada and the USA, whose identities have been based on their origins as the "nations of immigrants", the arrival of large numbers of non-European immigrants has coincided with political and economic changes which have led to a reassessment of the relations between the immigrant and native-born populations (Inglis 1997: 267). In Sweden, as well as in other Western European countries today referred to as "immigrant countries", such reassessment consists of a range of ongoing processes with no predictable future. Most importantly, they take place in everyday life and in political arenas in which different groups of immigrants, refugees and the native-born try to affect legal policies, negotiate meanings, and manage their daily contacts.

Different fields of research into these processes are delineated in this book, from the perspectives of ethnologists, anthropologists and sociologists. It by no means exhausts the approaches to challenges of belonging in diaspora and exile, but it presents a range of relevant scientific interests and shows their interrelatedness. The essays in the first part build on the rich tradition in Scandinavian humanities and social sciences of dealing with immigration, ethnicity and multiculturalism. Different contexts and different aspects of identity formation processes are discussed, connected by the underlying question of the relation between the given and the negotiable identification categories that immigrants and people in exile deal with. That is why this part of the book is entitled *Between embodiment and imagination: Imposed and negotiated identities*.

Regarding immigration research in Scandinavia, the focus has, generally speaking, been on ethnic identification dynamics, recognition of ethnic claims and integration of immigrants. As pointed out by Jonathan Schwartz, members of diaspora groups have most often been seen against the dominant discourse of integration, and publicly marked by the rhetorical presence of "integration problems". The making of diaspora without the strictures of integration has so far seldom been recognized as significant (see Olsson 1997,1999). Contributors to the second part of this book entitled *Beyond integration: Transnational connections* do not have integration as their primary concern. They are interested in transnational processes, as well as in processes of segmentation within groups often identified as homogeneous. By presenting new material and posing some new questions, they add a dimension to immigration research that has been less explored in Scandinavia. Their primary concern is to shed light on some cultural and political aspects of immigrants' and refugees' experiences and concerns that reach beyond the national borders of the countries they live in. In doing so, they find the concept of diaspora useful, since it directs attention towards dynamic and flexible connections between members of ethnic groups who are spread across national borders due to their specific histories of migration, but who establish links because of common cultural, economic and political concerns. The four essays in the second part are therefore well captured by a laconic definition of diasporic consciousness, but also of transnationalism in the widest sense, stating that *it is the connection elsewhere that makes a difference here.*

The authors interested in transnationality as the significant context of identity formation in diaspora and exile do not claim that all immigrants are *transmigrants* – immigrants fully rooted in their new country but maintaining multiple linkages to their country of origin (cf. Glick Schiller et al. 1995). They do not claim that everyone in the countries of origin is affected by transnational activities either. Yet, they share the conviction that the creation of transnational social fields can be conceptualized as a distinct phenomenon, different from other patterns of immigrant adaptation.

To clarify the notions (cf. Ong 1999: 4): *transnationality* is the condition of cultural interconnectedness and mobility across space, while *transnationalism* refers to the cultural specificities of global processes, marked by the multiplicity of uses and conceptions of "culture", as well as of "identity".[1]

In a general sense not related exclusively to international migration, *trans* in the term transnationality implies both moving through space or across lines, as well as changing the nature of something:

> Besides suggesting new relations between nation states and capital, transnationality also alludes to the *trans*versal, the *trans*actional, the *trans*lational, and the *trans*gressive aspects of contemporary behaviour and imagination that are incited, enabled, and regulated by the changing logics of states and capitalism (Ong 1999: 4).

These aspects of transnationality call for analytical tools suitable for reconsidering the meaning of locality and making visible the relational nature of contemporary economic, social, and cultural processes that stream across spaces. Concerning migration and transnational actors' quotidian reality, a new analytical framework for understanding has been named *transnationalism* (Glick Schiller et al. 1992).

The general notion of transnational actors might, of course, imply such very different actors as corporate capital decision makers, politicians mobilizing "their" diasporas, editors of television programmes, or organized smugglers and terrorist groups. This volume deals with refugees and labour migrants, many of whose cultural and political concerns are transnational and can be assessed through the concepts of diaspora and transnationalism. Their transnational social spaces

> consist of combinations of sustained social and symbolic ties, their contents, positions in networks and organizations, and networks and organizations that can be found in multiple states. These spaces denote dynamic processes, not static notions of ties and positions. Cultural, political, and economic processes in transnational social spaces involve the accumulation, use, and effects of various sorts of capital, their volume and convertibility: economic capital, human capital, such as educational credentials, skills and know-how, and social capital, mainly resources inherent in or transmitted through social and symbolic ties (Faist 2000: 199–200).

Transnational experiences and diasporic identities

In the research agenda defined by Nina Glick Schiller and co-authors (1992), a central position is occupied by the analysis of the manners in which transmigrants – caught between the experience of transnationalism and the dominant discourse of migration (most importantly integration) – construct their racial, ethnic, class, national, and gender identities. That is in accordance with an understanding of identities as historical and undergoing constant transformation.

In the research on transnationalism that focuses on (re)construction of place and locality, old anthropological understandings of the place-boundedness of cultural and social units have been reconsidered. It has shown that the notions of community, organic culture, region, or centre and periphery may obscure as much as they reveal (cf.

Clifford 1997: 245). "The concept of space is itself transformed when it is seen ... in terms of the ex-centric communicative circuitry that has enabled dispersed populations to converse, interact and even synchronize significant elements of their social and cultural lives" (Gilroy 1994: 297).

A high degree of human mobility and the emergence of new virtual neighbourhoods (through telecommunications, films, video, satellite television, and the Internet) have contributed to the creation of translocal understandings. Nevertheless, the translocal understandings are anchored in places, with a variety of legal, political and cultural determinants. The need for a new conceptual framework in which the refugees and diaspora people's deterritorialized and transnational social relations can be described has been answered by shifting the interest from immigration and integration/assimilation to transnational networks and communities. In that context, the notion of *diaspora* provides useful analytical tools, since it can be conceptualized *as social form, as type of consciousness,* and *as mode of cultural production* (cf. Vertovec and Cohen 1999). When referring to social forms, the notion of diaspora is suited to the investigation of social relationships, political orientations, economic strategies, as well as the sub-national and supra-national networks and patterns of power, communication and conflict that are not governed by the modern nation state. Diaspora as a type of consciousness encompasses a sense of identity based on a variety of experiences generated among contemporary transnational communities. Furthermore, it is considered to be the source of resistance through engagement with and visibilty in the public space. Finally, diaspora as a mode of cultural production inolves the production and reproduction of transnational social and cultural phenomena, in terms of syncretism, creolization, bricolage, cultural translation and hybridity.

> Diaspora provides valuable cues and clues for the elaboration of a social ecology of cultural identity and identification. The pressure to associate, remember or forget varies with changes in the economic and political atmosphere. ... The celebrated "butterfly effect" in which tiny, almost insignificant forces can, in defiance of conventional expectations, precipitate unpredictable, larger changes in other locations, becomes a commonplace happening

if we can adopt this difficult analytical stance. The seamless prop-
agation of cultural habits and styles can be rendered radically
contingent at the point where geography and genealogy begin to
trouble each other (Gilroy 1994: 209).

Research into identities based on new perceptions of locality, virtual
neighbourhoods, translocal understandings and forms of loyalty and
belonging, allows timely and important insights into how different
migration-based communities are constituted and denied, extend-
ing to different people and populations on varying terms and at
different times. However, Östen Wahlbeck's insight is of great importance, the need to take into consideration previous research and
theories of ethnic relations, international migration and forced migration when using the concept of diaspora (cf. Wahlbeck 1999).
Both exclusionary and inclusionary structures and policies in the
country of settlement, and the diasporic group's continuous transnational relation to the country of origin are relevant. Wahlbeck
warns against the danger that the concept of diaspora, with its pre-
occupation with immigrant (or refugee) *communities* and their relationship to the country of origin, may disregard the host society and
the power structures involved in majority–minority relations. "If
this happens the introduction of the concept leads back to culturalist
and other social and psychological theories in which immigrants are
largely seen as choosing to integrate or not, and exclusionary structures and ideologies, like racism, are not seen to play any significant
role" (Wahlbeck 1999: 36). Wahlbeck's work on Kurdish refugees in
Great Britain and Finland shows that their exclusion from the wider
society is not necessarily a product of their own diasporic consciousness. On the contrary, it is one of the reasons for the formation of
Kurdish diaspora.

This can be related to Aaron Turner's (2000) claim that with regard
to these kinds of social processes, it does not make sense to presume
that people are part of any community or group. "It makes more
sense to ask how it is that groups and communities are constituted
as significant at different times and what the significance and participation of different people and practices in these processes implies"
(Turner 2000: 59). The focus on social constituting configurations
and the identity formations they entail shifts the understanding

17

from local contexts and people as examples that allow us to understand wider cultures or communities (cf. Turner 2000: 59) to an examination of the ways in which social relationships and cultural identities are constituted.[2]

Like the tendency of "community-inventing", it is equally important to resist the tendency to equate diasporic identities with disaggregated, positional, performed identites in general (cf. Clifford 1997: 272). Diasporic subjects are distinct versions of modern, transnational intercultural experience, and diaspora discourses cannot be understood if not related to their specific histories.

> Thus historicized, diaspora cannot become a master trope or "figure" for modern, complex, or positional identities, cross-cut and displaced by race, sex, gender, class, and culture. … Identifications not identities, acts of relationships rather than pregiven forms: this *tradition* is a network of partially connected histories, a persistently displaced and reinvented time/space of crossings (Clifford 1997: 266, 268).

Definitions of diaspora

Assessing the usefulness of diaspora as a concept, Dominique Schnapper (1999) shows that the dispersion of people who cling to a sentiment of their unity in spite of a geographic breakup has existed since antiquity, but in different forms and with different meanings. The birth of nationalist movements and the formation of modern nations gave it a new, essentially pejorative, meaning, since nationalist movements made people who affirmed transnational loyalties suspect. Today, the weakening of the nation state's power and – in some cases – of national patriotism has given a positive sense to behaviours and identifications linked to the existence of diasporas (cf. Schnapper 1999: 227). As pointed out by Jonathan Schwartz (1998), the idea of diaspora is a salient metaphor in today's social scientific discourse and analysis, closely connected to representations of postmodern reality, where displacement is prevalent and communities are no longer perceived as "rooted". The notion of diaspora has been used to describe many types of displacement: immigrant ghettos as well as refugee groups, intellectuals in political asylum as well as "hyphenated" identitites of, e.g., the second-generation Hispano-Americans or German Turks. Schwartz observes that this implies the ambiguities of experiences captured by the notion, but also the ambiguities a researcher is made aware of when trying to read the traces of such experiences against a theoretical background.[3]

Academics use the notion of diaspora to characterize transnational ethnic groups, or practically any population which is considered "deterritorialized". Intellectuals and activists from these populations have found in it a positive way of constituting a "hybrid" cultural and political identity (cf. Vertovec and Cohen 1999: xvi–xvii). But talking about disapora became trendy and its expansion has resulted in analytical confusion. Cultural studies oriented to diasporic authors celebrate diasporic creativity in cultural production. Anthropology interested in grass-roots globalization processes sees diasporic networks as sites of resistance to capital and hegemony, and diasporic identities as empowerment against essentializing categories. Much, of course, is in the eye of the beholder, i.e., in the theoretical frames that guide interpretation. In a more down-to-earth manner, diaspora might be viewed as "making the best out of bad circumstances" (Clifford 1997), as a more or less successful attempt to reconstitute a community outside the natal or imagined natal territory, and within a space of cross-cutting determinations.

In the introductory volume of the University College London Press "Global diasporas" series, Robin Cohen tried "to give consideration to all the credible meanings of diaspora" (Cohen 1997: x). He proposes a typology of diasporas (victim, labour, trade, imperial and cultural), but admits that it is more unambiguous than the history and development of diasporas. By analysing historical and recent examples, he points to the overlapping of thus categorized diasporic experiences, and the possibilities for many ethnic groups to be classified in several categories consecutively, or even at the same time. Descriptive, historically informed definitions seem to be less useful for future research.[4]

Generally speaking, the term diaspora refers to members of an ethnic group who live away from the country in which they or their ancestors were born, but maintain strong ties with it. It is an immigrant group whose proportion in numbers and activities makes it visible and its activities felt in both the actual and the ancestral country. The significant elements are *ethnic, birth, group, away* and *ties*, but always in their specific historical meanings and constellations.

Regarding the elements of an ideal typical diaspora (cf. Safran 1991) – dispersion from an original "centre", the maintenance of memory or myth about the original homeland, the belief of not being fully accepted in the host country, the idea of return, commitment to maintenance or restoration of the homeland, and the group consciousness and solidarity research on diasporas shows that each and every one of these elements is relevant, but that they rarely come all together in the existing examples described by researchers.

A more interesting task than judging whether one definition of diaspora is better than the other, is to investigate the experiences of people living in what I would call *diasporic* conditions. Using an adjective instead of a noun hints at *processes* of their identity formation, and keeps the research interest open towards a wide range of experiences of "living away from home". These experiences might come from regular transnational practices, but also from a "mythical" relation towards the ancestral country. They can be dependent on belonging to a group, but they can also rely of subjective understandings of individual actions. The actions and representations coming out of such different experiences can all be assessed as "recent articulations of diasporism" (Clifford 1997: 244), or "versions of diaspora-consciousness" (Gilroy 1994: 208). Of course, the invocations of diaspora theories, diasporic discourses, and distinct historical experiences have to be differentiated in research.

Such an inclusive approach informs the editorial policies of *Diaspora: A Journal of Transnational Studies*, published by the University of Toronto Press since 1991. As noted in the information for authors, it welcomes essays that explore the concepts and practices underpinning the terms contained in the semantic domain of the journal's title: "nation", "nationalism", "diaspora", "exile", "transnationalism", "postcoloniality" and "ethnicity". All aspects of the subnational and transnational phenomena challenging the nation-state, as well as specific diasporan communities, existing or emerging, are considered relevant. Here diaspora is clearly associated with transnationalism. As posited by the journal's editor: "Diasporas are the exemplary communities of the transnational moment" (Tölöly-an 1991: 4). However, the notion of diaspora is narrower than the notion of transnationalism. First of all, it implies a *group* identity (for many authors, indeed, it implies the existence of a *community*). The salience of political attitudes (and often political activities) for di-aspora groups may not be shared by some transnational individuals and communities. Memories and myths of a lost homeland that sometimes mark diaspora groups, are also not relevant for the trans-migrants who link their country of settlement and country of origin into a single social field. The ideas about physical return to the homeland characteristic of many diaspora people would not make sense for transmigrants in this analytical construction, since they already live (also) in their homeland.

Inter-ethnic and transnational contacts of people do not point in a single historical direction; some are individually chosen and some are imposed on entire ethnic groups. Immigrants and refugees could be conceptualized as *labour and victim diaspora, old and new immi-grants* or *old and new ethnic diaspora groups*. However, the pair of terms *diaspora and exile* – as the most simple in this connection – is chosen in this book to remind the reader of radical differences be-tween the situations of choice and the situations of non-choice.

Diaspora versus exile?

In the original Greek meaning, *diaspora* denotes migration and col-onization, and does not imply traumatic losses. In contrast, exam-ples from African, Palestinian and Armenian, but first and foremost from Jewish history, have been used to point to collective traumas characteristic of communities in exile. Still, as the Hebrew word *galut* can mean both "exile" and "diaspora", it is also worth stressing that any allegorization of group identities is problematic inasmuch as it deprives those who have historically grounded identities of the power to speak for themselves and remain different (cf. Boyarin and Boyarin 1993: 697). This holds for the Jewish communities that Daniel and Jonathan Boyarin (1993) write about, but also for all other groups in diaspora and exile.

In this volume, the general terms *diaspora* and *exile* thus do not imply singular or stable identities. On the one hand, diaspora people are seldom either "cosmopolitan" or "nationalist". There are decisive differences within ethnic diaspora populations, most visibly along educational and political lines. On the other hand, refugees are not necessarily "lost" and underprivileged in their effort to re-establish life. Former assets and individual resources might inform crucial differences in the experience of exile. However,

> to think of exile as beneficial, as a spur to humanism or to crea-
> tivity, is to belittle its mutilations. Modern exile is irremediably
> secular and unbearably historical. It is produced by human beings
> for other human beings; it has torn millions of people from the
> nourishment of tradition, family, and geography (Said 1984a: 50,
> quoted in Schwartz 1998).

In another text on exile, Edward Said points out that even if it is true that anyone prevented from returning home is an exile, some distinctions can be made between exiles, refugees, expatriates, and émigrés. While exile originated in the age-old practice of banishment, producing stigmatized outsiders, refugees are a creation of the twentieth-century state. "The word 'refugee' has become a political one, suggesting large herds of innocent and bewildered people requiring urgent international assistance, whereas 'exile' carries with it ... a touch of solitude and spirituality" (Said 1984b, quoted in Malkki 1995).

Exile in this volume denotes the refugees' *escape* from oppression, most radically from threats to their lives. People become refugees in order to have the possibility of choice regarding the basic existential issues. It is thus wrong to forget (or even dismiss) the reasons for migration – escape being different in nature from many other reasons – and theoretically prioritize the potential benefits of exile. The state of migration and marginality cannot be easily perceived as "a promise" by the people who fled their homes in order to stay alive – at least not in the short term and not by many of them (Povrzanović and Jambrešić Kirin 1996: 9). The fact that, indeed, many a refugee might have experienced some subsequent benefits of exile should not overshadow the losses and the emotional burden they bear. Many victimized people – as explained by Charles Westin in this volume

– suffer traumas that cut too deep through their lives, making them incapable of a new start. Others are not believed when they talk about their suffering, as in the distressing example that Eva Norström writes about.

Diasporas discussed in this book include labour migrants who stayed in the host country, as well as their children, most often referred to in research as "second-generation immigrants" or "people of immigrant background". People who were doomed to flee from their home countries because of political persecution or war, often maintain an intellectual, cultural and spiritual sense of belonging to their homeland, too (Clifford 1997). Especially at the begining of their refugee experiences, the homeland they do not live in any more is very likely to remain a crucial place of emotional attachment and decisively defines their strategies of identification.[5] Yet, there are no simple answers to the questions about the time-span and the requirement necessary for the development of diasporic consciousness among refugees, or for turning an exile community into a diasporic community. Research presented in this volume reveals specific historical contexts in which particular lived experiences gain their meaning, and may be shared with others.

Regarding analytical differentiations between diaspora and exile, an important context is also the meeting of labour migrants and refugees of the same ethnic affiliation. If legal and social differences are easy to suppose, what about cultural and political differences? And what is the importance of other lines of division (most visibly age and education) cutting through both of these groups? The latter question points to some important analytical points in discussing both exiles and diaspora people.

As pointed out by Ralph Grillo[6], it is the common features of the two groups that are striking, and not the differences between them. Most importantly, the common feature concerns heterogeneity of (or diversity within) those two groups. Also, there is the reduction in status clearly marked in the case of refugees – where frequently educated people find themselves unemployed or having to do menial work – but which is becoming much more common nowadays in the case of labour migrants as well. Common, too, are the concerns about education and language. Economic ties, politics, associational activities, education, marriage and *rites de passage* are all social fields of great significance for the formation of transnational communities of both diaspora people and refugees. Finally, individuals and groups can drift from one status or category to another. For Grillo, the principal issue is the way in which studies of transnationalism – whether referring to refugees or immigrants – sometimes assume homogeneity instead of dealing with difference. There are many different ways – between different transnational communities and within any given transnational population – of relating to transnationalism depending on age, generation, gender, ethnic identity, religion, education, "stage" of migration, as well as the political and economic conjuncture at the time of exit or entry.

Transnational loyalties

People coming to Sweden as refugees in the 1900s were, in the majority of cases, offered the possibility of sharing the benefits of the country's welfare system. Potential benefits in the form of social and economic security, and social promotion via education have been recognized and realized by many refugees. They have been treated as citizens-to-be, and many took Swedish citizenship after five years of living in Sweden. However, since Sweden does not recognize dual citizenship, many also met emotional difficulties in legally withdrawing from their original nationality. Only a couple of years earlier, they could not have imagined themselves living out of their home towns, and only a few have no family ties left behind.

Benedict Anderson (1994) observed that passports tell us little about people's loyalties or habitus. In that regard, the example of a middle-aged Croatian woman living in Sweden since she married a diaspora Croat at the age of eighteen, is illuminating. She is embarrassed about not having a Swedish passport (she never applied for one, although she could have had it for some thirty years by now). She does not want her Swedish colleagues at work to know about it, for she feels that such a distance – even if purely legal – from the society that always made her feel welcome could be understood as ingratitude, even as some kind of "forgery". At the same time, she is one of the leading activists in a Croatian ethnic club in her town.

This is an example of not enforced, but freely chosen and emotionally true, autochthonous double loyalty, which does not depend on dual citizenship in the legal sense (or legal matters in general). Analytical categories delineating *either-or* loyalties might be helpful in the process of defining research aims. Yet, when imposed on people's lives, they might miss the basic logics of social and cultural dynamics if, as in the case described above, there is no *either-or* conflict within the person herself. Generally speaking, transnational practices employed by immigrants oppose the necessity of choosing between two national loyalties, but prove their belonging to both.

Small-scale illegal trade, such as smuggling a couple of bottles of home-made spirits from the homeland, is of little economic, but great cultural importance. Many Swedish citizens hold two passports although it is not legal. Again, they do not see themselves as jeopardizing the host country's social and political stability. For them the homeland passport might be an instance of limited practical, but of high symbolic value.

Not only individual immigrants, but also groups of immigrants can only rarely be decribed in clear categorical terms. Regarding the salience of ethnic belonging, their "reactive" and "linear" ethnicity (Portes 1999: 465–466) can be in a constant interplay. Fieldwork in these matters is crucial, for only field insights can provide a sound ground for understanding *how* ethnic belonging depends on social and political contexts. Supporting ethnic clubs and offering mother-tongue tuition, the Swedish state has done much to keep the immigrants' ethnicities "linear" quality characteristic of non-conflict circumstances. In those circumstances, ethnic belonging and the emotional attachment it bears go without saying, and are not a basis for political mobilization. "Reactive ethnicity" – in the sense of heightened significance of ethnicity as a mechanism for self-defence and collective reaffirmation against discrimination in the host country – might not be of primary relevance for most immigrants to Sweden. Yet, it was the pattern for, e.g., Croats in Sweden who tried to be visible as non-Yugoslavs (or anti-Yugoslavs) until Croatia has been recognized as an independent state in 1992. It certainly was the pattern for Serbs and Albanians in Sweden who organized open-air demonstrations in 1999 – the former condemning and the latter greeting the NATO bombarding of today's Yugoslavia. There are contexts within contexts, and in these examples they are informed by transnational loyalties reflecting integration and disintegration processes far beyond the borders of Sweden.

Multi-sited ethnography

"Diasporas are common, 'global' experiences, but they continue to be expressed in 'local' and special ways" (Schwartz 1998: 757). The contributors to this volume put forward the crucial role of field insights in the efforts to theorize the complexities of identity formations as situated in practice. For in doing so, they cannot see refugees as people "lost in their illusions of the past" or as "homesick people" who supposedly fail to organize the world out of a new centre: such an understanding reveals not only political, but also conceptual disorientation (cf. Povrzanović 2000: 158). They cannot agree to the caricaturing stereotype either, of "the lonely *gastarbeiter* in his dingy room" (Anderson 1994: 322), which is disturbing since it is promoted by an influential scholar like Benedict Anderson. Along with such stereotyping, Anderson also slips into surprisingly fierce statements and politically reductive stereotypes of "the malign role" of some diaspora groups, supposedly strong enough to "push" Western states into "fateful, premature recognition" of "breakaway states" formerly belonging to Yugoslavia (Anderson 1994: 327). He asks the reader to "consider" them, but refers neither to any research, nor to any other published source. (See Stubbs in this volume for a more elaborate discussion of the same example.)

Although "diaspora", "immigrants", "refugees" and "asylum seekers" are used here as general terms, they do not essentialize people to whom they might be applicable. In some essays, detailed pictures are presented of different attitudes cutting through the groups called "Bosnian refugees" (Povrzanović Frykman), "Croatian diaspora" (Stubbs and Povrzanović Frykman), "Turks in Germany" (Necef), or "Macedonian citizens in Copenhagen" (Schwartz). Others (Alsmark, Norström and Westin) reveal experiences of living in diaspora and exile from the individual's point of view. They depict identity formation processes from a close perspective while situating them in general cultural and political contexts. They prove that research which promotes individual perceptions, attitudes and responses from within groups is valuable in gaining scholarly insights, as well as insights that inform politics and policies.

Fieldwork – necessarily multi-sited and preferably long-term – enables insights into non-homogeneous practices within the more settled diaspora groups. When it comes to refugees, the dynamics of remembering and forgetting that varies with changes in the economic and political atmosphere (Gilroy 1994: 209) is best assessible through fieldwork, too, and so are the repercussions of escape from violence as the central feature of refugee experiences (cf. Povrzanović and Jambrešić Kirin 1996). Only by recognizing field reality as an appropriate court for understanding the various levels of power and struggle (Nordstrom and Martin 1992: 14) can a researcher obtain detailed answers about the multiple and often contradictory experiences in diaspora and exile.

An appropriate methodological outline of a "multi-sited ethnography" has been proposed by George Marcus (1995). He suggests the researchers should "follow" the *people* (migrants/exiles), *thing* (commodities, gifts, money, works of art, and intellectual property), *metaphor* (signs, symbols and images), *plot, story* or *allegory* (narratives of everyday experience or memory), *life* or *biography* (of exemplary individuals), or *conflict* (issues contested in public space). In this dynamic view of identity formation processes, Marcus suggests the tracing of a cultural formation across and within multiple sites of activity by way of methods designed around chains, paths, threads, conjunctions, or juxtapositions of locations. He thus stresses the need to locate the discussions within a transnational framework where changes involve many locations at the same time.

The contributors to this volume who deal with identifications embedded in transnational contexts would certainly agree also with Östen Wahlbeck's statement that "field research covers several different methods and the researcher has to be a methodological pragmatist and must use every possible method which can furnish more knowledge" (Wahlbeck 1999: 192). While other authors engage in more common, standard methods of anthropological research, Jonathan Schwartz relies on "NGOgraphy" when meeting informants and taking an active role in their transnational networks. Paul Stubbs engages in what he calls "netnography" when gathering ethnographic material on various websites and in e-mail discussion groups.

Between embodiment and imagination: Imposed and negotiated identities

There is something deeply disturbing about the internationally accepted terms like *processing refugees* (most recently applied to the plight of Kosovo Albanians) and about the supposed "normality" of the life in refugee camps, which blurs the fact that collective tragedies represented by the media are always personally experienced.[7] Even the term *humanitarian catastrophe* directs the attention rather to *humanitarian workers* who might have problems in organizing their work efficiently, than to the victims.[8] Exoduses and political exiles are not instances of bad luck, but results of injustice and violence imposed on different scales. The individual story of Ahmed encountered by Eva Norström can thus be read as a memento directing the reader's attention to the bottom line – or the very starting point – of any scholarly discussion of "refugee crises" and related issues, that is, to survival.

Eva Norström reveals a single life history and faces the reader with an insider's experience of being reduced to the position of an asylum seeker. Dissecting the Swedish asylum policy, Eva Norström does not try to generalize an individual and hopefully non-standard life history. She wants to share the perplexity of her own encounter with Ahmed and the humbling experience that every sensitive researcher is bound to understand when touching upon what is really at stake for any professional dealing with "refugee issues": the bodily experienced personal suffering of people we write about. Norström's critique of technical reasoning, which avoids a discussion about subjective elements such as personality, experience and other factors when judging the fear of an asylum seeker, is significantly related to Liisa Malkki's (1995) reflections on refugees and exile, as well as to Valentine E. Daniel's and John Chr. Knudsen's (1995) important insights regarding mistrusting refugees.

However, Eva Norström's essay not only points to the complexity and serendipity of individual experience that recurrently escapes the fixed and clear analytical categories. It also reminds us of the fact that what helped him to avoid the tragic end of a web of non-choices, was the individual, personal engagement of people for whom he was not just a name filled in a form to fit into a certain legal category.

In the essay on the approaches to the study of exile and traumatization, Charles Westin offers a macroperspective on "the refugee emergencies and mass flight situations that have struck Europe since the collapse of Yugoslavia, and that have haunted Africa for many decades", but also recognizes the need to give a detailed account of personal experiences. He exemplifies the traumatic reaction of a young woman who was a victim of the expulsion. Both Westin and Norström describe and analyse starting positions of people who came to Sweden to rescue their lives, and whose traumas seem to be depriving them from even trying some immigrant paths of adaptation.

Charles Westin allows us a closer look at the symbolism that is invoked by political violence, torture and gross violation of people's integrity. He also shows that, as long as therapeutic work is directed to the individual, ignoring the wider context of community, state and broader social issues, the likelihood of restoring the individual's meaning of life is minimized (cf. Daniel and Knudsen 1995: 7). Concerning the examples discussed in his essay, Westin claims that "though carried out with best intentions, the reception and resettlement programmes continued, and even reinforced, the personal crises produced by the expulsion".

The woman whom Westin quotes extensively in order to show proportions of suffering and disturbances in exile, and because of exile, is a Ugandan-Asian. Her narrative provides for a dramatic contrast to another Ugandan-Asian woman in Sweden presented by Gunnar Alsmark. While the woman met by Westin found it extremely difficult to overcome her traumatic experiences and has not been able to come to terms with her fate, the woman met by Alsmark successfully manages to weave her many identifications together into a non-conflicting whole.

Presenting herself as a Ugandan-Asian Muslim *Swede*, Masooma Rahim seems to have no problem in living a context-bound bricolage of identifications. She is eager to point out her non-standard crossings of the category boundaries inside and outside her family, ethnic, and religious networks. For her, Islam is not only a source of spiritual strength, but also a key to transnational contacts within the global *umma* of Muslim believers. Her plural, syncretic identity is an excellent example of what I would call "impersonated multiculturalism" (multiculturalism in the sense of lived experience, not political programmes) as a part of many immigrants' and refugees' everyday life (cf. Olsson 1999: 19). Yet, many imposed, ascribed or accidental aspects of identity remain beyond individual reach of influence. Personal identifications and expectations similar to Massoma Rahim's may be left unrecognized either by their communities or by society. Her "success story", as Gunnar Alsmark calls it, will be completed only if she is welcomed, appreciated and esteemed as a teacher by her Swedish-born (and all other) pupils and their parents.[9]

"Diasporic cultural identity teaches us that cultures are not preserved by being protected from 'mixing' but probably can only continue to exist as a product of such mixing" (Boyarin and Boyarin 1993: 721). However, the understanding of diasporas and transnationalism differs from the usual notions of "hybridity" as it is defined within cultural studies. New mixtures and new forms of syncretism might be celebrated, but it is equally important to show – as in Alsmark's example – how individuals and social groups become competent in, and improvise from, *existing* structures, cultures and languages.

> Fluency of movement and switching codes between a number of discrete cultures and social organizations is perhaps a more subtle and telling form of adaptation than syncretism. To see large numbers of people pulling off this particular trick may truly signal that we are entering a global age (Vertovec and Cohen 1999: xxvi).

It is axiomatic for researchers in the humanities and social sciences that identities are actively made and remade, that they should never be essentialized, but conceptualized as a process of becoming. Although such processes are always historically situated, we also agree on not seeing the "past" and "present" as stable, structurally fixed models shaping social action, but as models generated in everyday practice (Malkki 1990: 49). The interest in everyday life as the arena of identity formation processes is an important aspect common to Gunnar Alsmark's and Magnus Berg's essays. It is the everyday life where the

Swedes might meet – sometimes on a very personal basis – their old and new immigrant compatriots.

Yet, unlike in Alsmark's essay, Magnus Berg presents the image of Muslims in Sweden as heavily burdened with mediated popular Orientalism, and not at all standing for individual freedom and choice. Berg does not deal with Muslim immigrants' and refugees' experiences, but offers a thought-provoking insight into some pre-given frames of people's identity formation processes. When it comes to everyday Orientalism, these frames are of another kind than the legal frames described by Eva Norström. But the fact that they are less visible and less restrictive does not make them less present or less influential in people's interactions.

The (peaceful) everyday context might be the site of recognition of the relational character of identity, where people might see the other's otherness as an invitation for contact. Still, while discussing everyday Orientalism among the Swedes who meet Muslims of different ethnic backgrounds on a daily basis, Magnus Berg makes us question the optimistic belief in the coincidental creativity of everyday life. It may, after all, not always provide for an arena of constant negotiations of daily value judgements and more profound images of identity and belonging for people with mutually foreign experiential frames of reference. Berg shows that the most commonly used option of "seeing the other" is a benevolent effort to get along, but that it at the same time seems to be incapable of relating to the otherness of the other in a way that enhances understanding. The strategy of "focusing on the individual", and not on his or her orientalized otherness, can bring people together. Yet, "the problem with this strategy", Berg warns, "is that it does nothing but try to disregard the Orient as the Orient and the Orientals as Orientals. It turns to an individual, but at the same time it separates the individual from those cultural and historical contexts that Swedes are unfamiliar with". The fact that more than 250,000 Muslims live in Sweden, that Islam is the second biggest religion in the country, and that, e.g., Muhammed and Ahmed are among the four most common names given to children recently born in the town of Malmö (*Sydsvenskan*, 2 April, 2000), underlines the importance of Berg's work.

Beyond integration: Transnational connections

The authors contributing to the second part of the book are interested in transnationality as the significant context of identity formation in diaspora and exile. They delineate politically informed aspects of home- and origin-related strategies of identification. The politicized networks and connections reaching beyond national borders entail potentials for new forms of citizenship, solidarity and emancipation that may have positive outcomes similar to the one presented by Gunnar Alsmark. At the same time, they entail a construction of difference which might not help to resolve politically dangerous stereotypes like the ones discussed by Magnus Berg. They might even help to breed the seeds of new wars resulting in exoduses and traumas similar to those which Eva Norstöm and Charles Westin write about.

Researchers observe the continuing significance of nation states in most immigrants' and refugees' daily lives. Also, the forces that sustain national allegiances have proved stronger than any countervailing trends (Smith 1991: 143).[10] However, the density and importance of new networks, organizations and practices that criss-cross the globe require research that supersedes conventional state-centric perspectives. The new interplay of global and local, of international and domestic issues, often does not fit into the national politics of particular nation states. In relation to national identity, transnationalism can be a cause of divided loyalties, but also a basis of social capital. Some transnational communities influence political and diplomatic relations between their host and homeland states. In the age of information, social and political movements are organized and mobilized across national borders (cf. Cohen 1997).

To what extent do states create, shape, hinder and transform transnational practices? By discussing the concepts of nationality, ethnicity and citizenship in relation to immigrants, Mehmet Ümit Necef addresses problems that are central to the literature on transnationalism, namely the political implications of the "deterritorialized nation-state" (Basch et al. 1994). In his essay on the Turkish debate on the national allegiance of the Turks living in Germany, Necef investigates diaspora as the site of political engagement. Within the "hot" disputes on the definition of "authentic" Turkishness and the preferable homeland politics, Necef discerns three competing discourses on the place of Turkish immigrants in the host societies: the Turkish "nationalist" discourse, the "integrationalist", and the Islamist discourse. He presents the first two in detail, and shows how sensitive issues of dual loyalty polarize the most visible and the most widely dispersed immigrant group in Western Europe. In Necef's essay, the tension is illustrated between the highly questionable assumption that immigrants will demonstrate an exclusive loyalty to the state they live in, and the assumption that they neccessarily engage in "long-distance nationalism" (Anderson 1983).

Jonathan Schwartz's essay on ethnic communities from the Republic of Macedonia in Copenhagen touches upon similar questions. It can be read as an ethnographic assessment of James Clifford's (1997) claim that by the very character of their multiple belonging, diasporas can never be truly essentialist, thus never truly nationalist either. Schwartz's valuable ethnographic insights show that this claim is at the same time true and false. In that regard, there are examples of radically different attitudes among different diasporic groups, but also within groups usually seen as homogeneous. With regard to their public engagement in the host countries, some diaspora groups can be characterized as "low profile", while others are "high profile" – visible and loud in public spaces, often promoting their original nation's interests or supporting nationalist political claims. Still, when speaking of "low profile diasporas", Schwartz does not imply that the mobilizers of those diasporas voice moderation. "Their organizations of the civil society in the metropole promote *cultural rights*, but most often they are *national rights*. The line between 'cultural' and 'national' is perhaps just as ambiguous as the cartography of the various Balkan nation states. In the multicultural diasporas, however, cultural rights and national aspirations are made to feel congruent as they seldom are in the multicultural homelands."

Schwartz has been engaged in long-term research (for over two decades!) within ethnic communities from Macedonia in Copenhagen, as well as in Toronto and Melbourne. He kept in touch with their social contexts and significant contacts in Macedonia, too. In his contribution to this book, he puts several pieces of evidence together, found in those diverse, separate sites, believing that "a form of social scientific validity ought to emerge by virtue of the time-span" and by virtue of such multi-sited fieldwork. Schwartz claims that "studying ethnic communities in greater Copenhagen, and perhaps in any large metropole, requires the identification of dispersed segments – literally diasporas – as the familiar urban neighborhood approach is rendered increasingly obsolete". Indeed, his essay enables an understanding of local internal divisions because it makes clear the crucial role of their transnational aspects.

Schwartz's essay is at the same time an example of a worthwhile dialogue with older research on immigrant groups that was focusing on integration.[11] He traces the continuity of dance events, as institutions, from the nation state that once was Yugoslavia. Still punctuated with events celebrating contested national holidays, today they are in the first place "keen markers in the making of diasporas".

My own contribution stands against presumptions about ethnic groups in the countries of immigration or exile forming ethnic *communities* in unproblematic ways. The Croats in Sweden provide a complex example. There were refugees of an earlier, post World War II generation, labour migrants in the 1960s and 1970s, political exiles in 1971, and most recently refugees in the 1990s. Various patterns of identification processes and their implications open up for different kinds of research focus, especially on the importance of migration links and networks prior to exodus, and the tension between immigrants and refugees coming from the same country.

Although local community experiences and traditions make for a variety of groups that might or might not see themselves as belonging to the Croatian nation in an essential sense, national identification was radically heightened by the war in the 1990s within Croatian diaspora people throughout the world. I seek to explain the differences of narrative and other strategies through which symbolic spaces and collective images of ethnic and national belonging are produced by Croatian immigrants who have lived in Sweden since the 1960s and refugees of the same ethnic affiliation who came in the 1990s, mostly from Bosnia-Herzegovina. I assess the cultural impacts of war that seem to be decisive for self-perceived differences among people who share ethnic affiliation, but not the experiences of war and exile.

The concluding essay by Paul Stubbs also deals with the Croats, but in a completely different way. Here critical perspectives on social consequences and determinants of globe-spanning technologies are presented, and the globalized media's impact on ethnic community dynamics is discussed. Paul Stubbs seeks to elaborate upon the work of Arjun Appadurai (1996), through a specific focus on the construction of particular kinds of diasporic affinities dependent on the rapid growth of computer-mediated communication as one aspect of modern media. New public spheres are created through the use of the Internet and computer-mediated newsgroups. Paul Stubbs makes them at the same time the sites and the objects of his study.

Stubbs adopts Appadurai's (1996) notion of *ethnoscape* in order to asses the specificities of diaspora and computer-mediated communication. He stresses the "underdetermined nature" of the Croatian ethnoscape, in terms of relative unpredictability or logic of associations. Most importantly, he addresses the theoretical implications of notions such as *multiple diasporization, virtual ethnicity* and *virtual community*, and directs a sharp critique towards ideas about "a new divide" opening up between *cosmopolitanism* and *nationalism.* Stubbs shows that the work of collective imagining which may be found within diasporic public spheres cannot simply be juxtaposed to notions of "cosmopolitan", anti-nationalist identities, which are commonly presented as superior and non-contingent. His analysis discerns a complex discourse merging realities, images and narratives with its inventory of dominant themes and meanings. That discourse entails the possibility of challenging particular kinds of National narratives within diasporic public spheres. This is, holds Stubbs, "far less likely to come from really existing 'postnational movements, organizations and spaces' (Appadurai 1996: 177) than from the minutiae of understandings of, and consciously articulated disruptions to, the slippage from politically oriented National discourses to the sphere of everyday life."

Notes

1   Presenting the contested, yet quickly expanding field of "transnationalism", "transnationality" or "transnational social spaces" is beyond the reach of this introduction. The relevant references are abundant, but so far including mostly articles published in journals, notably in *Diaspora: A Journal of Transnational Studies.* The books by Basch et al. (1994), Ong (1999) and Faist (2000) should be mentioned,

as well as the collections edited by Glick Schiller et al. (1992), Smith and Guarnizo (1998) and Vertovec and Cohen (1999). The important work on transnational connections by Ulf Hannerz (1996) does not focus on immigrants and refugees, but provides insights into a wider context of global cultural flows and local reactions to an emergent world system. His theoretical questions on "culture", "the local", "community", "nation", or on "who are the globalizers" are of high relevance for topics dealt with in this volume. Arjun Appadurai's influential work (1996) is discussed at length in Paul Stubbs's contribution.

2   See Liisa H. Malkki's (1995) elaborate critique of "the refugee" as an epistemic object and as an object of knowledge, as well as of essentializing "the refugee experience" within "refugee studies".

3   The notion of diaspora "has been used to cover all sorts of expatriate ethnic communities that can somehow be identified as ethnic, racial, or religious categoric groups, and even indigenous minorities that are not (or are no longer) related to any external point of origin or 'center'. ... This conceptual enlargement has been undertaken by a number of ethnic, religious and/or racial groups themselves for a variety of legitimate reasons: to equip themselves with a 'hyphenated' identity in order to stress their uniqueness; to free themselves psychologically from the grip of a homogenizing 'nation-state' and a domineering cultural monocracy; and, on occasion, to vie with others in articulating their victimhood" (Safran 1999: 260–261). Khachig Tölölyan notes that a full explanation of "why such conceptions of diaspora – broader, more accommodating, more 'empowering' – have proliferated requires an exploration of the transformation of universities, the emergence of literary and cultural theory, the elaboration of theories of pluralism and multiculturalism, the change in American, Canadian and Australian immigration laws since around 1965, et cetera" (Tölölyan 1996: 16). See his article (Tölölyan 1996) for a survey of definitions of "diaspora", for analytical distinctions between "diasporan" and "ethnic communities", as well as for the reasons of proliferation and valorization of diasporas.

4   For an elaborate critique of Cohen 1997, see Safran 1999.

5   This is directly connected to the insight based on anthropological research, on the individual refugee's self-identity being "anchored more to who she or he was than what she or he has become" (Daniel and Knudsen 1995: 5). The same was shown by the ethnologists contributing to Jambrešić Kirin and Povrzanović (eds.) 1996.

6   At the conference "New Approaches to Migration: Transnational Communities and the Transformation of Home", University of Sussex, 21–22 September 1999.

7   A closely related example on *normality* in and of (*sic!*) refugee camps was notable in a *EuroNews* programme in mid-April 1999. The filmed images from a refugee camp in Albania where Kosovo Albanians were waiting to be sent to Western countries were accompanied by a comment saying that "although life in the camp seems to be normal", the refugees live with uncertainty. The "normality" was recognized in the fact that a woman could be seen washing clothes in a dirty plastic container.

8   Related to this issue is the general predicament of humanitarian workers, or "caseworkers". Daniel and Knudsen (1995) explain how "sadly, the demands of

states and state interests – even when channeled through the United Nations – exert a stronger force on the daily duties of the average caseworker than do humanitarian interests". The myriad national and international bureaucratic microstructures are primarily beholden to the state's interest, so "one ends up with caseworkers who are reduced to information-gathering and information-dispersing functionaries. They become men and women who have no real opinions of their own, and the information they gather does not inform them" (Daniel and Knudsen 1995: 5). The predominant media representations of refugees seem to follow this pattern.

9   In relation to the situation of "meeting the immigrants in the classroom", let me mention an example of goodwill on the part of Swedish authorities which is not necessarily "paving the way to hell", but certainly confirms how even in professional surroundings that are highly sensitive (and obliged!) to political decisions on multiculturalism and civil equality, essentializing categories applied to immigrants persist and, as it seems, remain unnoticed. In the Swedish reader used in the first grade of comprehensive school in 2000–2001 (Lena Hultgren, *Mini och den magiska stenen*, Almqvist & Wiksell Förlag, 1995), the two children characters' parents are presented. The three of them with Swedish names have professions. The fourth, called Mario, is just "from Italy". Running the risk of being picky, I would say that the obvious wish to "present reality" succeeded in revealing the fact that a considerable number of today's schoolchildren's parents in Sweden are immigrants. Yet, at the same time it reveals the reality of immigrants being ethnified in popular representations, and reduced to the identity of a non-Swede. Reading it as yet another instance of ethnifying, essentializing, exoticizing, or naturalizing orders of difference would mean overinterpreting this example, but it is by no means trivial. A revised version of that otherwise very well-made book, presenting an Italian father who is, e.g., a head of a clinic, would perhaps not present any statistically relevant reality, but it would prove an official effort in the direction of changing attitudes regarding the presupposed immigrants' (non)positions.

10   As elaborated by Anthony Smith, "national identity today is not only global, it is also pervasive. Though there are some situations in which it is felt to be more important than others, it may also be said to pervade the life of individuals and communities in most spheres of activity. In the cultural sphere national identity is revealed in the whole range of assumptions and myths, values and memories, as well as in language, law, institutions and ceremonies. Socially, the national bond provides most inclusive community, ... and the limit for distinguishing 'outsider'. ... Finally the nation and national identity, by commanding the basic political allegiance of citizens, have become the only recognized source of 'inter-national' legitimacy .... Such order as may be found in the community of states is premissed on the norm of the nation as the sole unit of political loyalty and action" (Smith 1991: 143–144).

11   It is Carl-Ulrik Schierup's and Aleksandra Ålund's (1987) comparative study on integration patterns of two groups of Yugoslav immigrants (Vlachs and Macedonians) in Sweden and Denmark.

References

Anderson, Benedict. 1983. *Imagined Communities: Reflections on the Origin and Spread of Nationalism.* London: Verso.

Anderson, Benedict. 1994. Exodus. *Critical Inquiry* 20: 314–327.

Appadurai, Arjun. 1996. *Modernity at Large: Cultural Dimensions of Globalization.* Minneapolis: University of Minnesota Press.

Basch, Linda, Glick Schiller, Nina, and Szanton Blanc, Cristina. 1994. *Nations Unbound: Transnational Projects, Postcolonial Predicaments, and Deterritorialized Nation-states.* OPA Amsterdam: Gordon and Breach Publishers.

Boyarin, Daniel, and Boyarin, Jonathan. 1993. Diaspora: Generation and the Ground of Jewish Identity. *Critical Inquiry* 19: 693–725.

Clifford, James. 1997. Diasporas. In Clifford, J., *Routes: Travel and Translation in the Late Twentieth Century*, 244–277. Cambridge, MA, and London: Harvard University Press.

Cohen, Robin. 1997. *Global Diasporas: An Introduction.* London: UCL Press.

Daniel, E. Valentine, and Knudsen, John Chr. 1995. Introduction. In Daniel, E. V. and Knudsen, Chr. (eds.), *Mistrusting Refugees*, 1–12. Berkeley, Los Angeles, London: University of California Press.

Faist, Thomas. 2000. *The Volume and Dynamics of International Migration and Transnational Social Spaces.* Oxford: Clarendon Press.

Gilroy, Paul. 1994. Diaspora. *Paragraph* 17(1): 207–212.

Glick Schiller, Nina, Basch, Linda, and Blanc-Szanton, Cristina (eds.). 1992. *Towards a Transnational Perspective on Migration: Race, Class, Ethnicity, and Nationalism Reconsidered.* New York: New York Academy of Sciences.

Glick Schiller, Nina, Basch, Linda, and Szanton Blanc, Cristina. 1995. From Immigrant to Transmigrant: Theorizing Transnational Migration. *Anthropological Quarterly* 68(1): 48–63.

Hannerz, Ulf. 1996. *Transnational Connections:. Culture, People, Places.* London: Routledge.

Inglis, Christine. 1997. Introduction. Identity in a Changing World. *Asian and Pacific Migration Journal* 6 (3–4): 267–273.

Jambrešić Kirin, Renata, and Povrzanović, Maja (eds.). 1996. *War, Exile, Everyday Life: Cultural Perspectives.* Zagreb: Institute for Ethnology and Folklore Research.

Jayawardena, Lal. 1995. Foreword. In Daniel, E. V. and Knudsen,

Chr. (eds.), *Mistrusting Refugees*, vii–ix. Berkeley, Los Angeles, London: University of California Press.

Malkki, Liisa. 1990. Context and Consciousness: Local Conditions for the Production of Historical and National Thought among Hutu Refugees in Tanzania. In Fox, R. G. (ed.), *Nationalist Ideologies and the Production of National Cultures*, 32–62. Washington: American Anthropological Association.

Malkki, Liisa H. 1995. Refugees and Exile: From "Refugee Studies" to the National Order of Things. *Annual Review of Anthropology* 24: 495–523.

Marcus, George. 1995. Ethnography In/Of the World System: The Emergence of Multi-Sited Ethnography. *Annual Review of Anthropology* 24: 95–117.

Nordstrom, Carolyn and Martin, JoAnn. 1992. The Culture of Conflict: Field Reality and Theory. In Nordstrom, C. and Martin, J. (eds.), *The Paths to Domination, Resistance, and Terror*, 3–17. Berkeley, Los Angeles, Oxford: University of California Press.

Nuscheler, Franz. 1995. *Internationale Migration: Flucht und Asyl*. Opladen: Leske + Budrich.

Olsson, Erik. 1997. Att leva nära en flygplats. Chilenska migranter mellan hemland och värdland. *Socialvetenskaplig tidskrift* 4(1): 43–63.

Olsson, Erik. 1999. Etniska gränser och transnationella gemenskaper. In Olsson, E. (ed.), *Etnicitetens gränser och mångfald*, 11–26. Stockholm: Carlssons.

Ong, Aihwa. 1999. *Flexible Citizenship: The Cultural Logics of Transnationality*. Durham and London: Duke University Press.

Portes, Alejandro. 1999. Conclusion: Towards a New World – the Origins and Effects of Transnational Activities. *Ethnic and Racial Studies* 22(2): 463–475.

Povrzanović, Maja, and Jambrešić Kirin, Renata. 1996. Negotiating Identities? The Voices of Refugees between Experience and Representation. In Jambrešić Kirin, R. and Povrzanović, M. (eds.), *War, Exile, Everyday Life: Cultural Perspectives*, 3–19. Zagreb: Institute for Ethnology and Folklore Research.

Povrzanović, Maja. 2000. The Imposed and the Imagined as Encountered by Croatian War Ethnographers. *Current Anthropology* 41(2): 151–162.

Safran, William. 1991. Diasporas in Modern Societies: Myths of Homeland and Return. *Diaspora* 1(1): 83–99.

Safran, William. 1999. Comparing Diasporas: A Review Essay. *Diaspora* 8(3): 255–291.

Said, Edward. 1984a. The Mind of Winter: Reflections on Life in Exile, *Harpers* Sept.: 49–55.

Said, Edward. 1984b. Reflections on Exile. *Granta* 13: 159–172.

Schierup Carl-Ulrik, and Ålund, Aleksandra. 1987. *Will They Still be Dancing? Integration and Ethnic Transformation among Yugoslav Immigrants in Scandinavia.* Göteborg: Almqvist and Wiksell.

Schnapper, Dominique. 1999. From the Nation-State to the Transnational World: On the Meaning and Usefulness of Diaspora as a Concept. *Diaspora* 8(3): 225–254.

Schwartz, Jonathan. 1998. Visions of Diaspora in Contemporary Social Science. In Haxen, U., Trautner-Kromann, H., and Goldschmidt Salamon, K.L. (eds.), *Jewish Studies in a New Europe,* 757–769. Copenhagen: C.A. Reitzel.

Smith, Anthony. 1991. *National Identity.* London and New York: Penguin.

Smith, Michael Peter, and Guarnizo, Luis Eduardo (eds.). 1998. *Transnationalism from Below.* New Brunswick and London: Transaction Publishers.

Tölölyan, Khachig. 1991. The Nation-State and its Others: In Lieu of a Preface. *Diaspora* 1(1): 3–7.

Tölölyan, Khachig. 1996. Rethinking *Diaspora*(s): Stateless Power in the Transnational moment. *Diaspora* 15(1): 3–36.

Turner, Aaron. 2000. Embodied Ethnography: Doing Culture. *Social Anthropology* 8(1): 51–60.

Vertovec, Steven, and Cohen, Robin (eds.). 1999. *Migration, Diasporas and Transnationalism.* Cheltenham and Northampton: Edward Elgar Publishing.

Wahlbeck, Östen. 1999. *Kurdish Diasporas: A Comparative Study of Kurdish Refugee Communities.* London: Macmillan.

Part 1

Between embodiment and imagination:
Imposed and negotiated identities

To see the other

Eva Norström

Once the realisation is accepted
That between the closest human beings
Infinite distances continue to exist
A wonderful living side by side
Can grow up, if they succeed
In loving the distance between them
Which makes it possible for
Each to see the other whole against the sky
(Rilke)[1]

Introduction

Swedish law stipulates that an alien, refugee or other person, who is
in need of protection in Sweden, has a right to be issued with a
Swedish residence permit. The term refugee in the *Aliens Act* (1989)
refers to a person who is outside the country of his/her nationality
on the grounds of a well-founded fear of being persecuted, for reasons
of race, nationality, membership of a particular social group, or
religious or political opinion, and who is unable or, owing to such
fear, is unwilling to avail him/herself of the protection of that country. This applies irrespective of whether persecution is at the hands
of the authorities of the country or these cannot be expected to offer
protection against persecution by private individuals (*Aliens Act* 1989,
chapter 3 section 2). The term refugee is defined in accordance with
the 1951 Geneva Convention relating to the status of refugees and the
1967 protocol relating to the status of refugees. These two international instruments govern refugee status at the universal level. A total
of 136 states are parties to one or both of these instruments. Aliens
in need of protection who do not meet the criteria for refugee status

are issued with a residence permit on specific grounds defined under the *Aliens Act*, e.g., due to well-founded fear of being sentenced to death or corporal punishment or being subject to torture or other inhuman or degrading treatment or punishment; due to an external or internal armed conflict; because of sex or homosexuality (*Aliens Act* 1989, chapter 3, section 3).

A *Handbook on Procedures and Criteria for Determining Refugee Status under the 1951 Convention and the 1967 Protocol relating to the Status of Refugees* was issued in 1979 for the guidance of governments.[2] For many years, the *Handbook* has been accepted as a reference by Swedish immigration authorities. Later, in the amendments approved to the 1989 *Aliens Act*, the Parliament decided that the *Handbook*, as well as the conclusions from the UNHCR Executive Committee, should normally be used for guidance.[3]

In this paper I illustrate the generally accepted principles of the *Handbook*, mainly through paragraphs 37 and 40, with one asylum seeker and relate what happens to him in the process of determining his case.

Paragraph 37 establishes that the phrase "well founded fear of being persecuted" is the key to the definition. It reflects the views of the authors of the Handbook regarding the main elements of refugee characteristics. Fear is subjective, and thus the definition involves a subjective element in the person applying for recognition as a refugee. "Determination of refugee status will therefore primarily require an evaluation of the applicant's statements rather than a judgement on the situation prevailing in his country of origin." Paragraph 40 acknowledges that you cannot separate the evaluation of the subjective element from an assessment of the personality of the applicant. Psychological reactions of individuals may differ under identical conditions. "One person may have strong political or religious convictions, the disregard of which would make his life intolerable; another may have no such strong convictions. One person may make an impulsive decision to escape; another may carefully plan his departure."

In order to evaluate the subjective element, there are certain factors to take into consideration, such as the concepts of personality and dissimilar narrative traditions. How you perceive yourself is basically formed during your childhood, and if you are loved, feel safe, can trust the persons you depend on, you will probably become a secure and trusting person. Your perception of who you are, the meaning of your life and what is expected of you are related to your surroundings and internalized to become something you consider self-evident (Frykman and Löfgren 1987).

But the self is also accidental, heterogeneous and depends on a variety of cultural beliefs, values and forms of life (Rose 1996:6). In Western societies, for example, our political beliefs rest on a commitment to "respect for the rights and powers of the citizen as an individual" (Rose 1996:1) Here the value of self is connected with concepts like autonomy, identity, individuality, liberty, choice and fulfilment, concepts which are clearly cultural.

Another consideration is that traumatic experiences at any age can affect a person so deeply that s/he may suffer from permanent physical, emotional, and even spiritual injuries. Since any event is separate from any one verbalization of it, various ways of translating a traumatic experience have to be considered. The notion of post-traumatic stress disorder (PTSD) is central here, since it refers to the pattern of inconveniences or symptoms a person might suffer from after a traumatic experience, e.g., at the risk of life or physical integrity (*DSM* 1988). PTSD might affect the way people act in an interview situation. It is not until one has worked through a trauma that it is possible to describe this experience in words without reliving the trauma. This means that persons interviewing asylum seekers have to understand that people with traumatic experiences might limit what they tell in order to protect themselves from reliving the trauma. This does not indicate that they are untrustworthy. In cases of emotional denial it might seem as if the asylum seeker has no feelings at all in relation to what s/he is telling. This does not indicate untrustworthiness either. Torture implies that a hostile surrounding consciously hurts an individual. Inability to communicate is one of the damages of torture (Firnhaber 1998: 24; see also Westin in this volume).

I now wish to introduce Ahmed. I tell his story, as I have perceived it, in linear form. But that is not how he told it. It was rather like a puzzle which began as he said "I like the police officers there", when passing the local police station. I have excluded information about geographical facts, precise time references and other information that I consider may facilitate his being identified. I am well aware of the fact that this might leave the reader with unanswered questions. The Swedish authorities have had access to the same material as I have.

Ahmed

My first encounter with Ahmed, a man then in his thirties, was on a cold and clear autumn day in 1996. He met me at the railway station in a small town in Sweden. We spent a whole day together while he told me all about his life. (We made an agreement. He was willing to give me access to his experiences over time, hoping that it some-how will be useful for other asylum seekers.) This was not easy for him. Everyday activities interrupted the difficult parts of our day as we travelled back and forth in time. During those moments we were here and now as he showed me the paintings he was working on, cooked us a meal, talked about friends (for whose sake he has decided not to commit suicide), his job and life in general.

I was curious, respectful, even scared because Ahmed is one of those people who have met with complete evil, who have been rejected in the worst possible ways and who have again and again vainly tried to reconstruct new lives. I was not sure I wanted to know and at the same time I had to make myself understand as much as possible. I actually felt as if there is a key to life in the mere presence of a man of Ahmed's calibre.

Ahmed was born in the early sixties in a small Middle-East town as a stateless Palestinian.[4] The family was poor and at the age of nine Ahmed was working after school to be able to buy some things he wanted, for example, a football. He was safe within his family. But in his early years he learned that his people were not safe, when, for example, he saw more and more of those who went to war in Lebanon coming home in wooden boxes.

Ahmed did well at school and finished with high grades at the age of nineteen. Because of this, he was offered a position at the School of Technology in the capital. He declined the offer without realizing that this was going to affect his entire life, and instead he studied economics and operated a small shop, both part-time. In addition, he studied English at a cultural centre.

His decision not to study at the School of Technology caused the Security Services to investigate his political views, and he says he soon knew that he was "registered", which meant that everything he did was observed and registered by the Security Service. One day when he was on his way to the Cultural Centre to return an English book he had borrowed, two men stopped him and ordered him into a car, parked in the front of the centre. He was blindfolded and beaten. He was taken to a prison where he was accused of espionage for Israel and threatened with death. More than eight months of imprisonment with regular physical and mental torture followed (the methods are described later in this chapter). Finally a friend found out where he was and paid the equivalent of US$ 7,000 to have him released.

As discussed by Charles Westin in this volume, torture breaks down the tortured person physically and mentally, deprives him/her of the drive to act, crushes his/her identity and language and violates his/her integrity (see also Westin 1989). During the time that followed his release, Ahmed felt depressed. He said he could not manage the situation at all. For the first time in his life he had serious misgivings about his ability to control his own life. He was behind with his studies and he was uncertain about his future, but in order to support himself he went back to the shop and eventually also resumed his studies.

Before long his university professor contacted him. The professor had been appointed to a ministerial post within the government. The new minister offered Ahmed, now 25, a position in his ministry. Ahmed told him about his time in prison and what he was accused of. After considering, the minister still wanted Ahmed to work for him. It did not take long for Ahmed to realize that the Security Service was thoroughly checking what went on at the ministry. He felt extremely insecure and worried because of his earlier experiences. When the minister entrusted Ahmed with the task of handling his correspondence, Ahmed felt that the situation at work became even more unpleasant. He realized he had to resign from his first qualified job. He went back to his shop once more.

In the early nineties the situation in the country was tense. The regime expected "spontaneous demonstrations" to celebrate the president. As an owner of a shop it was Ahmed's duty to see to it that there were pictures of the President in the shop and outside it. The police came to the shop and told him that his window dressing was not acceptable. He made some changes but before long the police were back to point out new shortcomings. Ahmed was taken to the police station. He was questioned and thereafter brought to a military prison. Investigations followed, although he was neither suspected of anything nor charged with anything. He was not allowed to contact his family or anyone else. He did not even know where he was.

During this second term in prison the torture was crueller than during the first. "I went through very high levels of torment." Ahmed talked about being oppressed, hit and humiliated. "Fear was my only company during this period. It was very easy for them to torture and insult a person. Nobody knew where you were."

For three months Ahmed was kept in a one-square-metre cell underground. It was dark. He could not stretch his limbs and he never saw daylight. There was no toilet available. Once a day he got watery soup. He was frequently tortured. He was then moved to another cell, which he shared with 74 other people. This cell was not big enough for the prisoners to lie down to sleep. Instead they sat with their backs against one another. There was a toilet in one corner of the room. Once a day the prisoners were allowed to go out and at that time the toilet was cleaned. Ahmed was often ordered to do that. Sometimes he threw up what little he had eaten and on a couple of occasions he fainted. "Each night we sat tensely wondering who would be fetched for torture." At least once a week Ahmed was called to "interrogations". He told me that "the first blows are the worst. After that you are numb."

During the time Ahmed was in prison, the president decided to give amnesty to some prisoners. Ahmed was brought out of prison blindfolded and driven to the central parts of the city where he was released at 2 a.m. The military secret police told him they did not like the amnesty, that he was not allowed to talk about his experiences and that they would see him again. Ahmed was informed that he had lost certain fundamental rights. He had suffered many physical injuries from the torture and eventually went to see a doctor for treatment to his knees, feet, wrists and shoulders. His groin had to be operated on.

Ahmed was obliged to report to the police twice a week. Almost always he was kept there for hours. He was always frightened and concluded that his only chance to stay alive was to leave the country. In order to finance this, he sold his shop. There was no possibility for him to get a travel document legally so he bribed a civil servant. When he was ready to leave he went to a private travel agent and within 48 hours he obtained a visa to Russia.

He left for Moscow where he stayed in a hotel. He sold merchandise to tourists, avoiding Russians and fellow countrymen. But agents from the embassy of his earlier country of residence found him. The agents said that he had to go to the embassy within three days or they would see to it that he was sent back. They accused him of collaboration with the Israelis and of espionage. His life was threatened and he knew that this threat was for real as the Security Service of his country had murdered suspected opponents before.

The threats continued for about a month and then he decided to leave Russia. When I asked Ahmed how the agents knew where he was, he laughed and said I was naive. "The whole of the Middle East is involved in the arms trade and the Mafia, and in every hotel in Moscow there are people who find out the nationality of the guests and sell the information."

Ahmed paid a smuggler who disappeared with his money. He made a second attempt when he paid the smuggler US$ 2,500 and was told to go to a harbour, from where he would be sent by a small ship to Scandinavia. The smugglers refused to take him on board unless he gave up his travel document. Ahmed did not want to do that but as a life has less value than a valid travel document he burned it in front of the smugglers so that they would know it was no use robbing him. The ship was destined for Denmark but there was a big storm so they waited in a bay and then they headed for Sweden. The highly dangerous trip took eight days and when they arrived in Sweden 391 persons of the 427 who had boarded the ship were still alive.

Ahmed applied for asylum, mentioning that he had been tortured, that the deferment to doing military service he had earlier enjoyed had expired after he left, and that he was not willing to return to his country of origin because he feared being persecuted. He lived in a refugee reception centre where he shared rooms with asylum seekers from Bosnia-Herzegovina and Kosovo. During this time, they got to know each other well and he learned to speak what was then called Serbo-Croat before he learned Swedish. One of the things he observed was that there seemed to be a general conception amongst the asylum seekers that there was no correlation between the reasons people had to seek asylum and who actually got it. The decision-making seemed to be unpredictable but not corruptible.

The Immigration Board rejected his application on three grounds:

1. It was not considered possible that his activities in Moscow were of a kind that would attract the interest of the authorities.
2. His failure to report for military service was not sufficient grounds to grant asylum.
3. The destruction of his travel document was considered as withholding vital information of consequence for assessing his right to asylum in Sweden.

There is no reference whatsoever to the torture he had endured or the time he spent in prison without trial. He could not understand this. He knew his life was in danger if he was sent back and he had nowhere to go. It is significant that the country Ahmed left has not signed the 1984 Convention against Torture and other Cruel and Degrading Treatment. Ahmed felt altogether abandoned.

He became desolate and could see no meaning in life. He was living the torture over again in both day and night dreams, he had a feeling of distance to other people, no sense of the future, insomnia, difficulties in concentrating etc. (Dyregrov 1992). He had clear symptoms of PTSD, and received regular treatment at the regional hospital's psychiatric ward. He frequently went to a little stream to fantasize about drowning himself. Instead he took all the sleeping pills he had. One of the staff at the reception centre was worried about him and went looking for him, which is how his life was saved.

Through his lawyer Ahmed made an appeal to the Aliens Appeals Board (AAB). This appeal was made at a time when Ahmed was wavering between hope for a functioning life in Sweden and a longing for death. He constantly carried with him his version of the cyanide ampoule, a bottle of turpentine. His lawyer enclosed three certificates from the regional University Hospital where it is confirmed that he had been seeing a psychiatrist regularly for a year, that he suffered from PTSD and that the risk of a new suicide attempt was to be taken seriously. Not long after this, he made another serious attempt to end his life. Aiming for an instant death, he drank his bottle of turpentine. He was saved at a hospital, but it has left him with permanent injuries to his digestive system.

The Aliens Appeals Board declined his application for the following reasons:

1. AAB found it remarkable that a man who has been in prison should be offered a position at a Ministerial Department.
2. Furthermore, the AAB found it remarkable that Ahmed did not mention the obligation to report to the Security Services twice a week until he appealed.[5]
3. AAB did not believe he could have obtained a passport through bribes.
4. AAB held it against him that he did not have any valid travel documents, which made it difficult to control his travel route.
5. The fact that he burned his passport in Riga was interpreted as a deliberate attempt to withhold vital information.

The AAB did not evaluate the risk of further suicide attempts, nor did it weigh Ahmed's experience of torture or the risks he faced if returned. He made a new application on his own.[6] He argued against the AAB grounds for rejecting his appeal for asylum. Among other things he wrote: "After an adventurous weeklong journey when we all thought we would die, we arrived. We had to answer routine questions from the Immigration Board with no chance to explain anything." (The Immigration Board uses a form with questions that have been decided on beforehand.) AAB once again rejected his application, referring to the fact that he only answered their rejection but did not put forward any new proof of his need for protection.

During his stay in the reception centre, he had got to know some Swedes who belonged to a church in the town where he lived. They saw his despair and tried to help him in various ways. They hid him from the police, and gave him a job in a second-hand shop where he could feel safe. They wrote to the AAB that they could not accept that Ahmed's reasons for seeking asylum were not even discussed.

They encouraged him to contact Amnesty International in London, who referred him to the Swedish section. In their short reply, the Swedish section told him that that Amnesty understands that his situation is difficult but that their principal task is to inform about the political situation in different countries, and that they unfortunately do not help individuals seeking protection. They enclosed their annual report about the country he had left, and referred him to the Swedish Refugee Advice Centre (a non-governmental organization), who replied that they could do nothing.

The right to legal aid ceases to exist after the Aliens Appeals Board's decision on expulsion. (Legal aid may be granted again if the AAB orders a stay in an expulsion order.) It was Ahmed's friends who gave him economic guarantees for legal advice. The new lawyer contacted the UNHCR regional office in Stockholm, who regretted that they could not be of any assistance to Ahmed.

Driven by despair, Ahmed wrote a long detailed letter including a thorough description of life in prison, his fear of being persecuted if he were sent back, and his feeling of abandonment. The letter contains a list of the methods of torture used on him: hitting the foot soles with cables; the car tyre method, which means you are hung in a car tyre and hit with copper sticks and cables; lashing with belts or bull penis whips; forced medication (tablets and injections in various parts of the body); psychological torture ("I was strung to an electric chair, but the electricity was never switched on").

His new lawyer took action to have Ahmed thoroughly examined at the Centre for Torture and Trauma Survivors (CTD) for the first time during the two years since his arrival. Two specialists in forensic medicine, one specialist in psychiatry, and one bachelor of psychiatric medicine examined him. These four specialists found that his claim to have been tortured was well founded. They stated that the association between the information about the methods of torture, the threat of future torture and the methods Ahmed used to put an end to his life have a high correlation in research material on PTSD and suicidal behaviour.[7] Furthermore, they warned of the danger of new suicide attempts.

In a petition to the AAB the lawyer reminded the authorities of their obligation to deal with the matter of torture in Ahmed's case.[8] He also addressed the matter of suicidal behaviour as a ground for a permit to remain in Sweden.[9] In due course, the expulsion order was stayed and finally Ahmed obtained permission to remain in Sweden on humanitarian grounds. In accordance with Article 1D of the 1951 Convention relating to the status of refugees, Ahmed was issued with a travel document for refugees.[10]

At this point the Immigration Board declared its intention to make a note in the travel document stating that Ahmed's identity was not established. Ahmed's lawyer handed in four original documents confirming his identity and also asked the Immigration Board to see Ahmed's father, who was visiting Ahmed and whose identity was not disputed. (Ahmed resumed contact with his parents shortly after he was granted permission to stay in Sweden.) The Immigration Board replied that they had difficulties understanding how seeing Ahmed's father would help to identify Ahmed. Ahmed and his father called on a public notary and the local police where they were met with a helpful attitude. It was made clear that Ahmed is Ahmed – yet the Immigration Board decided not to make any note about his identity. When Ahmed applied for citizenship afterwards, his application was declined because the Immigration Board does not consider his identity established.

Conclusions

I chose a method of interviewing which indicated an acceptance of receiving pieces for the puzzle in the order they were delivered. I am well aware that this method, like any other method, entails a risk of over-interpreting the given information. I am also aware that I cannot sufficiently assume what it is like to be Ahmed, but – at least –

he has read and accepted my paper. I did not see him in order to make a quick evaluation of him nor to get a ready story to believe. With these starting-points I wish to share my reflections about Ahmed and what has happened to him.

In the *Handbook* (1988, paragraph 37), the authors write that determination of refugee status will "require an evaluation of the applicant's statements", but Ahmed is a witness who was not heard properly. In the reasons for rejecting his applications for asylum, there are no references to the information about the torture he has endured. Furthermore, there is no reasoning about the grounds of his fear of being persecuted once more, the threats from the security police, the prevailing situation in the country he left, and his Palestinian identity. It should be noted here that Ahmed is far from the first asylum seeker from this country, where torture is known to be used frequently and systematically.

In the rejections of Ahmed's application there is no attention given to the specific ways of narration that prevail in the area from which he comes. There is no reasoning about how to judge his experience of torture. In fact, he is met as if the torture had never taken place. In the denial of this existential threat lies a parallel to his situation as a *persona non grata* in his country of origin.[11] He perceived the threat of being expelled from Sweden as a direct threat to his life.

In studying Ahmed's and other asylum seekers' cases I detect a pattern in relation to the difficult and yet fundamental question of "well-founded fear of being persecuted". The pattern is to submit to technical reasoning[12] and to simply avoid a discussion about the subjective element in the person (e.g. in relation to paragraph 40 in the *Handbook*), the personality, self, experience and other factors relevant when judging the fear of an asylum seeker.

It is obvious that Ahmed's environment contained enough love to give him positive self-esteem and also role models to encourage him to use his personal drive to take responsibility for his own life. As a 19-year-old he had enough belief in himself to find and manage a job after school and this capability to be responsible in relation to his undertakings stays with him through all his experiences. He has lived through a series of crises.[13]

He has first-hand knowledge of the methods a persecuting state uses and of Mafia methods. His reactions in relation to his experiences are normal. He has never been psychotic and he has never questioned who he is. His defence mechanisms function well. The disbelief he shows in himself after the first time in prison is a symptom of PTSD, a normal reaction to the trauma of torture. His wish to die was brought about in Sweden and is a normal reaction to a situation where the very threat to his life is made almost invisible or at least trivialized (on the boat where 36 people were thrown overboard, he did not choose to jump). It is the first time the existential doubt "is it worth while?" appears. His attempts to commit suicide were not a cry for help. His intention was to die.

He seemed to manage everyday life, work, paint, and see friends (of whom I met two). Although he held a low key, he was not detached but authentic, focused and at times he showed a good sense of humour. He was generous in his sharing with me. He was not doing this for nothing, as he hoped his experience would be used to make it easier for other people in similar situations. He had access to his internal emotional memories of the terrible situations he had lived through and survived. He was now able to talk about them with me without reliving them, like scenes from extreme horror movies, which he by now could decide himself whether to view now or later, well knowing they will always stay with him. He had the ability to draw me into a deep existential perspective.

I do not dispute that the Swedish authorities on a general level are eager to stand by the Human Rights conventions, to show solidarity and generosity and to be fair and efficient. One purpose of the system is to regulate immigration to Sweden in a fair and efficient way whereby each applicant is heard without any bias from the civil servants and where all relevant facts are recorded and evaluated. But what comes out in practice is not always consistent with these ambitions. In some cases it is hard to find any proof of willingness to analyse what has actually happened to the asylum seeker and even less willingness to understand his/her fear of being persecuted in the future. In this paper I do not deal with explanations as to the discrepancy between ideals and practice.

I have told you about Ahmed and how he had to deal with the existential questions of who he is and for what purpose he is living.

The witnesses to his struggle were not to be found within the system created to protect the persecuted, but amongst his Swedish friends, medical personnel and one lawyer. They were the people who saw him. They could not help him to make sense of the decisions to reject his application, but they were confirming witnesses and since his ability to create deeper relationships was intact, he was able to make the conscious agreement to endure life as it is.

Acknowledgements

A number of people have been kind enough to read and comment on the manuscript. These were Ingrid Johansson, Kjell Jönsson, Hugh McCullum and Michael Williams.

Notes

1   The text quoted comes from the letter Rilke wrote to Emanuel von Bodman on 17 August 1901: "Aber, das Bewußtsein vorausgesetzt, daß auch zwischen den nächsten Menschen unendliche Fernen bestehen bleiben, kann ihnen ein wundervolles Nebeneinanderwohnen erwachsen, wenn es ihnen gelingt, die Weite zwischen sich zu lieben, die ihnen die Möglichkeit gibt, einander immer in ganzer Gestalt und vor einem großen Himmel zu sehen!"

2   The Handbook was issued in response to a request from the Executive Committee of the High Commissioner's Programme at its 28th session. The criteria set out in the Handbook relate to the 1951 Convention and 1967 Protocol and do not cover the wider concept of the term refugee adopted in regional legal texts (Handbook 1979: 1).

3   *Government Bill* 1996/97: 25, *Parliamentary Committee Report* 1996/97: SfU5, *Official Letter from the Parliament* 1996/97: 80. See Sandesjö and Björk 1995, as well as the Aliens Appeals Board's publications on practice in aliens' cases.

4   *Aliens Act* (1989:529) with amendments October 1997, Chapter 2, sections 2 and 3 also applies to stateless persons, as was also the practice before the amendments to the law in 1997. In this paper I do not discuss how the various states in the region look at the question of statelessness and citizenship of the Palestinian refugees.

5   One of the characteristic effects of torture is that the victim has problems concentrating and remembering. When an applicant adds facts to his grounds for seeking protection s/he is often accused of "escalating" the story and the added facts are turned against the asylum seeker as proof of untrustworthiness (Firnhaber 1998: 24).

6   When a decision has come into force the alien can make a new application for asylum. The application may be granted if it based on circumstances which have not previously been examined in his/her case and if the alien is entitled to a resi-

dence permit under chapter 3 Section 4, or it would be contrary to requirements of humanity to expel the alien (*Aliens Act* 1989: 529).

7   For a systematic discussion of the relationship between torture methods a person has experienced and the method s/he uses when attempting to commit suicide, see Ferrada-Noli 1996.

8   If substantial grounds exist for believing that the applicant would be in danger of being subjected to torture if returned to his or her country of origin, the application for asylum should be granted according to chapter 8, section 1, of the 1989 Aliens Act.

9   The grounds for when the risk of suicide should lead to permission to remain are to be found in Government Bills 1984/84:144 and 1988/89:86, Official Reports SOU 1983:29, SOU 1988:1 and SOU 1994:54.

10   United Nations Relief and Works Agency for Palestine Refugees in the Near East, UNRWA, had already accepted Ahmed as a refugee, which gave him immediate access to the privileges of the 1951 Convention when granted permission to stay in Sweden.

11   I would like to stress that for the tortured individual, torture is an experience touching the foundation of the individual's social and political existence. For the torturer, in most cases a civil servant, torturing is a routine instrument for enforcing power (Westin 1989).

12   The subjective element is discussed in Wikrén and Sandesjö 1995: 134 ff. With reference to the Handbook paragraphs 37–42, they maintain that the applicant's fear is to be accepted as well founded when there is reason to presume that s/he will be subject to persecution if returned. This interpretation of the 1951 Convention and 1967 Protocol is disputed. In contrast to UNHCR, Hathaway (1992) and Grahl-Madsen (1966) share the opinion that the refugee definition never contained both a subjective and an objective element. Instead, they claim that the authors of the Convention and the Protocol had in mind an objective trial of the asylum application with consideration taken for current and future risks for the applicant. Wikrén and Sandesjö (1995) draw the same conclusion as most Western European states, namely that the objective elements are predominant in an evaluation of an asylum claim. The most important factor is the risk of persecution if the applicant is returned. If the applicant has already been the subject of persecution, this is an important indication of future risk of persecution as long as the same regime or the same circumstances prevail. It is recommended that the presumption for future persecution should not easily be abandoned and also that proof of earlier experiences of persecution should be taken as evidence of future risks.

13   Here defined as "a necessary turning point, a crucial moment, when development must move one way or another, marshalling resources of growth, recovery, and further differentiation" (Erikson 1968).

References

Aliens Act 1989: 529 with amendments, October 1997.

DSM (Diagnostic and Statistical Manual of Mental Disorders). 1988. 3rd edition. American Psychiatric Association.

Dyregrov, Atle. 1992. *Katastrofpsykologi*. Lund: Studentlitteratur.

Erikson, Erik H. 1968. *Identity: Youth and Crises*. New York: Norton.

Ferrada-Noli, Marcello. 1996. *Post-Traumatic Stress Disorder and Suicidal Behaviour in Immigrants to Sweden: An Epidemiological, Cross-cultural and Psychiatric Study*. Stockholm: Department of Clinical Neuroscience, The Karolinska Institute.

Firnhaber, Rudi. 1998. Följdverkningar av tortyr får inte vändas mot den asylsökande, *Kantt, tidskrift från Kantt, kansliet för tortyr- och traumaskadade* 1–2.

Frykman, Jonas, and Löfgren, Orvar. 1987. *Culture Builders: A Historical Anthropology of Middle-Class Life*. New Brunswick and London: Rutgers University Press.

Government Bills 1984/84: 144, 1988/89: 86, and 1996/97: 25.

Grahl-Madsen, Atle. 1966. *The Status of Refugees in International Law, part 1*. Leyden: Sijthoff Publications.

Handbook on Procedures and Criteria for Determining Refugee Status under the 1951 Convention and the 1967 Protocol relating to the Status of Refugees. 1979 (1988). Geneva: Office of the United Nations High Commissioner for Refugees.

Hathaway, James. 1992. *The Law of Refugee Status*. Vancouver: Butterworths.

Official Letter from the Parliament 1996/97:80.

Official Reports SOU 1983: 29, SOU 1988: 1 and SOU 1994: 54.

Parliamentary Committee Report 1996/97: SfU5.

Rose, Nikolas. 1996. *Inventing Our Selves: Psychology, Power, and Personhood*. Cambridge: Cambridge University Press.

Sandesjö, Håkan, and Björk, Kurt. 1995. *Utlänningsnämnden – Praxis. Utlänningsnämndens och regeringens beslut. 1995 års utgåva i urval*. Gothenburg: Publica.

Westin, Charles. 1989. *Tortyr och Existens*. Gothenburg: Korpen.

Wikrén, Gerhard, and Sandesjö, Håkan. 1995. *Utlänningslagen med kommentarer*. Gothenburg: Publica.

Approaches to the study of exile and traumatization

Charles Westin

This article consists of three parts. The first section looks from a macroperspective at the refugee emergencies and mass flight situations that have struck Europe since the collapse of Yugoslavia, and that have haunted Africa for many decades. The second part exemplifies the traumatic reaction of a young woman who was victim of the expulsion of the Asian community in Uganda in the early 1970s. It puts the resettlement process in Sweden of Ugandan Asians in context. In the third section, a closer look is taken at the symbolism that is invoked by political violence, torture and the gross violation of people's integrity.

Refugee-producing conditions

In May 1999, Serbian forces were driving Albanians out of Kosovo. Hundreds of thousands of Albanians crossed the borders to Albania and Macedonia. Persistent reports appear of mass executions and systematic rape of which Serbian forces are said to be guilty. Nobody knows how many Albanians are displaced in Kosovo itself. The United Nations has been unable to act resolutely to put an end to the crisis. In this situation NATO (North Atlantic Treaty Organization) stepped in with the intention of making Serbian forces retreat from Kosovo by targeted air raids against military installations in Yugoslavia. The NATO strategy, however, has not brought about the expected results. Instead of putting an end to the ethnic cleansing policies, the NATO strategy has rather reinforced them.

In the complex Yugoslav ethnic mosaic, the province of Kosovo is special in the sense of being clearly bi-ethnic – Albanian (90%) and Serbian (10%). The Kosovo emergency is a clear case of systematic ethnic cleansing, the objective being to turn Kosovo into an ethnically Serbian province. The Yugoslav government, supported by a vast majority of the Serbian people, have no intention of ceding Kosovo, or of granting the province greater autonomy under its Albanian majority. In Serbian national mythology Kosovo is the heartland and cradle of Serbia. It is non-negotiable territory.

The refugee situations in sub-Saharan Africa and Europe have differed in many respects. On the whole, the number of refugees has been considerably larger in Africa for a much longer period of time. Moreover, the conflict hotbeds generating refugee movements and massive displacements are spread over virtually the whole of the continent, whereas in Europe the post-war conflicts have been confined to specific regions. During the Cold War it was the border regions between NATO and the Warsaw Pact (Hungary, Czechoslovakia, Poland) from which refugee movements emanated. Since then the regions of crisis have been located in the Balkans, primarily the former Yugoslavia, and the Caucasus. The causes of mass flight situations, however, are pretty much the same. It is about violations of human rights on a massive scale, ethnic cleansing, breakdown of the state and internal conflict.

At the core of the international refugee phenomenon is a basic asymmetry of power relationships. The Declaration of Human Rights pertains to individuals. When human rights are violated, the victims are individual human beings. Perpetrators are also individuals. The Nuremburg trials established that those found guilty of crimes against humanity are personally responsible for these offences and hence liable to punishment even in cases where the offender *only* followed orders issued by superior commanding officers. On the other hand, when we are speaking about violations of human rights it is also important to note that perpetrators act as *representatives of the state*, or of some organization or body controlled by the state. The conditions that produce massive displacements and refugee flows are invariably situations in which individuals are wronged by collectives, where the collective in most cases is the state, some of its bodies or organizations supported by the state. However, the OAU (Organization of African Unity) definition of refugees also recognizes non-state actors as perpetrators giving rise to legitimate refugee status.

To deal with large refugee flows is a major task facing the international community today. According to the "Protocol relating to the Status of Refugees", which modifies and generalizes the 1951 Geneva Convention, a refugee is basically defined as a person who

> ... owing to a well-founded fear of being persecuted for reasons of race, religion, nationality, membership of a particular social group, or political opinion, is outside the country of his nationality, and is unable to or, owing to such fear, is unwilling to avail himself of the protection of that country.

Most of the world's refugees and displaced persons are found in Africa and Asia, and, more recently, since the wars in the former Yugoslavia and the conflicts in the Caucasus region, also in Europe. The vast majority of the fifty million refugees and displaced persons are either within their country of origin or have crossed the border into a neighbouring country. A smaller share have made their way to a third country within the region. In relation to the magnitude of the global refugee population, the numbers who have sought refuge in other continents appear almost insignificant. In Africa more than nine million are seeking refuge, mainly in neighbouring countries. Close to eight million refugees are of Asian origin, and approximately eight million refugees are of European origin.

To understand the current international discourse on refugees, we need to look back to the European post World War II years. The charter of the United Nations was drawn up, the Declaration of Human Rights was written, and Europe was burdened by tens of millions of displaced persons, many of whom were stateless, released concentration camp victims and slave labour who had been forced to work for the Nazi war production schemes, and people who were forced to abandon their homes because of border changes – Germans, Poles, Finns, Hungarians, Romanians and many others. It was well into the 1950s before the problem of the many displaced, stateless and homeless victims of World War II eventually sorted itself out through the persistent work of the UNHCR (United Nations High Commissioner for Refugees).

As a result of the talks at Yalta and Potsdam in 1945 concerning the political outcome of World War II, the boundaries between the Soviet Union and several central European states were redrawn. Within less than a year after the conclusion of the war, friction between the Western powers and the Soviet Union developed into a major rift. This created a new refugee context of people escaping from the Communist-run countries. Initially there were passages through the Iron Curtain. In time, however, they were closed one by one. During the early stages of the Cold War, Western Europe was generously committed to refugee reception. It was only natural in view of the horrors, forced displacement and genocide that had taken place during World War II. This attitude was possible because the number of refugees escaping from Eastern Europe was small. It was hard to get out of the Communist countries. Borders, airports and communications were rigorously controlled. Those who did manage to reach the West were automatically granted asylum.

On rare occasions, certain borders to the West opened up temporarily. In 1956, two hundred thousand Hungarians fled when the Soviet Union put down the freedom movement. A similar outflow of refugees took place from Czechoslovakia in 1968 when the Soviet forces put an end to the liberal reform policies initiated by the Czech leadership. Then again, after the 1981 *coup d'état* in Poland temporarily putting a stop to Solidarity, a new wave of refugees made their way to Western countries. For most of this period it was easier for Yugoslav dissidents to escape to the West because Yugoslavia was never controlled by the Soviet Union. As from the mid-1960s, the government of Yugoslavia encouraged labour migration to Western countries as a way of coping with the country's economic problems.

Since most countries of Western Europe accepted large intakes of manpower from peripheral regions of Europe and former colonies at this time, the small trickle of refugees was treated within the general labour migration framework. Repatriation was out of the question. Integration into first countries of asylum was sometimes an option. Resettlement into a third country was normally the most favoured solution. A primary objective of the UNHCR was to work out durable solutions to the refugee problem that had been overshadowing Europe.

In European migration history, the early 1970s represent a turning point. Labour migration was stopped almost simultaneously in all of Western Europe at the same time as refugees from Third World countries started to appear in Europe. The first Third World refugee emergency to affect Western Europe was the expulsion of the 70,000 Ugandan Asians in 1972. A year later, the *coup d'état* against the Allende regime launched a flow of asylum seekers to Europe from Chile. A few years later again, people, many of whom were of Chinese ethnic origin, fearing the Communist takeover in Vietnam in 1975 fled in overcrowded vessels to Hong Kong, Thailand, Malaysia and Singapore. During the 1970s there was, moreover, a trickle of asylum seekers who came by their own steam from the Middle East. Many were Kurds, some were Syrian Christians.

Asylum seekers from Third World countries that were not too distant geographically (the Middle East) or culturally (South America) thus began to find their way to Western Europe. At this time, that is to say the 1970s, the numbers reaching Europe were still small and the receiving countries could handle the situation quite easily. As immigrant communities were gradually established in the receiving countries, networks between the receiving and sending countries evolved. Inevitably, as a logical consequence of the migration network dynamics, family reunifications started to increase during the early 1980s.

The frozen East–West divide came to an unexpected end in 1989, when all Moscow-controlled puppet regimes in Europe had been replaced. Two years later the Soviet Union itself collapsed. Its former republics claimed independence and international recognition. Unfortunately, the prospects of future peaceful coexistence in Europe were soon thwarted by reports of brewing conflict in the Caucasus region and Yugoslavia.

The Yugoslav wars have led to a wave of refugees seeking asylum outside the war zones. The number of asylum seekers is constantly increasing. Despite the well-documented atrocities involved in the *ethnic cleansing policies*, a majority of the displaced Bosnians and later the hundreds of thousands of Kosova Albanians are not officially regarded as convention refugees. The majority of them have fled from *generalized violence* due to ethnic conflict (Dacyl 1996) rather than from individualized persecution for the five reasons stipulated in the

1951 Geneva Convention. This implies that they lack the formal legal grounds to be entitled to the same level of protection from the international community as convention refugees.

The European scene was dominated for more than forty years by the stalemate of the Cold War and in the following years by ethnic conflicts in ex-Yugoslavia and the Caucasus. During the same period, Africa, on the other hand, has undergone a difficult transformation from a colonial order characterized by authoritarian European minority rule in practically every country to political independence and African majority rule. By and large, the theoretical, political and legal discourse on refugees has been fashioned by the European experiences, and more specifically by the early post-war/Cold War period,[1] not by the African or Asian experiences.

One cannot really discuss trends in refugee policy that apply to the African situation without saying something about the historical, social and political context. The extraordinarily large flows of refugees in sub-Saharan Africa have been triggered by a combination of factors relating to environmental conditions, demographic structure and population development, economic resources and ethnopolitical conflicts. The desertation of the Sahel belt in the interior of western Africa, caused by overgrazing, population increase and a series of severe droughts, has given rise to an increasing migration pressure towards the coastal regions in the west and south. Environmental refugees are projected to increase in numbers throughout Africa in the foreseeable future. During the most recent decades, however, the really large flows of refugees have been sparked off by ethnic and political conflict, initially between liberation movements and colonial powers, and thereafter between different ethnopolitical factions *within* the boundaries of given states. Only a few instances of controversy have led to a state of armed conflict or war *between* states.

Practically all sub-Saharan state boundaries are artificial in the sense that they do not coincide with ethnic, cultural, linguistic, religious or national groupings that have developed out of Africa's own historical experiences.[2] These boundaries are at the same time *permeable*, people cross them back and forth without being intercepted by border control authorities, and *permanent* in the sense that no state is prepared to voluntarily concede part of its sovereign territory to a neighbouring state in order to create ethnic, linguistic or national homogeneity. Most states, then, are multiethnic. Boundaries divide one and the same ethnic community between different states but also place different ethnic groups together within the confines of one multiethnic state formation.

In the African context, each new outburst of ethnic violence and each *coup d'état* has tended to bring out even greater numbers of displaced persons than in previous crises. In round figures, the refugee flows of the 1960s were of a magnitude of tens of thousands of persons. By the 1970s the volumes had risen to hundreds of thousands, and since the 1980s we are speaking literally about millions.[3]

Basically there have been three approaches to dealing with refugee influxes: settlement in the first country of asylum, resettlement in a third country (second country of reception), and voluntary repatriation. Some refugees move through all three positions. For African refugees, resettlement overseas has seldom been an option (Oucho 1996) but even resettlement in third countries within the region is unusual. Settlement in the first country of asylum or repatriation have been the available solutions. Local populations in receiving countries have shown remarkable signs of tolerance and solidarity with fleeing victims of colonial oppression in earlier decades and of ethnopolitical violence in the most recent ones. One explanation for this is that state borders do not coincide with the much older ethnic and tribal boundaries. Refugees from one country will be treated kindly by ethnic or tribal compatriots on the other side of the border. So while the deviation of state boundaries from ethnocultural boundaries is part of the problem, it has as yet also been part of the solution.

The refugee problem in Africa has reached such proportions that it may only be solved through the concerted efforts of the international community. The only realistic long-term approach seems to be to address the root causes of the conflicts and conditions that generate refugee flows, and then to find appropriate solutions to them. This requires rethinking the entire problem. In the final analysis it means coming to grips with the problems of democratization, equality, justice, rule of law, and economic development. It will have to involve the implementation of literacy and civic education programmes, and, in a more utopian vein, devising institutionalized

64

forms of dealing with ethnic or tribal conflict. The efforts of the international community need to be directed towards finding diplomatic solutions to acute conflicts, and in the long term securing peaceful coexistence between conflicting factions and groups. Finding solutions to the refugee crisis, then, will involve much more than finding ways to handle refugee flows once they are on the move, or of directing aid to concentrations of refugees.

Traces of ethnic cleansing in the mind of a young woman: A case study of expulsion and resettlement

This section shifts the perspective from the macro to the micro. I will recapitulate the story of a young Asian woman as she related to me her traumatic experiences resulting from the expulsion of the Ugandan Asians in 1972 and her involuntary exile in Sweden. Her story, however, needs to be put in context.

Uganda is a country of central Africa that since the 1960s has experienced decades of political turmoil, internal warfare and refugee emergencies. The territory of present-day Uganda was taken by the British as a colony in 1890. It included several kingdoms. The most powerful kingdom was Buganda on the northern shores of Lake Victoria. The British turned the territory into one administrative unit, arrogantly naming it *U*ganda. At an early stage, Indians from Punjab were brought to British East Africa as indentured labourers. In the wake of this manpower migration traders from Gujarat moved in and settled in the colony. While the British were in political control and also controlled the land, the *Asian* community, as it was termed, gradually assumed control over trade and the economy.

African majority rule under Milton Obote succeeded the British when Uganda gained political independence in 1962. Members of the Asian community were given the option of becoming citizens of Uganda, or of maintaining their status as British protected persons. Many of the Ugandan Asians had worried about their position as a minority when Uganda gained political independence. Initially the transition of power, however, did not affect the Asian community negatively. After some time the Asian leaders felt more relaxed about the situation.

In 1971, Idi Amin seized power in a military coup. At first the Asians welcomed the fall of Obote because they were concerned about the socialist course pursued by the Obote regime. One year later, Amin announced that people of Asian origin would have to leave the country within three months. Amin's declaration came as a surprise to most Asians. Some, of course, had been aware of the coming crisis and had moved their economic assets out of the country. Amin's motives were to secure African control over the economy. By scapegoating the Asian community he could divert attention from the brewing conflicts between the many divisions of the African majority population. Nation-building and state formation was, and still is, extremely complicated in Uganda because of its many complex divisions – ethnic, linguistic, religious, cultural and historical. The expulsion of the Asian community was a clear case of ethnic cleansing, although the term had not been invented at the time.

Practically the entire Asian community of 70,000 persons was forced to leave Uganda before the three-month deadline was up. British-protected persons, about half of the community, were accepted by the United Kingdom. The other half, citizens of Uganda, were deprived of their passports and made stateless. People had to abandon their homes and leave material possessions behind. Jewellery, bank books and money that some had managed to scramble together and bring along were stolen at military checkpoints. The maltreatment and abuse that some suffered at the hands of Ugandan military forces, the loss of friends and material possessions, the splitting of families, and the insecurity of the future was something that most individuals and families went through. Internationally organized airlifts transported the Asians to UNHCR-run refugee camps in Europe, and from there they were dispersed to various *third countries* for resettlement. Neighbouring countries had refused to accept the Asians, and repatriation was out of the question. Some 800 stateless Asians from Uganda eventually ended up in Sweden.

In the resettlement camps in Sweden, the Asians had to start their lives from scratch. They were subjected to a standardized treatment and confronted with uniform demands. They were taken care of by the authorities to such an all-encompassing extent that they were more or less deprived of their sense of agency. There was little they could do to influence their situation. They were forced into a state of collective submission, of being treated as "patients", of being out of control. In this sense, then, the reception programme mirrored the expulsion programme.

The Asians whom I have followed over the years reacted in individually rather different ways to the trauma of expulsion. The ways of coping with the trauma interfered with the task of establishing a life in the new society. Still very much in a state of shock, most people seemed to passively accept the "treatment" they were subjected to. Others were more self-reliant and tried to set out on their own, although not always successfully. Still others used a more systematic and goal-oriented strategy of trying to learn the subtle rules that apply in Swedish society by identifying the "hidden script". A fourth category represents those who were really desperate, persons who had been unable to cope on a personal level with the stress and strain of the past months, and the traumatic loss, not only of a way of life but of an entire community.

To shed some light upon personal problems of adjustment after a process of ethnic cleansing, I will quote from a lengthy conversation with a young woman finding herself in a serious psychological crisis. Only a few people could voice troubles as serious as the ones she describes. The point is, however, that her story captures qualities of the mental experiences that most of the expelled Asians suffered, although very few of them actually lost touch with reality. I have edited her story and altered the factual points.

> When I went to Älmhult I was quite alone. I was educated and I had always had time to do things. In Uganda I used to teach. I am a very active type of girl. I always like some sort of mission in life. When I went to Älmhult, suddenly, for the first time I used to feel very depressed. I used to sit alone and I used to cry too much and I went many times to the labour exchange to get a job, but they strictly told me that I could never get a job until two years, not even in a factory. And he just behaved very rudely to us. I tried to convince him but I couldn't convince him. He just used to joke and that's all. And finish off as if, you see, it was not his job to give us jobs. It was as if he was a man who is having his own land where I went to ask him to give me some sort of fruit. But he didn't want

it, and I think that many people started hating us Asian people. They told first of all that there is no value of education in Sweden. You must not continue your education in university, you must take some sort of training.

And then I delivered my child and then I brought my child home. Then, suddenly, you see, the depression became so extreme. I was sitting at home, and I felt as if my legs were shivering, and I started hating my child and I started hating everyone. I became so afraid that I was in great danger. Someone must protect me, and I wanted to see people because I didn't see so many people in Älmhult. I never saw anyone. I was so afraid and scared that I went running to my husband. I told him you must stand and do something because something very wrong is happening to me. It's becoming more and more wrong. I'm in danger. And I was telling him to please hold me very tightly. And he held me, but even then I felt that something was running from me. Someone, my own self was running away from me. My own self didn't want to talk to me, and then I wanted myself and then I ran to see myself in the mirror that I was still the same. There was nothing changed, but then I felt there was something changed in my mind. I couldn't sit or stand. I was so anxious that I ran to the window and then I ran to another place and then I ran. I was going running because I thought that something was running away from me. And then suddenly at night I went to sleep. And I became so sick. I felt as if my breath was being stopped. And at once the first idea came that now death is coming to me. And I asked my husband to ring for the ambulance at once. I thought that the oxygen was finished in me. And I need oxygen. He was so nervous and my baby was crying too much, my child daughter. I didn't give her milk that night I remember. Then I went and rang the ambulance myself. The ambulance came and when they picked up my stretcher I really thought that this is my coffin which I am going on. It's only that my eyes are open, that's why I can see everything, otherwise I am dead. When they took me to the hospital the doctor checked me and he told me that everything was all right, but that I was afraid. And, you know, suddenly I was changed and I was happy. In one minute I stood up. I had a little fever, and then they wanted to give me a sleeping tablet, but I didn't want the sleeping tablet because I thought that my brain was going to be stopped, and I told them that I didn't want a sleeping tablet because I am going to die.

I wanted someone to stand near me, two-three people, because I wanted to see people, that was my only interest now. I didn't want the light off. I wanted too much light in my room. And I wanted contact with the people. I must see people coming and going. I didn't want my room to be empty without nurses. I thought I was going to die or I was in danger.

I was kept there for eight days and I came back home at twelve o'clock in the morning. But suddenly in the evening at four o'clock I felt again that depression, and then I took my baby and myself to my one friend and I didn't tell my husband. He realized that something was wrong but he didn't stop me. If you like you can go to your friend he said, and I went to sleep in her house because I wanted to see the people, many people. And I slept in her house, but at night at two o'clock it felt as if my hands were dying very badly. And my heart was sinking down and down. I felt as if someone was putting me down in a well, in a very dark well. And I started shouting. I shouted calling to my friend to please come quickly and go and call to my husband because something is again happening to me. He came and he was so disappointed, but he started talking to me and he was talking and talking and talking until I became a bit better. But then it started attacking me again and again until I had to come to the hospital and they told me that I was scared of something.

I stayed nearly for one month or more than one month, it was nearly two months. It was a hospital where mothers, women who deliver children, can go and rest. And I stayed there for one month but I was so sick there that I couldn't eat. I forgot to talk my own language. I forgot to talk the Swedish language. I forgot all my teachings. My mind was so paralysed that I couldn't think anything. I thought that now life is beginning. I am nearly twenty-three years old, why am I so old when I am beginning my life? It felt as if I was sixty, seventy or eighty years old. I felt very old because I knew that I was dying. I wanted to be very small. But the main thought in my mind was that my hands were dying. Whenever I had an attack the only attack was in my hands. Someone had either cut my hands or my hands were dying. And I think it was unconsciously because I had no work and nobody recognized my abilities. And unconsciously I felt that my hands could not do anything. And I really felt something in my hands, you know, the blood circulation. I could hear the sound of blood circulation. My blood pressure was very low, and my hands became so cold that I wanted to cut my hands to feel that they were not dead. I wanted someone to press my hands very hard, my hands, because I thought they are not my hands. They became strangers for me. I used to lick them all the time, I used to press my fingers by opening and closing my hands. Whenever I looked at my hand my husband used to hold my hand at once and say, don't look at your hands, and he used to hide my hands. Then I started looking at other things. I wanted to avoid my hands. I worked so hard, so hard you know, until I controlled this feeling of my hand. But one thing entered in me. I felt that I had become very old. I was always crying. I was crying for happiness because I was never happy. I felt so sorry. Why am I in this world?

I thought it was very good for me to transfer to Växjö because I could see some people. And if I have some friends, they come to my house. I would forget my disease. I knew that I was not well. My heart is crying, but I am not nervous. But when they go away, suddenly I feel that at once I am changed. It was like two colours, black and white, as if they are changed at once. I became black. So I came to Växjö and I tried to improve myself. I felt that I was not nervous but I was always crying. I have been crying too much. I have been crying whenever I see the face of any woman, or man, I just think that I must cry. I just see the face and I start crying. Because I wanted that they should say, you are not in danger. I thought that someone was attacking me. I think it might be because the people didn't treat us well, like the man at the labour exchange, like many people. There was always this fight. When I was sick there was really a fight between two personalities. One was very angry with me, and said that you are insulting me, you are disgracing me. The other was saying that you have nothing. Look at your hands. Your hands are dying. The other was making me very scared of many things, especially the other personality was laughing at me. You have come to Sweden and what did you do? You have got your certificates and everything and nobody wants to talk to you.

And then I improved my health, but slowly, slowly. I started avoiding that whether you are young or you are old. It's nothing to do with me. I could control it after a long time. When I am crying, suddenly I just close my mouth, or I start talking to anything, to the wall or to someone else. Or I start opening the book, or I start jumping or I start running to avoid this mental thing. I controlled it too much. But only now I still become sad sometimes for all that ever happened. I become so sad and only then I feel like crying. This is not finished and I feel only alone, and I think that I have now confidence that I will do something, because then I made a mission against those people who are not treating us well. And that made my mind change, that you have something to do. And my hands started working.

When I was sick in Växjö I started hiding from everyone, even from my husband because then I didn't want them to say that I was nervous or mentally sick because it was a great wound to my personality, to my pride. I started crying, because crying was my only interest. That was my last certificate of my own personality that I could show them. That was the only thing left in me. I felt very happy when I was crying because I hadn't been able to cry for some time. I was so shocked. So I feel when I am crying, I feel that I really have something, some ability.

Suddenly one night I changed. I slept well the whole night and I slept for many days. The thing which was running away from me slowly, slowly came to me. My shadow came back to me. I felt that it is not me who wanted to come in me but it is my own personality, she wants to come back to me. Now she is attracted because she knows I have some treasure. So I thought that I was standing now, slowly, slowly and slowly I started going too much outside, meeting people. The blood is very hot in me, warming me, and I wanted to run too much, because I was paralysed for a long time. I couldn't walk mentally. I often met Lisa Larsson. I feel that someone is giving me a shield. I am being attacked but there are many shields like Lisa. And I thought that now I will not die alone.

I don't like cities where there are very few people. I have no interest in the beauty of the city. I am only interested in people, in a crowd of people. Älmhult is a very small city, but I didn't understand that, because in Uganda even in very small cities there were so many people and we had social life. When I was sick I thought that Älmhult and the whole of Sweden is a graveyard. People are so quiet. They never laugh and I thought they never talk. And I thought they are always sad. I thought the people are very slow. Whenever I passed by a graveyard, I always used to find my grave because the idea of death really entered in me as a truth. I accepted it as a truth. I talked too much to Lisa. I wanted to know that it hasn't only happened to me. I wanted to know that it did happen to others. And the doctors and Lisa said, yes it has happened to others also. Then I used to take a breath, that thank God, it happened to everyone.

Now I feel I have got an experience of life and that even a strong personality can lose the strength. A bird in a cave cannot fly. I think that bird might lose its ability to fly. I was brainwashed. All the time in Älmhult I was brainwashed by sitting all alone. I saw everything. I saw my hands. I saw my abilities day and night but I saw nothing that I can apply all these things to. I think it was only that I was brainwashed very strongly by a deep silence. Just imagine that you are given a telephone and you have this telephone connection with whole world and you are locked in a room. Day and night you ring everywhere. The phone gives the connecting tone but there is no answer.

I will not dwell upon the psychiatric aspects of this case. But we may note that the crisis this young woman experienced was probably due to the fact that she suppressed the trauma of the ethnic cleansing and expulsion and the grief it brought to her. Others did not deny the trauma and the grief they felt. They suffered too. I have made a point of telling her story because the extremes of her crisis make the experiences everyone went through more comprehensible and tangible. One conspicuous fact is that hardly any Swedes with whom the Asians were in touch were prepared to listen to them and to try to understand the existential problems brought about by the ethnic cleansing, expulsion, flight and resettlement in an alien society.

There are at least six themes running through the young woman's story: the trauma of the expulsion; the feeling of not having her capabilities recognized, the loss of worth, and of being denied her dignity; loneliness, silence, and a linguistic isolation; the loss of traditional female support in childbirth; the manifestation of somatic reactions to the mental stress; finally, as a hint in passing, stigmatization by skin colour.

The fact is that the woman's story pertains to essential determinants of identity: basic trust; a sense of competence, ability, and dignity; a sense of coping with one's life conditions; and a sense of community with others. She touches upon aspects of identity that are internally defined by herself as well as those externally defined by others, thus being moored in society and culture. She points to existential problems affecting all of the refugees, although they may not have talked freely about them to Swedes or amongst themselves. By now it is a rather hackneyed phrase, frequently employed as an explanation though not necessarily meaning a thing, to refer to events such as these in terms of culture conflict. Yet, this is what it was all about. People's subjective identity, for the Asians having been shaped within their communities in Uganda, was simply not compatible with the external definition imposed upon them in their exile in Sweden. Though carried out with the best of intentions, the reception and resettlement programmes continued, and even reinforced, the personal crises produced by the expulsion. Meeting her many years later, it is obvious that this young woman found it extremely difficult to overcome her traumatic experiences. She has been haunted by memories of the past over the years in Sweden. She has not been able to come to terms with her fate.

For most of the Asians it was not until one had regained one's sense of agency that Swedish society took the shape of a possible setting for their futures. A first test occurred in 1979 when Idi Amin was overthrown by Tanzanian forces and had to flee himself. Ugandan Asians in third-country exile were faced with the question of whether return was possible. Due to the chaotic political situation and internal conflicts that were to last another seven years, the Asians in Sweden realized that return was impossible. After Yoweri Museweni seized power in 1986, and law and order were gradually restored, the question of return arose again. Some families did eventually *resettle* in Uganda, but there was of course no Asian community to *return* to. Those who did venture back to Uganda had to start again from scratch.

Most of the Ugandan Asian refugees recognized that life would be much safer in Sweden than in Uganda. For many years, they felt secure in Sweden. For a majority, the traumatic experiences brought about by the expulsion gradually faded in significance. In 1993, however, the awakening was painful. The mosque that Ugandan Asians had established in the town of Trollhättan was burnt down by racist activists. So even the Asians have become the targeted victims of fanatic neo-Nazi organisations. The increase of racist actions and the spread of xenophobia in Sweden is reawakening a sense of fear that the Ugandan Asians experienced during the ethnic cleansing crisis in 1972, but couldn't dream they would have to re-experience after twenty years of exile in the "safe" haven of Sweden.

There is virtually always a traumatic side to involuntary exile. On the whole, the Ugandan Asians who were expelled seem to have fared reasonably well. They were soon in the hands of UNHCR, and they were accepted as refugees in quite a few Western countries. Moreover, they were linked up with influential international networks connecting Indian and Pakistani diasporas in other parts of East Africa, the United Kingdom, various European countries, the United States and Canada with the Indian subcontinent. The Ugandan Asians are a good example – if ever there was one – of a transnational minority. Once the acute phase of resettlement was over, the networks could be utilized for a range of purposes – business, marriage partners, cultural needs etc. These support systems undoubtedly made the exile somewhat easier for a majority of the Asians. Food supplies, books, films, clothing items and various other cultural necessities could be imported and distributed within a short time. For some persons, as in the example above, the uprooting from the country in which they had been born and raised was extremely painful. These painful memories were not fundamentally relieved by the gradual establishment of an organizational and semi-political infrastructure for the (Ugandan) Asian communities in Sweden. Some people were entirely at a loss, their self-identity shattered by the exile forced upon them. The meaning of their lives seemed to have been taken away from them. The point that I want to make is that even for people who were not abused physically, who were not imprisoned, and who did not lose family members, the memories of ethnic cleansing, expulsion and exile were still a heavy load.

The human body: Central dimensions
of extreme traumatization

The young woman whose story I have quoted in the previous section points out how she felt that her hands were withering away, and how she felt that her body was ageing at a very rapid pace. She understood the symbolic significance of these experiences. In this section, I will explore further effects of traumatization on the body and identity of refugees. To do so I will examine a most extreme example of abuse, maltreatment and asymmetric power relations, but not in terms of the PTSD (post-traumatic stress disorder) discourse. Instead I will approach the question from a social psychological and existential point of departure. How should the really gross violations of personal integrity in *torture* be understood to affect identity? What are their somatic correlates?

Swedish doctors, conducting routine medical examinations of refugees from South America and the Middle East in the mid-1980s, estimated that approximately one fourth of the refugees then accepted in Sweden were victims of torture, or had been subjected to political violence aimed to abuse and degrade them (Amnesty International 1984). I do not know how the doctors arrived at this estimate, and with the benefit of hindsight I believe today that the estimate should be questioned. However, at the time it was generally accepted. If only five percent of the refugees were torture victims, the total numbers would still be high. This, however, is not the issue here. First, some words need to be said about the phenomenon of torture.

Torture is an interrogation staged by officials normally backed up by the authorities in power: the security police, intelligence agencies or specially assigned units placed under the direct control of the political and military leadership of the state. It is an interrogation in which the detainee is subjected to extreme physical pain and extreme psychological abuse. Quite frequently interrogation in torture is made to resemble a judicial trial. However, as we know torture parodies a legal examination of the facts. It ridicules basic values pertaining to human rights. Yet it is deadly serious. In war, or in an acute political crisis in which the very foundations of the legitimate political system are believed to be at stake, torture will undoubtedly be resorted to even by democratic states if the security of the state is believed to be secured by information extracted in torture.

People who have been subjected to torture, isolation and other forms of extreme stress, brutality and abuse in political oppression are (normally) understood to be severely traumatized. They present a set of symptoms which are difficult to treat within the regular public health services. At the same time, however, it is evident that some victims manage to lead normal lives after their ordeals. Little is known about what factors help them to cope with their traumatic experiences. Little is known about the long-term effects of torture.

Mental and physical wounds resulting from torture are the seque-lae of the, conceivably, most extreme violation of human integrity. A drastic psychological defence that may come into force is a dissociation of the body from the mind on a symbolic level. This rift between body and mind seems to continue in some victims for years after the ordeal. Various symptoms may be understood as outcomes of this defence. Chronic pain lacking identifiable physiological foundation and problems of muscular coordination represent elements of a somatic language in which the body makes its existence known in an effort to bridge the rift to the mind.

Clearly torture is about pain, but it is also about violation, humiliation, abuse, insecurity, suspense, isolation, unpredictability, deprivation and endless ways of breaking people's minds. Mental torture denotes a wide range of psychologically devised techniques employed to derange the victim's mind. Subjecting people to sensory deprivation, or to sensory hyperstimulation, is known to bring out hallucinations and a loss of one's sense of reality. Forcing the victim to witness the physical torture of others with the explicit instruction that his answers will determine whether the treatment will be discontinued or not usually gives rise to overwhelming feelings of guilt and a mistaken sense of responsibility for the sufferings of the other. Subjecting the victim to grossly abusive treatment, in which one common denominator is the penetration of the body, and thus of the physically tight boundaries of personal integrity, is another element of mental torture. The bodily apertures – the mouth, the anus, the genitals, the ears and the eyes – are particularly exposed regions of penetration. The most painful experience of all, according to recurrent testimonies, is the mock execution. Having prepared oneself for one's imminent death – which then does not set in – means being thrust into an agonizing and confusing existential void. Here, the basic fabric of the mind and identity is penetrated.

The mind and the body cannot, and should not, be regarded as separate entities. They are facets of the same totality – the human being. The pain one experiences when electric current is led through the body sets off a physiological course of events affecting the peripheral as well as the central nervous system. The individual also reacts psychologically to the violating treatment with a number of emotions – insufficiency, fear, despair, shame, aggression, guilt, and anxiety. Against the devastating feeling of anguish, and against the overwhelming feeling of powerlessness, psychological defences are mobilized. In turn, these defences give rise to mental attitudes having repercussions on self-conceptions and identity, as well as on bodily carriage.

An overall perspective is necessary. But what does it imply? How does one bridge the dualism of the body and the mind, impressing our manner of thought, and again founding the subdivision of disciplines and professional fields? Two courses of analysis exist, both of which have to be entered; setting out from the body and moving towards the mind, and thereafter, moving from the mind back towards the body again. The concept of individual identity is a crucial tool if we are ever to understand what traumatization is about.

Few concepts in the behavioural and social sciences have proven to be as fruitful as identity. The concept enables us to coordinate a large number of apparently different phenomena studied by widely disparate fields of scholarship. Identity deals with a range of matters from in-depth psychological studies to anthropological inquiries into cultures and societies. The price for this conceptual span, however, is a certain vagueness and lack of theoretical precision. Identity is dissected into a variety of subdivisions and constituent parts. Various aspects of the concept are distinguished. Various perspectives of analysis are presented. Less frequently, in comparison, are the parts recombined into models representing identity as a dynamic process.

How does the serious violation in torture affect the individual victim's identity? In order to answer this question we need an idea of what identity accomplishes and how it operates. We need to assemble its various parts. Identity is a process, I contend. If the acts of violation to which a victim of torture is subjected impairs his identity, then these violations will have reverberations long after the acts themselves took place. We need a metaphor which may provide us with an inkling of what identity is about and how it operates.

Identity may be conceived of as an instance in which consciousness generates propositions telling me (and others) who I am, who I perceive the other to be, what I perceive her/him to believe about me, what (s)he thinks I believe about her/his conception of me, what I believe (s)he believes I believe. In a metaphorical sense, then, identity may be conceived of as a "grammar" – as clauses which structure its elements in some order. It should be possible to distinguish between a surface structure of identity in terms of markers, impression management, identity administration and negotiations on the one hand, and the deep structure pertaining to basic drives such as sexuality and the need for distinctiveness on the other hand.

The interesting though seldom discussed concept of *idential* was proposed by the Dutch psychiatrist David de Levita (1965). This concept alludes to all those identifying particulars in an individual that may be an identity to him and for him. One might put it that the identials are the stuff or material of identity. We recognize three kinds of identials. *Intentionally attained identials* pertain to membership in groups, collectives, and organizations. Formal and well-established organizations, which have arisen in response to needs, wants, and demands in society, come to mind, but also more casual attachments, temporary whims of fashion that vanish as quickly as they appeared.

Intentionally acquired identials are usually bound to supplementary roles constituting the structure of interaction. One of the roles in a constellation simultaneously presupposes and determines the other – husband and wife, teacher and pupil, parent and child, superior and subordinate. In normal everyday life, the supplementary elements of roles may be subtle. A person develops social skills in relating to others and handling novel social situations. Subjective identity always depends upon the direct or indirect confirmation of others.

The *unintentionally ascribed identials* pertain to sex and gender, date of birth, ethnicity, and skin colour. Sometimes religion and social class count in this category as well. Even names may be regarded as unintentionally ascribed identials. In other words, these are the given categories with which an individual is furnished at birth, and can do very little to change. These categories are crucial with regard to self-definitions and definitions of the other.

Identials, then, refer to a series of structural properties and roles.

They refer to what is essential, and to what is beneath or behind the presented or apparent being. They pertain to the substantive, not to say the substantial aspects of being with roots in the deep structure. These identials are the stuff and material of identity. In other words, we may refer to them as the "substantives" or "nouns" of identity. They constitute identity's kinds and categories. They pertain to its contents.

We may also distinguish "adjectives", "pronouns" and "verbs" of identity. The adjectives relate to the contents of identity too, but in a descriptive, and, above all, in an evaluative sense. A *positive* self conception, a *sound* self-confidence, a *secure* identity, along with their polar opposites, are familiar examples. The "verbs" of identity refer to the processing aspects of identity. Every individual shows unmistakable and distinguishing physical traits in facial features, bodily structure, and voice. The human body develops and ages. It changes with time. Yet the individual "gestalt" remains. The unique configuration of traits transcends the ageing processes. The same applies to identity. A unique configuration of self-determinations has a continuity withstanding the ravages of time. Statements about somebody's identity, whether self-definitions or definitions imposed by others, make use of practically any verb. What I suggest, however, is that literal statements of identity in ordinary language may be rephrased in clauses using one of the three crucial identity verbs; to be, to have, and to do.

The first verb – *to be* – applies to temporal relations. It subsumes the totality of memories of the past and intentions directed towards the future. The verb *to have* pertains to spatial relations and to processes of externalizing and internalizing identities in interactions with the social and material worlds. The verb *to do* concerns the relations of movement and action. It is the category of the body. Continuity and change throughout the course of a person's life, tensions between the internal and external fixed points of identity in interaction, and transcending and creative actions are the very foundations of existence and identity. Time, space and action, then, are basic dimensions of identity.

What does the verb *to have* imply? Superficially it suggests owning, possessing, and claiming. In a deeper sense it is the category related to the subsistence and continuity of life. Thus, *to have* represents everything that is necessary for life to have its course. It represents the externalization of identity in objects and things with which one surrounds oneself, in short, socio-matter. A number of things are invested with meaning especially significant to my identity. But I invest my identity in people close to me as well – family, kin, friends, colleagues, and antagonists. In this respect, a reciprocal, sometimes even a symbiotic, system of identity confirmations evolves.

One significant aspect of identity externalization applies to one's domicile. One's home is saturated with identity meaning. Its in-grained everyday objects, used and employed, represent root-fibres to the semi-conscious aspects of human existence, to stability and continuity. Various formal and informal social networks, bonds of friendship and neighbourhood relations make up local society. Recognition and casual contacts, continuously confirmed in mutual greetings, fuel identity externalization.

The physical surroundings – the well-known buildings and familiar streets – are points of fundamental importance when it comes to getting one's bearings and finding one's way through existence. The close scenery represents fixed bases in existence, serving as a background for memories and recapitulations of personal biography. External points of identity fixation materialize tradition and renewal. They bring out continuity across the generations. People interact with their material and social environment. They shape it, but are also fashioned by it in turn. They conquer the world at the same time as they are absorbed by it. In these processes society and culture are reproduced.

What does all this mean in the refugee context? The victims of torture are deprived of their physical and social environment. They are deprived of the last protective coat between their bodies and the torturer's implements. When the fixed external points are wrenched away, the internal ones are weakened. One consequence of being arrested, imprisoned and tortured is that survival becomes linked to flight and thereafter *exile*. The price is that much of the social fabric of identity is (temporarily) lost.

In normal circumstances of life, one has an approximate and intuitive idea about the span of remaining time allotted to oneself – granted that accidents or unforeseen events do not extinguish one's life suddenly without warning. Experiences of life, added on every day, are stored in memory and increase in importance. They constantly create new opportunities for identity. Some memories fade out and are replaced. Others maintain their luminosity throughout the years. The verb *to be* represents the fact that experiences lived through during the course of life are the constant subject of interpretation and reinterpretation. Personal biography is constantly rewritten. Being driven away from one's home and expelled from one's country, the victim of ethnic cleansing or torture, implies that the presence of death floods one's mind without any forewarning. It means that normal anticipation, long-term plans, and preparation for actions to be realized are lost within a short lapse of time. An intuitive feeling of the extension in time of one's future life-span is reduced from tens of years to a matter of days and hours, at the very worst stages, to minutes and seconds. The future is cut off. Pain, isolation and the complete indifference of the assailant, contribute to the fact that the victim's grasp of his past is undermined. Memories fade away.

What is the significance of the verb *to do*? It is the category of action and creativity. Life is a process in which a person moves out to the world and incorporates it. Identity is a lifelong activity and creative process. Actions affect, and are in turn affected by reflection, planning and considerations of means and objectives. Action is transcending. Identity is proved in action.

Torture is an extreme experience in which a person's agency and freedom of movement are restricted to the greatest possible extent. The victim is at the mercy of the other, effectively prevented from defending him- or herself through action. Only the psychological defences are inaccessible to the torturer. To steel oneself is to equip oneself symbolically with an armour of muscular tensions guarding the internal and vulnerable regions of the body. As this defence is gradually broken down, the defences are moved further in. One of the most devastating long-term effects of torture is ambivalence in action, to say, that is, to want one thing and at the same time to want the opposite, to commence upon a goal-directed action but to back out of it immediately.

Identity processes as described by the verbs *to have*, *to be* and *to do* represent transformations from the deep structure of drives and needs to the surface structure of identity matter and identity stuff. Torture is an attack directed against all levels of identity – the identials and interactional conditions of the surface structure, the drives and delineations of the deep structure, and the processes which transform the deep-down conditions to the surface where they become salient, apprehensible, and evident.

I have attempted to show how violations of personal integrity tatter and tear essential aspects of one's self conceptions and identity. Violation of integrity in torture is all-encompassing. It surpasses any other demeaning, degrading and humiliating treatment. There is not one value or symbol that it refrains from employing to insult, offend, or defame the victim. Not only are the acts of violation the deliberate destruction of individual identity, these acts undermine the identity process as a whole, that is to say, the "grammar" of piecing together the experiences of life to self-conceptions and self-definitions. The links between process and content are broken. The attacks directed against intentionally acquired identials have repercussions on the processes which deal with "having". The attacks upon intentionally attained identials injure the processes which deal with "doing", and the attacks directed against unintentionally ascribed identials undermine the processes related to "being".

In order not to succumb to the extreme stress and pain in torture, an ultimate defence is resorted to. This is to dissociate the mind (or soul) from the body, if you like, the veritable deconstruction of the *identity* of psyche and soma. A long-term effect of torture is chronic pain, and frequently, diffuse aches: headaches, pains in one's feet, shoulders, back, neck, and other parts of the body. These pains for which discernible lesions to bodily tissue rarely are objectively identified, may be interpreted as "reminders" of the body's existence. Post-traumatic pain of this kind may be interpreted as an expression of the frail links remaining between the body and the mind. Pain functions as the interconnecting agent. These post-traumatic pains may, however, also be interpreted as the embodied experience of violations to integrity.[4]

The post-traumatic throes that many victims of torture present may be interpreted as a symbolic expression of the fact that the intimate bonds between the body and the mind still exist. Obviously pain in the victim's feet is an outcome of the prolonged and frequent beatings of the soles of the feet, a treatment sometimes designated as "falanga". These pains, however, may also be regarded as an indication of the violation to individual integrity. The soles of the feet represent the body's area of contact with the ground, suggesting being grounded in reality. Symbolically, the inability to walk implies problems of making decisions about matters in everyday life. Pains in the neck are caused by muscular tension. But they also have symbolic meanings. A person who feels pride in himself keeps his head high. Stooped heads are an image of subservience and oppression. Heads bowed down or turned away may express feelings of shame. Backaches, from which many suffer today, have a number of neurological and physiological causes. However, the stooping back is also a symbol of heavy burdens, suffering and fear. In the world of symbols, a straight back represents boldness, courage, and straightforwardness. The dispirited person, the fragmented identity, is expressed somatically in a hunched-up carriage. Feelings of guilt are embodied in a glassy stare or by the averted eyes. Resolution suggests itself in somatic stability – a firm handshake, a determined gait, and distinct facial expressions. Problems of coordinating bodily movements suggest a lack of integration in the mental sphere. On a symbolic level a bodily spinelessness, indistinct facial expressions and gloomy eyes represent a fragmented identity.

Enjoying a sense of self-respect and competence, being in control of one's life and being able to integrate life experiences, along with their polar opposites, may be seen in, and on, the human body. The young Asian woman whose story was related in the previous section was not a victim of torture as such. However, her trauma manifested itself in ways that are similar to those found in the extremes of torture.

Notes

1   See the 1951 Geneva Convention on Refugees which specifically points to the European scene. This geographic clause was not altered until the 1967 Protocol on the Status of Refugees.
2   Africanists in general agree that one root cause of the severe conflicts haunting the continent date back to the arbitrarily drawn boundaries settled by the European imperial powers at the Berlin conference in 1878. These boundaries were inherited by the independent successor states that formed in the wake of colonialism

from the end of the 1950s to the mid-1970s. The transition of power was itself a destabilizing factor.

3 More than one million persons of Mozambican origin fled to Malawi at the end of the 1980s. The 1994 crisis in Rwanda triggered a flow to Zaire and Tanzania of 1–1.5 million persons within a matter of weeks (Rutinwa 1996). By the end of 1994 a total of 2.5 million Rwandan refugees had sought asylum in neighbouring states (Anacleti 1996).

4 These acts of violation represent attacks upon the victim's soul, identity and mind. The functional defences to which one has access in normal conditions of life are usually quite insufficient in torture. Bettelheim (1986) desribes in a classic text how prisoners in Nazi concentration camps resorted to defences on a very primitive level of functioning. He details the defence known as "identification with the aggressor". The most far-reaching of these defences is to turn oneself into nothing. Being nobody one no longer can be intimidated. In other words, this mode of existence corresponds to total apathy, merely an inch from death. Testimonies have been given by people who against all odds survived the terrors of the concentration camps. Deep down, in the very core of their souls, they must have had some small spark of a will to live. In these individuals apathy was not all-encompassing, just almost. In the most critical of situations they must have managed to mobilize their very last reserves, judge the situation correctly, and, with a good share of luck, survive.

References

Amnesty International. 1984. *Tortyren på åttiotalet*. Stockholm: Nyblooms förlag.

Anacleti, Odhiambo. 1996. Regional Responses to the Rwandan Emergency. *Journal of Refugee Studies* 9(3): 303–11.

Bettelheim, Bruno. 1986. *Surviving the Holocaust*. London: Fontana.

Dacyl, Janina W. 1996. International Responses to Refugee Flows from Former Yugoslavia. In *Temporary Protection – Problems and Prospects*, Report No. 22. Lund: Raoul Wallenberg Institute, University of Lund.

de Levita, David J. 1965. *The Concept of Identity*. Paris: Mouton.

Oucho, John O. 1996. Refugees and Displacement in Sub-Saharan Africa: Instability due to Ethnic and Political Conflicts and Ecological Causes. In Adepoju, A. and Hammar, T. (eds.), *International Migration in and from Africa: Dimensions, Challenges and Prospects*. Dakar: PHRDA.

Rutinwa, Bonaventure. 1996. The Tanzanian Government's Response to the Rwandan Emergency. *Journal of Refugee Studies* 9(3): 291–302.

Masooma – a Ugandan-Asian Muslim Swede

Gunnar Alsmark

Some years ago I met a young, dark-skinned woman, who in perfect Swedish presented herself in the following way: "I am Masooma Rahim, a Swedish Ugandan-Asian Muslim, and a woman, living in Lund and learning to become a schoolteacher in Malmö." During the next hour she talked about herself and her life in Sweden, as a Swede, challenging our prevailing picture of what a Swede looks like.

> My belonging is mixed. I am a Muslim. I am an Indian. I am a Swede. I am married to a Kurd. And I am an Oriental too, who lives in the West. No one expects me to be just one person!

I was delighted, because this statement confirmed my own ideas about Swedishness, and encouraged my more political ambition, that a Swede can appear in many different ways – and colours. At the same time I was a little bit confused. How on earth did she manage to combine such a seemingly multiple identity, containing so many belongings, loyalties etc? Or maybe her identity was not at all multiple, but very solid and homogeneous.

To sort it out, at least a bit, I asked her to help me in my perplexity. We did a series of deep interviews, over almost a year, with the possibility of deepening the themes we were talking about during the previous meeting, and to find completely new topics as well. It was a very rewarding, but at the same time time-consuming method, and complicated when it comes to the analysis. The method is built upon trust and friendship; you open up a door to more subtle things in a person's life history, you make people tell stories they have not told before; they confess and reveal, exposing themselves in a very open, sometimes unconscious way. And it all ends up with an article, where all the nice chats are suddenly mixed together into new and revealing contexts. It is a shocking experience to see oneself scrutinized and classified – displayed and valued.

And it is, in some way, a shocking experience for me as a researcher to see all my guesses and speculations in print, being well aware of the huge lack of knowledge that still remains, even after five or six deep interviews. What you have done is only to scratch the surface of a person's life and identity, and you both know it. Of course you can always console yourself by saying that this is not her real biography, it is not necessarily about real events or true statements. It is just a narrative, constructed in a specific context here and now. True or false are not interesting considerations. But the problem is, as far as I can see, that we are not satisfied with that. In spite of all its shortcomings, we are tempted to use our, say five, ten or fifteen interviews in more general terms, as if the results are valuable for a whole ethnic or national group of people. This is a delicate problem, especially when we are dealing with immigrants and refugees, because our statements very often have an impact on the politicians and their policies.

All this reminds me of the story Barbara Meyerhof related in the introduction to her wonderful book *Number Our Days* (1978). She comes to the urban Jewish ghetto and meets an old woman who asks about her study. "What do you want from us?" she asks. "I want to know as much as I can about your way of living, about your traditions and values and so forth." "That sounds good," the old woman says. But after a moment of silence she adds: "And what can you do for us?"

How often can we ethnologists, social anthropologists, sociologists and so on answer this question in an honest and constructive way? Very seldom, I guess. On the other hand, and this is important, we sometimes do research not for the sake of the informant, but for society as a whole. It happens that we come across things which are not pleasant for the people in question, or things that they deliberately try to undercommunicate or hide, such as criminality, political oppression, tax-dodging, child abuse and so on.

Enough about this methodological and ethical part of my work.

Back now to Masooma Rahim and my search for her identity. Or shall I say cultural identity, since my interest has been on how she gives her identity cultural forms in her everyday life. Identity in the more narrow sense of the word, which means the person's own subjective view and perception of the self, is also important, but a matter for the psychologist as well as for the ethnologist. Here I am looking for interesting, interdisciplinary cooperation in the future.

Coming so far, we can present two different, but closely related approaches to cultural identity, going for both the collective and individual levels. The first one, apparently the easier one to grasp, focuses on cultural forms. Refugees in exile do this or that. The second one, and the trickier one to investigate, focuses on the processes. How have things become what they are? Here we concentrate more on *who* and *how,* rather than on *what.* This latter approach is about power, hegemony, oppression, subordination etc. Or just to give an example: we can describe what is cultural heritage (traditions, food, fairytales and so on), but we can also describe the process behind these cultural forms; who decides what traditions (foreign or native) are good and exhibitable – or bad and threatening. In short, heritage politics.

Until now, very little has been done on *how* identities are generated in the interplay between individual and structure in a Swedish context. We still look too much at immigrants and refugees from a harmonizing perspective, even when we present different lifestyles within the community. Still we smooth things over, maybe in order not to provide the racists with weapons. Or because we are afraid of or listening too much to the gatekeepers of political correctness, a group that has been growing over the past ten years.

In the following, I would like to present some thoughts based on my study of Masooma, thoughts which might be of some interest for our discussion about people living in exile or in societies they were not born into (Alsmark 1997). I mentioned that Masooma challenged the common presumption of what it means to be a "real", "genuine" Swede. Swedishness is for many immigrants a very important part of their identity, regardless of their constitution and the colour of their skin – and regardless of the fact that most of the people in Sweden still have great problems accepting such a broad view of the concepts of Swede and Swedishness. Black, Muslim, of Uganda-Asian origin, married to a Kurd from Turkey, is not what we first think of when we talk about Swedishness. But we should. Now, and even more in the future. Swedishness has many features, many faces – and I am very much concerned with this kind of learning process for how to broaden the concept of *a Swede*.

Like Masooma, many refugees have lived in Sweden most of their lives. They speak Swedish perfectly, they know most of the cultural codes – and yet they are constantly asked where they come from, and praised for mastering our language so well. Or answered in English! Especially when their skin is coloured. I wonder how long it will take until Swedes become colour-blind when it comes to tolerance and cultural acceptance.

Masooma is not only a Swede, from my point of view. She is also a very active and purposeful person, which challenges another very common notion of refugees as people to be pitied, helpless victims in a cold and hostile country. But the *hell of exile* is just one picture, not at all false for some of the refugees, but very often exaggerated and one-sided.

Migration researchers of today have a more balanced attitude towards this victimizing of immigrants. At least, in general. On the left-wing side, a victimizing and patronizing view is still very common, although it is not all-prevailing any more. But unfortunately this is the case among politicians. Here I am talking from almost twenty years of experience. *Taking care of* is the core of Social Democratic politics, which is just another word for creating clients – and specialists as well, let us not forget! A great many interesting studies have been done on this part of identity formation, not least by researchers who are immigrants themselves (Gür 1996; Rojas 1993; Rojas 1995; Ålund 1991).

Even if one is an unemployed client, living on the welfare system, one is still an active subject. That is not always easy to understand or accept. As claimed by Lash and Friedman (1992), *both modernists and postmodernists have had as the cornerstone of their theory some notion of the irrelevance of identity, of subjectivity, of the social actor or agency.* It is still very much so, as soon as we go outside ethnology and some other, closely related disciplines. In economics and social sciences, for instance, a dominating macro-structural approach leaves very little room for subjectivity. A very common and simplistic attitude in the public debate talks about society as the overriding problem. The immigrant or the refugee is a victim, not at all to blame for his or her situation. I would like to go behind this kind of reductionism, in its blooming in the 1970s, but still very common when it comes to immigrant issues. Of course, structural explanations are of importance, but not to an extent where one neglects individual strategies or believes that they can exist in a logical and causal way only within the frame of a structure. We have to look for contradictions, irrelevancies, irrationalities and transgressions. And we need penetrating studies on, for instance, the everyday life of unemployed immigrants. For although they are out of work, they are far from being inactive. For many people cultural identity is only partly related to their situation on the labour market, especially among youngsters of today, immigrants as well as ethnic Swedes.

To sum up a little, we can see how the concept of identity is due in some way to the political and ideological background of the researcher, and to the prevailing scientific discourse of his or her discipline. This is nothing new, of course, but my point is that, in spite of all our talk about reflexivity, we very seldom take this into consideration.

In this context I find the concepts of *diaspora* and *exile* somewhat complicated. How long does a person live in exile? The whole of his or her life? Or almost not at all, if you find your new country good for you and your family and have no intention to repatriate. It might be an appropriate concept for the parents from, say, Chile, but what about their children, even if they were born abroad? Some people, like the Jews, have learnt how to live with a portable home country, with a special ability to feel at home abroad – or *être diasporique*, as Bernard-Henry Lévy put it. This seems to go for the Ugandan-Asians as well. I never thought of Masooma as living in exile. Nor did she.

I think we have to use the concept very carefully, while it encompasses a tone of patronizing, of external labelling in terms of *us and them: you are an exile, a foreign bird in our forest*. To me diaspora and exile are nationalistic concepts, dooming people to be outsiders forever. Most problematic is "diaspora", the latest concept *à la mode* in academic circles. Originally, it refers to the dispersion of the Jews from Palestine after the Babylonian captivity. In a broader sense it signifies "the spreading of a people originally belonging to one nation or having a common culture" (*Collins English Dictionary* 1979: 409). In relation to this essentialist view of people in exile who belonged to a common culture in their home country, questions like *who* talks about exile and diaspora, *how* and *when*, and for what *purpose*, are important to me. So too are all scientific concepts, terms and expressions, colonizing our knowledge of the world in specific ways and categories.

What concepts like exile and diaspora do analytically, in a positive way, is that they focus on the transnational aspects of a person's identity formation. Today, when we can see a tendency to overemphasize political, social and economic aspects in explaining especially suburban immigrant youngsters' way of living, sometimes totally neglecting culture and ethnicity as explanatory factors (or reduced to so-called *cultural racism*, Sander 1995), we need to "go abroad", to cross the national borders of Sweden in subtle and diversified ways (Alsmark 1996).

Identity – religion

When it comes to identity formation, Masooma's biography puts things in perspective. Let me briefly present some interesting aspects. First of all – being an immigrant is not a quality, it is a process. And it is a process which is not at all unilinear. As far as Masooma is concerned, from the very beginning, she identified herself as a Muslim. But it was not until she was twelve, and made a journey together with her mother to Damascus, that she become very religious. Among other things she started to wear the veil as a public expression of her religion. After a while, however, she got sick and tired of always being on the retreat, of always finding herself defending Islam, even when she did not want to. So she abandoned the veil and other more formal parts of the religion (praying five times a day, for instance). From being very formalized, Islam turned out to be a kind of inner conviction, a strength and a guiding rule for all kinds of situations, in her life. So in one way she became less religious, in another more.

Today she is in many respects critical of the Shia-Muslim community in Trollhättan, where many of her relatives live, although she often visits their mosque. Yet she does so not so much for religious purposes, but because she wants to meet her family and friends, and to broaden her social network. "When I want to pray, I very often go to the cathedral in Lund," she says. "That's a perfect place for contemplation."

The mosque as a kind of "people's house", a room for devotion, a social welfare office, an education centre, a culture centre, an information centre, in short, a place where a collective spirit of community is created, has been described by Pia Karlsson in her study of Swedish mosques (Karlsson and Svanberg 1995). It is important to look for arenas that provide a highly condensed importance for a person's identity formation – either because you fully accept the ideas and the ideology, or because you partly confront them, forming alternative interpretations.

According to Eva Hamberg, professor of immigration research at the Faculty of Theology in Lund, four different ways in which migration may affect the religious beliefs and religious practices in exile can be distinguished. In some instances they appear to remain more or less unchanged by migration. In other cases, religious commitment and participation decline. One of the reasons for this may be that in the new country the immigrants lack the social network on which the plausibility of their religious world-views depends (which is not the case of the Ugandan-Asian refugees in Sweden, by the way). Under other circumstances, migration may instead lead to an increase in religious commitment, or even to a radical change in religious orientation. The latter is the case when immigrants convert to religious groups of the sect type (Hamberg 1998: 70).

Identity – modernity

Back to Masooma Rahim. The longer I knew her, the more full of inconsistencies she seemed to be. But at the same time she was able to put all these parts together, giving them logic and meaning. And

I did not find it contradictory when she challenged current theories about postmodernity, being premodern, modern and postmodern at the same time. In some way, she seemed to be a perfect person representing the postmodern quest for an answer to the question "who am I?" Searching, wondering. *A nomad of the present,* to quote Alberto Melucci (1992). And she was very modern in her stressing of individualism, of doing what *she* wanted to do. She refused to accept the Ugandan-Asians' rule of endogamy, and married a Kurd. When her extended family met, she constantly crossed the male-female border, one moment sitting where she should, among the women, the other moment among the men together with her father, and what is more, she was not at all quiet, but took part into the discussions, just like a man.

But, if Hoffman-Axthelm (1992: 200) is right when claiming that "in the name of identity, laws of the species were to be abolished, traditions and corporate chains cast aside", Masooma is, in many respects, also premodern. Her family is very important to her, and so are collective traditions. Islam means a lot to her, too. Actually, religion is the organizing principle of whole her life, mentally and practically.

The concepts of premodern, modern and postmodern do not seem to be very useful for my analysis. They work when we discuss general tendencies in society over time, but they create problems when we try to understand the identity formation of an individual.

Identity – ethnicity

> The word "ethnicity" certainly is not helpful, since it seems to be associated more strongly with the belief in measurable differences by descent and thus obstructs a clear understanding of the newer theories (Sollors 1986: 36).

As shown by Werner Sollors (1986), ethnicity in the United States is a matter not of content but of the importance that individuals ascribe to it. It is important to adopt this approach in Sweden as well. To make it more clear, I would like to refer to Herbert Gans (1974), who called attention to the ways in which modern ethnic identification works by external symbols rather than by continual activities that make demands upon people who define themselves as "ethnic". With the concept of *symbolic ethnicity* Gans tries to build a bridge from the assimilation point of view (straight-line theory) over to the pluralistic one (the bump-line approach, as Gans calls it). A person's ethnic belonging is kept apart from his or her everyday life. Nathan Glazer and Daniel Patrick Moynihan, the authors of the book *Beyond the Melting Pot* (1963), influential in the sixties, wrote a decade later "that the cultural content of each ethnic group in the United States seems to have become similar to that of others, but the emotional significance of attachments to the ethnic group seems to persist" (Glazer and Moynihan 1975: 8).

As far as Sweden is concerned, I tried to find out whether there was a dominant attitude in the ethnic community of the Ugandan-Asians, an attitude with a strong emotional significance. A cultural code which like a compass needle governs the way of life, not for all of the people, but for most of them, with a great variety of deviations from the main direction, but nevertheless, overarching.

Alladin Anwar, Masooma's uncle, leader of the Islamic centre in Trollhättan where the Muslims have built their own mosque, made the following statement: "According to the Koran you shall be loyal to the country where you live!" And that this was not just empty talk was revealed very strongly the day after the mosque in Trollhättan was burnt down by three Swedish youngsters, some years ago. When many members of the Muslim community called for revenge, Masooma's uncle pleaded for calm and reconciliation. And that is how it turned out.

Masooma also mentioned an all-embracing rule which she learned from her grandmother. "Remember, Masooma," she said, "we lived two generations in Uganda. We learned how to eat bananas. But we never learned how to be clothed in banana leaves." And Masooma underlined this, saying to me: "I think we Indians strongly believe that, wherever we go, we should take the best from the society – and let the rest be!" This statement does not express what it seems to do. A total freedom of choice, in a very postmodern way of living. On the contrary, I would warn against a tendency to ascribe too much logic and reflection to a person (like Masooma), doing something because of a certain ideology, a certain intention, an already existing identity. It may seem to be that way, but coincidences and chances often govern life.

As a whole she tries to live her own way, far from the mainstream of the Ugandan-Asian community to which most of her relatives belong. But there is not an absolute gap between Masooma and her family, as far as integration is concerned. In spite of differences in ambition, almost every foreigner in Sweden, immigrant or refugee, tries to adjust to the dominant culture, and at the same time preserves traits from his or her original culture. In this respect we see a difference in degree rather than a difference in kind.

Possibly there is a difference in attitude towards the majority society. One attitude might be an offensive preservation of the "culture", claiming mosques, private schools, economic support for home language tuition, for "ethnic" programmes on radio and television, for newspapers and so on. The other attitude is to play down such demands, keeping a low profile in relation to the dominant culture, as Masooma seemed to do.

I question those parents who ask for Muslim schools. This is not a solution. Rather the contrary. Then you isolate yourself more and more from society as a whole. A better way is to educate the teachers, giving them a new way of looking at pupils with other cultural and religious backgrounds than the Swedes.

This is theoretically speaking. In practice, however, the border between these two attitudes often seems to be rather blurred. The Danish researcher Flemming Røgilds talks about *ambivalence* rather than *symbolic ethnicity* as a result of the relationship between modernity and identity (Røgilds 1995: 142), which might be a more appropriate term.

Individualism versus ethnicity

Generally speaking, ethnic identity among the refugees in Sweden is problematic. It differs from group to group, or rather from individual to individual. Here I just want to present two tendencies of identity making in Swedish society today, in many respects counteracting each other.

The first one strongly emphasizes the individual, and equal rights and opportunities. This official policy has parallels in the United States, where great emphasis has been placed on consent at the expense of descent definitions, where achieved rather than ascribed identity has been strongly favoured, and where "self-determination" and "independence" of ancestral, parental and external definitions have been encouraged (Sollors 1986: 37). This policy has a very special impact on, for instance, social work with children, where we often argue that we have to take our point of departure in the child itself, in the individual, not in the family as a whole. For us the interest of the individual is always at the centre, and should be, according to a lot of people. They think that focusing on the family creates a risk of keeping the child bound to old patriarchal, non-democratic, sex-discriminating patterns.

With such a view, however, we ignore the very specific ethnic and social conditions of the child and simultaneously demolish an important part of its identity. And we deny the possibility of other alternative values of a childhood than our own. It is, in fact, a highly ethnocentric position.

The second force with an impact on immigrants and refugees identity formation is *ethnification,* growing more and more intense during the last decade. We can see how Turks, Kurds, Finns, Bosnians, Serbs, Croats, Kosovo Albanians, to mention just some, try to expose their "own culture", their own rules, values and demands, in exile.

What we do know very little about is the extent of this movement. How many Turks, Kurds, Finns and so on in Sweden are involved in this kind of construction of a partly new ethnicity in exile? As far as I can see, there is a very clear tendency towards ethnification on the part of the researchers themselves. They talk about Kurds, for instance, as a well-defined group, about Kurdish "culture" with specific traits and content, in a very essentialist way, in spite of the fact that this might only be true for a rather small core of traditionalists, maybe ten to twenty percent. But what about all the rest, for example, those who are Bosnians by nationality, but not by culture? Or those who try to get rid of the fetters of ethnicity, creating a "cultural hotchpotch".

Syncretism

With few exceptions, these two forces are always combined within the same ethnic group. Masooma claims that among her own relatives, many of them do not want to be integrated, at least not to any great extent. Some isolate themselves, some stick to their own people and enjoy the pleasant and often uncomplicated life their culture and traditions provide (as did her sister and brother), some have no guts, no ambitions, a kind of attitude more related to their personal character than to their ethnicity.

"Ugandan-Asians stick very much together", Masooma says. "Only the very purposeful will succeed!" In this very specific case, success does not mean assimilation, in spite of what many people think – native Swedes, as well as Ugandan-Asians. Assimilation is not what my research shows either. On the contrary, Masooma is a very good exponent of *syncretism*. In developing her own identity, ethnicity is very little of a hindrance to her, but an asset. Her identity is trans-cultural, not only within the Swedish context. Like all the other Ugandan-Asians, her social network is almost global, with narrow contacts with Ugandan-Asians spread all over the world. This is, I guess, as much a result of the ethnic background as of the religious one. Muslims challenge the equation between culture and community in two ways, as Gerd Baumann presents it in *Contesting Culture* (1996). "One of these results from the vast cultural variety within this local *community*, the other from the global spread of the multicultural *community* or *umma* of Muslim believers" (Baumann 1996: 122f.).

This gives the concept of *Swede* an even more extended significance than discussed in the beginning. For a growing number of Swedes today, born within the borders of the nation or abroad, Swedishness contains a national, official culture, and an ethnic, religious, political, and so forth, culture, which is both local and global at the same time. How people selecting from all these different components are able to construct a more or less well-functioning identity – and most of them do – is a challenge for researchers. "Well-functioning" is of course a relative expression in this connection. I do not mean "without problems", for life for all of us is partly a struggle, full of disappointments, reverses, and sorrows. At least it is so for most of the refugees. But there are also good times in their lives, moments of joy and happiness. Success stories are not rare, as Masooma is a good exponent of.

What I criticize is the tendency to overemphasize the problematic part of the situation for people living in exile. With such a point of departure, one has difficulties in seeing how people make a consistency out of their life, in one way or another, and in seeing them as a whole.

In order not to be misunderstood, I will once more point out that Masooma in many respects is unusual. She seems to handle the conflicts modern–traditional and individuality–ethnicity rather well, and very much due to her parents who are very understanding. Certainly they do not always agree with the things their daughter does. Sometimes they do not understand her claim for independence. But they respect her, which means that they relieve her of living a double life. Not in full, of course, but far beyond what many first- and second-generation youngsters have to do. Many reports tell us that a rupture with their parents' way of living is common, and far from being unproblematic. Mainly this seems to be urban–rural oriented. Yvonne Mørck (1998) presents many telling stories from interviews she conducted with youngsters from different ethnic groups in Copenhagen. A Turkish-Danish girl says that parents belonging to the first immigrant generation, coming from rural areas in Turkey, often are afraid of losing control of their children. For them traditions are of great importance, giving them identity and continuity in a new situation, in many ways difficult to manage. It requires a large amount of inner strength and security to let the children choose their own way of living, which often means far away from that of their parents. And the same can be said about the children. Their position between cultural continuity and loyalty towards the family on the one hand, and their search for change and new formations do have their own pains and sorrows. It is hard to tell, says Mørck, when we can talk about constructive schizophrenia or disintegration and confusion.

By emphasizing *syncretism*, regarded as a general feature of the transformation of cultures into new combinations, I challenge the essentialist understanding of *us and them*, with clear-cut differences and borders. I very much agree with Edward Said, whose primary goal is not to separate, but to create liaisons. The most important philosophical and methodological reason for this is that all cultural traits are hybrids, mixed, impure and that it is now time for cultural analysts to re-establish this connection between analysis and reality (cf. Røgilds 1995: 236).

The concept of *syncretism* is not unproblematic. It suffers from the same weakness as *creolization*, because it seems to postulate a mixture of cultural and religious traditions which is whole and indivisible. According to this view, it might be easy to look upon a "hybrid" as a person who has lost his or her true belonging, nourishing a dream, or an ambition of once coming back to the "mother culture". In opposition to this, I would reject all these thoughts of absolutism and essentialism as well as the idea that the dilemma of the immigrants, and of people in diaspora, is to have just two choices, either to go back to their roots, or to be assimilated. What I have tried to illustrate with Masooma as an example is that people in exile learn to handle at least two identities, to speak at least two languages and to interpret and negotiate between them. As Stuart Hall has pointed out, culture, identities and roots are relational constructions (Hall 1992). Perhaps the concept of *liminoid experiences,* inspired by Victor Turner, best expresses what I want to say. The concept, developed from the original thought of *liminal ethnicity,* is characterized by the transgressing elements in this process (Turner 1983; Turner 1984). And this border landscape we want to examine is as much a mental landscape as a physical and social one (Røgilds 1995: 254). This fact makes it a real challenge to the researcher, because he or she too has to cross interpersonal as well as disciplinary borders in order to really understand what is going on in the formation of an identity.

The second weakness of the concept of syncretism is that it too often gives the feeling of a free choice, neglecting both the force of tradition, as I mentioned above, and the force of discrimination and racism. Regardless of what you want to be and what you think you are, the dominant attitudes within society towards immigrants and refugees are of extreme importance. How this has affected Masooma Rahim was a subject I tried to touch upon many times during the interviews. But this part of constructing her identity was almost impossible to figure out, at least for me as an ethnologist. Perhaps cooperation with a psychologist would be an example of the interdisciplinary teamwork proposed above.

References

Alsmark, Gunnar. 1996. Å ena sidan, å den andra. In Arnstberg, K.-O. (ed.), *Boja eller befrielse: Etnicitetsforskningens inriktning och konsekvenser*, 7–16. Botkyrka: Mångkulturellt centrum.

Alsmark, Gunnar. 1997. En svensk Uganda Indier. In Alsmark, G. (ed.), *Skjorta eller själ: Kulturella identiteter i tid och rum*, 62–84. Lund: Studentlitteratur.

Ålund, Alexandra. 1991. *Lilla Juga*. Stockholm: Carlsson.

Baumann, Gerd. 1996. *Contesting Culture: Discourses of Identity in Multi-ethnic London*. Cambridge: Cambridge University Press.

Collins English Dictionary. 1979. London.

Gans, Herbert. 1974. Ethnicity, Acculturation and Assimilation. Foreword to Neil Sandberg, *Ethnic Identity and Assimilation*. New York: Praeger.

Glazer, Nathan, and Moynihan, Daniel Patrik. 1963. *Beyond the Melting Pot: The Negroes, Puerto Ricans, Jews, Italians, and Irish of New York City*. Cambridge: MIT Press.

Glazer, Nathan, and Moynihan, Daniel Patrik. 1975. *Ethnicity: Theory and Experience*. Cambridge: Harvard University Press.

Gür, Thomas. 1996. *Staten och nykomlingarna: En studie av den svenska invandrarpolitikens idéer*. Stockholm: City University Press.

Hall, Stuart. 1992. The question of cultural identity. In Hall, S. et al. (eds.), *Modernity and its Futures*. Cambridge: Polity Press.

Hamberg, Eva M. 1998. Migration och religiös förändring. *Svensk Teologisk Kvartalskrift* 74: 66–70.

Hoffman-Axthelm, Dieter. 1992. Identity and Reality: The End of the Philosophical Immigration Officer. In Lash, S. and Friedman, J. (eds.) *Modernity and Identity*, 196–217. Oxford: Blackwell Publishers.

Karlsson, Pia, and Svanberg, Ingvar. 1995. *Moskéer i Sverige: En religionsetnologisk studie i intolerans och administrativ vanmakt*. Uppsala: Svenska kyrkans forskningsråd.

Lash, Scott, and Friedman, Jonathan (eds.). 1992. *Modernity and Identity*. Oxford: Blackwell Publishers.

Melucci, Alberto. 1992. *Nomader i nuet: Sociala rörelser och individuella behov i dagens samhälle*. Göteborg: Daidalos.

Meyerhof, Barbara. 1980. *Number Our Days*. New York: Simon and Schuster.

Mørck, Yvonne. 1998. *Bindestegs-Danskere. Fortællinger om køn, generationer og etnicitet*. Copenhagen: Forlaget Sociologi c/o Samfundslitteratur.

Røgilds, Flemming. 1995. *Stemmer i et grænseland*. Copenhagen: Forlaget politisk revy.

Rojas, Mauricio. 1993. *I ensamhetens labyrint*. Halmstad: Rojas och Brombergs förlag.

Rojas, Mauricio. 1995. *Sveriges oönskade barn*. Stockholm: Bromberg.

Sander, Åke. 1995. Rasismens varp och trasor. In *Rasismens varp och trasor: En antologi om främlingsfientlighet och rasism*, 132–167. Norrköping: Statens invandrarverk.

Sollors, Werner. 1986. *Beyond Ethnicity: Consent and descent in American Culture*. New York: Oxford University Press.

Turner, Victor. 1983. Liminal to Liminoid in Play, Flow and Ritual: An Essay in Comparative Symbiology. In Harris, J. C. and Park, R. J. (eds.), *Plays, Games and Sports*. Champaign, Illinois. Human Kinetics Publishers.

Turner, Victor. 1984. Liminality and the Performative Genres. In MacAloon, J. J. Rite (ed.), *Dramas, Festival, Spectacle*. Philadelphia: Institute for the Study of Human Issues.

Mediated Orientalism
and everyday Orientalism

Magnus Berg

The subject of this essay originates in two research projects: one completed (Berg 1998), and one ongoing. The completed project is based entirely on textual material. It consists of an analysis of several popular cultural productions – books and films – which all have something in common, as they present images of the Muslim Orient. It concerns a study of what, with reference to Edward Said (1993), might be called popular Orientalism. Within the framework of this essay, however, it would be more convenient to talk about popular Orientalism as mediated Orientalism in contrast to Orientalism in everyday life, which I am going to discuss later on.

The aim of the completed project was to examine these presentations of the Orient as Western mirrors or as areas where Western cultural ambivalences and contrasts might find their symbolic solutions. Ambivalences most frequently dealt with in the area of mediated Orientalism were those concerning questions of freedom and compulsion.

In certain cases, the Orient represented freedom and the West compulsion. Such stories are among the oldest in the material, and they are almost always historic depictions. Two good examples are David Lean's film *Lawrence of Arabia* of 1962, and Edith Maud Hull's classic *The Sheik*, the first sheik novel, published in 1923. In both of these cases, the oriental wilderness – the desert – is the place where the heroes may escape from strict demands of self-control and discipline laid down by an overly-civilized West and where they may establish contact with suppressed and, as described, authentic parts of their personalities.

Mostly, however, it is the task of the Orient to form the home of compulsion on this earth, and this compulsion is contrasted with the thought of the individual freedom in the West. Above all, this dichotomizing dominates the popular Orientalism of a contemporary date. The Orient consists in this instance, to a major or minor degree, of a patriarchal and compact detailed regulation of all areas of life. The patriarcharlism may be described as maximally stretched in its vertical dimension. From God in his heaven and all the way down to the more humble family tyrant, an unshakeable consensus rules, and from there a power is exercised against women and children. This symbolic order often appears in a modern disguise, but it is premodern by its nature and is characterized by firmness, unchangeability and lack of reflexivity which is usually designated as being the opposite of late modernity. The social roles are stable and are to be acted, irrespective of the individual's likes or dislikes. Value systems really deserve to be called systems, and they are both unanimous and uncontradicted.

The opposite of all this compulsion is to be found in the West. There the individual enjoys the freedom of creating his own life, and this is described as a good order. However, a somewhat deeper study of the textual material shows that this freedom has its price in terms of lost security and stability, difficulty in finding values that provide a base for a lifelong life, existential abandonment and all the pains arising from break-ups and discontinuity.

These contrasts and frictions are clearly demonstrated in Betty Mahmoody and William Hoffer's book *Not without my Daughter* (Mahmoody and Hoffer 1988), and more exactly in the descriptions of Betty's American existence, which is presented in a series of flashbacks from the hell in Teheran. In her American life, Betty swung in a most staggering way between completely disparate projects of life. One pole consisted of a subordinate, traditional working-class femininity and the other of a modern and independent female subjectivity in a middle-class framing, saturated by career power. When this American biography is sneaked into the noisy description of the alleged coldness of the Orient in relation to the freedom of the individual, the squeaking from these ambivalences is drowned. Next to the compulsion of the Orient, the late modern Western ambivalences take the shape of a completely normal life.

The Orient presented by mediated popular Orientalism can consequently be seen as a simple interior designed to facilitate Western identity work; an area where the modern Western drama can be acted out and lived and brought to a head. Observed from this perspective, the Orient of mediated Orientalism has no more than superficial points in common with what could be called the real Orient. From this perspective, the Orient of mediated Orientalism also seems politically innocent. Mediated Orientalism mainly concerns Western efforts to handle cultural ambivalences belonging to Western culture. The description of the area where this takes place is entirely secondary to these efforts. The West creates the Orient it needs to obtain a perspective on its own problems. This is not least evident from the fact that the same Western toil with ambivalences and contradictions has given rise to a succession of other fantasy lands. The folktales had theirs, science fiction productions theirs and horror movies theirs. These are circumstances that add a good portion of political innocence to mediated Orientalism; the concentrated search for identity which takes place in the Oriental fantasy land may indeed seem somewhat meagre and petty, sometimes even silly, but if so, that must surely be a problem concerning none other than us Westerners.

However, mediated Orientalism is not all that politically innocent. It also describes a perception of the world, in the most literal sense of the term. This perception is characterized by anything but innocence. A fundamental trait in almost all mediated popular Orientalism is the normalization of a symbolic world order, in which power and access to material resources are distributed according to unjust principles disguised as necessities fixed by law and where the West's global dominance is legitimized, at the same time as its moral innocence is defended by rough methods.

In the symbolic world order of mediated Orientalism, there is a truth that weighs heavier and forms the basis of all other truths: the West is, in every crucial aspect superior to (the rest, but in this case) the Orient. This truth can be proven in two ways.

Firstly, the Orient can be described straight off as the West's, in different aspects inferior, opposite. The Orient – a faraway place, to which it is awkward and dangerous to travel – is premodern, religious, despotic, patriarchal, stagnated, whereas the West is modern, rational, democratic and friendly, treating the sexes fairly equally and in a state of vital development.

The stories that are built around this direct dualism often take place in the past, and this fact is a pointer to what this Oriental form is a reflection of, for it shares basic characteristics with the world-picture of colonialism. What all stories of this design have in common with colonialism's world-picture are the distinct borders between what must be kept apart. Dualistic separation was colonialism's basic principle of organization. Its mental world was one of borders and distance: between metropolis and colony, colonizer and colonized, ruling and ruled, centre and periphery, accumulation and exploitation, consumption and exudation, progression and stagnation, civilization and different degrees of barbarism, the West and the rest.

Secondly, the Orient can be described in a way that in its basic traits negates the faraway and different Orient. The Orient is so close and similar to the West that the two are very difficult to keep apart. Betty Mahmoody's husband Moody lived and worked in the USA, in a way that, according to the author's metaphor, made him seem "as American as cherry pie". The Oriental countries that Western thriller and action heroes visit, display great outer similarities to the countries they have just left. This emphasis on similarity and proximity can be seen as a reflection of the postcolonial world, born from the breakdown of colonialism's systematic separations.

As this Oriental form describes the Orient as similar and close to the West, one should perhaps think of it with appreciation and confidence, since the emphasis on similarity and proximity would in all likelihood serve a global awareness and prevent fundamentalist orientations. This, however, is not the case. The similar and close Orient is actually only a phase in a movement that aims at separating the East from the West. It is as if a kind of fear of touching forced popular Orientalism to establish difference and distance a second after it had identified proximity and similarity. This manoeuvre has a clear but unspoken goal: the disapproval of the Orient as equal to the West, by exposing its true face, alien to that of the West.

*

Consequently, this is what can be said about the Orient of mediated Orientalism: it has been put together in order to reflect a Western cultural complex of problems. It aims at separating the East from the West and tries to assemble proof of the East's inferiority. It is basically a very simple construction, but which nevertheless attracts much interest. Judging from sales figures and public exposure, many people seem to want to take part in it and be absorbed by it. But, does this also mean that the mediated Orient plays an important part when people in their everyday lives take up their stance on the Orient of reality? It seems incredible that such a crude instrument would be able to function as a compass in a complicated reality. On the other hand, it is likely that it should not be completely uninfluential when people form their pictures of the world.

Questions like these form the basis of my project in progress. It can be described as a form of ethnographic continuation of the first one.

Its empirical basis consists so far of fifteen interviews with nineteen native Swedes, living and/or working in a suburban area of my home town Gothenburg. These interviews have been carried out by Åsa Andersson, an ethnologist in Gothenburg, who has also discussed them in an essay (Andersson 1996).

The purpose of the research is to try to form an opinion of the different sources from which these Swedes have obtained their knowledge about the Orient and also how this knowledge has been put together. Immigrants form approximately 80 percent of the population of the area, and a large proportion of them come from countries such as Turkey, Iran, Iraq, Lebanon, Somalia and Bosnia. In other words, what may be called the factual Orient is strongly represented.

This area shares characteristics with other Swedish residential areas that can be characterized as having a high density of immigrants. These characteristics tell of poverty and lacking resources. This is clearly shown in the local statistics. With an index of 100 for the whole of Gothenburg in 1995, the area can in round figures be described like this: average income 50, proportion of high income (annual income of over SEK 220,000) 25, seeking employment 140, early retirements 125, single-parent households 210, people with college education 40, proportion of families on welfare 370.

Most of the interviewed Swedes are unique in that they have a professional relationship with the inhabitants of the area, perhaps mainly with the youngest of these. Here one can find professions such as teachers, school hosts, day-care centre teachers, librarians, midwives and priests represented. There are also some who are pursuing different types of further education in the area and who thereby come in contact with mainly younger people of immigrant background. It is mainly in this group that the counterweight against middle-class dominance in the group of informants is found. The ones now at school occupied positions as construction workers, casual labourers and kitchen assistants before their unemployment, retraining or further education. As many as thirteen of the interviewed people are women. The oldest person among the interviewed – an unemployed man who formerly worked as a construction worker – is fifty-nine, the youngest – an unemployed woman who had a brief employment at a check-out counter – is twenty-five.

The references made by the Swedes when talking about the Orient can mainly be reported in three directions. First there are the daily experiences from the Oriental neighbourhood, which may be called everyday-life Orientalism. Another reference is the different training courses given to many individuals within their professions and aiming at a more comprehensible and useful handling of multi-cultural practice. A third reference is the mass media and popular culture that constitute mediated Orientalism.

The interviews are characterized by an anti-racist tolerance and a will to understand the multi-cultural situation in the suburban area. This attitude is quite often formulated in contrast to another form of anti-racism. It can be called The Anti-Racism of the Town Centre. The interviews contain a certain degree of acidity towards the middle-class people living where there are no immigrants – in the segregated Swedish urban landscape the town centres form such zones – but who nevertheless are the people who, in a self-confident way, bring together the leading rhetoric of anti-racism.

This is what a woman living in the suburb and working in one of its schools says:

> Well, somehow you want to stay here to show that there are, well, Swedes who want to stay here too. Because I often get angry when

they write a lot in the papers and they are on the barricades, it is: "Oh, we are going to bring refugees here, we are going to do it and..." But they themselves do not want to live here, those who are on the barricades. They should move here, to areas like this and really show that they are willing and honest. It is all right to live in Askim and say that we should welcome ... yes. (Askim is one of the most wealthy and mono-ethnic areas in Gothenburg.)

The anti-racism of the interviewed Swedes has as its basis a pushy multi-cultural practice. It makes heavy demands on those embraced by it, as the anti-racism of the suburbs must first of all be part of their lives and not a topic for conversation.

This is also the fact shaping the Swedes' experiences of the Orientals in the suburb: the efforts to get a complicated, multicultural practice into a working order. In the first place, there is an aim to find ways to cooperate with immigrants in their roles as neighbours and – most of all – as workmates, customers, clients and so on.

A way to achieve this would be to avoid topics of conversation which are thought to be afflictive, sensitive – topics where there is a suspicion that it might risk the interaction which enables the multicultural everyday life of the suburb. This balancing act is analysed by the ethnologist Billy Ehn in his book on "The floating boundaries of work" (Ehn 1981). He calls it peaceful ethnical coexistence.

Resulting from this, only a very limited quantity of knowledge about the above topics is transmitted through direct relations with the immigrants from the Orient countries. This does not mean that these sensitive topics are uninteresting to the Swedes. On the contrary, they talk a lot about them in the interviews. But, and this is the important thing, they do not talk about them with the immigrants of the suburb.

What are these sensitive topics? Have they anything in common? Yes, they are connected by their close relation to the all-embracing question of freedom and compulsion thematized by mediated Orientalism.

Questions about religion, for instance, are sensitive. Islam is quite often associated in a routine manner with submission and fanaticism. The status of the Muslim woman is sensitive, too. She is understandable in the light of Oriental, patriarchal compulsion. This is how one man reasons about this specific topic:

> Well, I suppose it's something I've thought about, that I probably take care not to, for example, sit and talk to a woman from a Muslim country, sit and talk to her, you know, because of some sort of fear or respect for what could happen if her husband showed up then, you know. So, I do have that kind of respect, you know.

A woman who has become acquainted with a number of people from Muslim countries in her work with children at day-care centres, also touches upon this issue:

> A: There are perhaps certain things you don't discuss with these friends, you know.
> Q: Such as?
> A: Certain parts of religion and certain parts of feminism perhaps, that you don't discuss.
> Q: Why not? Do you know straight off that your opinions differ that much?
> A: Yes, well, you feel that, don't you? When you've known each other for a while, you know what you can't discuss and that.
> Q: Do you think it's mutual that you avoid these questions?
> A: I don't know. No, it's hard to say. It's different with all of my friends. They're so different among themselves.

There is not much transethnical talk about Oriental solidarity and unity between family members and other relatives, and there is hardly any mention of younger people's respect for the elderly. In contrast to Islam and the question of the status of women, this is valued in a positive way. Considering the facts that more than half of the Swedish informants have experiences of divorce (their own or their parents') and that many of them, partly for geographical reasons, have fairly limited contact with their parents, this is perhaps not very strange. However, this positive valuation is only made, so to speak, at first glance. Many persons will, in fact, change their minds after having expressed their approval of the unity of the Oriental family and the age hierarchy. The emphasis is then placed on the feeling of confinement which presumably might occur, should the interviewed person be as firmly and hierarchially integrated into his or her own family. This feeling is portrayed in words by a female teacher in the area:

> At the same time as I can imagine that if I lived there and all my relatives came storming in as soon as something was up, I would probably feel that it was too much and that I had no integrity and nothing of my own, because I'm not used to it. It doesn't come naturally to me, but to them it's something positive. But that it should be completely transferred, that I don't know. It's OK for us to be a bit different, isn't it?

These issues are hardly taken up with the Orientals in everyday surroundings. Still, the interviews are full of references to them. The question then arises about the source of knowledge, as this knowledge is evidently the basis for people's viewpoints. Sometimes reference is made to knowledge gained from different training courses in connection with employment, but such knowledge is often used for modulating stereotyped, Oriental apprehensions. More often the references are related to mass media and popular culture, as and when the compulsion elements of the Oriental image are touched upon. Pictures of religiously excited Oriental crowds of people are obtained from television, and more penetrating reports on the patriarchal compulsion of the Orient are provided by popular culture.

The nineteen interviewed Swedes differ from each other in several ways, but they have one thing in common: with one exception they have all read *Not Without My Daughter*, or seen the film based on the book. It is the knowledge obtained from such sources that fills the gap created by the lack of cross-cultural communication in everyday practice.

*

So, a partial silence prevails in the suburb. And it is because of this silence that mediated Orientalism continues to be an important source of Orientalistic knowledge in fields reflecting modern, individual emancipation.

Considering this – and simultaneously keeping in mind that presented Orientalism reflects and inverts something that is very controversial, problematic and ambivalent in the suburb and in the West – it does not seem particularly strange that Swedes tend to consider suburban Orientals in the light of mediated Orientalism. This is something most Swedes are reflexively aware of and something they try to fight. The multicultural suburb is full of reminders that this is a sensible course of action. Some everyday-life observations give a certain support for mediated Orientalism, but many more contradict it.

> I mean, if you see women that you've thought or read about that they are really subservient, I don't really think they are, you know, I can't say that about this area. They are really women with spunk and who, well, put their foot down and are clever, very clever and many of them learn the language really quickly and so on. Then there is, of course, a group of illiterates who haven't been able to go to school and who stay at home, have a lot of kids and so on. But there are many, well, who don't have, who haven't shown that side with subservience at all, as you would have thought, but are very independent and that.

The knowledge that Orientalism of everyday life mainly brings about is the insight into the fact that people from Muslim countries are individuals, too, and that the Orient also is a very complex social and cultural system.

> We had help from a guy from Iran and he was going to have dinner with us. And there was another Iranian and both of them, I suppose, had said that they were believers and that. Then when we were going to eat, one of them asked if it was pork. So we said yes, and then we all laughed. And then he still ate it. And then the other, he was so pissed off, so he said "But didn't you say that you were a Muslim, that you wouldn't have that?" Yes, he was hungry, he said. Then the other one started "Well, then, you shouldn't go around saying that you're a Muslim if you eat that stuff. What do you do when you fast?" And he went on like that, you know. So that's what we've experienced ourselves, you know. It's as if they like to pressure each other, you should be a Muslim, you should

fast, and you should … they keep an eye on each other. Otherwise, I think they're like everyone else, maybe a bit more open than us Northerners, you know. Like when that guy Akbar, when he was quitting, he gave me a peck on the cheek, haha, and that's never happened to me.

Everyday-life Orientalism is far more complicated than mediated Orientalism. Their similarities are much fewer than their contradictions. In this situation it is almost impossible to consider suburban Orientals as mere reflections of mediated Orientalism.

In the struggle to avoid such tendencies, one very common strategy is presented in the interviews. It is called "focusing on the individual". It aims at trying to regard each person in the light of his or her actions and statements without relating these to ideas of underlying cultural patterns. It is a strategy that harmonizes well with the modern tendency to individual emancipation. Therefore it is not especially surprising that it is as common as it is.

Many people think that it works very well. Some, however, have problems with it, as for example one female receptionist. Her experiences of Oriental men's way of treating female white-collar workers have made her efforts "to focus on the invidual" considerably more difficult.

No, I know when I started here, I was sort of totally focused on my resolve that I wouldn't … I'm going to go straight into every person that enters, they're sort of an unwritten page. But time has changed me into something different, I have to say. And I don't really like that. I do not like the fact that the people who said that it would be like this were right.

In spite of these setbacks, it is still her opinion that "one has to focus on the individual". She is, as mentioned, not alone in this. A nurse tells about more successful attempts to maintain the same strategy:

But I mean my job, when I meet people here, then I focus on, we always focus on the children. I focus on the children. It's because of the children we meet, you know, and then it doesn't matter if you're a Muslim or a Christian or where you come from, but you focus on the children, the children's needs. So, I don't sit around thinking about it, you know.

A young unemployed woman, formerly employed as a kitchen assistent, formulates a similar standpoint:

> I can't see that, even if they come from Muslim countries, I can't see, she is from that place and everyone there is like that, if you see what I mean, instead I see them as individuals or from person to person, it varies, of course. No, I never say "well, you know, everyone from that place, they're a bit strange or act in that way, or ...". No, I don't.

None of the Swedes, however, is particularly explicit when they talk about this strategy, and it is not altogether easy to discover all the nuances of the words "to focus on the individual". But if you make a more literal interpretation of the words, then there is reason to discuss them critically.

The strategy of "focusing on the individual" is of course generous and sympathetic. It can certainly bring people closer together, but the question is whether it broadens the possibilities of presenting nuanced knowledge about the Other. The problem with this strategy is that it does nothing but try to disregard the Orient as the Orient and the Orientals as Orientals. It turns to an individual, but at the same time it separates the individual from the cultural and historical contexts that Swedes are unfamiliar with.

This can be looked at in two ways. First, the focus on the individual could in itself be regarded as a way of interpreting the Orientals in the light of the modern Western individualization process that Swedes are a part of. It is first and foremost in this perspective that the phrase "to focus on the individual" becomes meaningful. It presumes an individual who is understandable without knowledge of meta-individual traditions and cultural patterns. The individual has not been understood in that way through all time and in every place.

Secondly, it should be asked what the individual that one is supposed to focus on actually looks like. He or she is first of all a component of the peaceful ethnic coexistence. He or she is someone you meet mainly at work and who first and foremost activates those sides of his or her personality which facilitate the work procedure and social interaction at work, at the expense of other sides of his or her personality. He or she is also someone in whose company you avoid certain sensitive subjects. These sensitive subjects are religion, the relationship to the opposite sex and to your own family and moral issues – that is, questions that are very important to every human being, irrespective of where he or she comes from and what cultural shape and adaptation these subjects might have had there.

This individual is a rather "thin" figure. Not only does he or she lack connections with basic and broadly human existential issues. He or she is also cut off from all occurences of the past, which happened independently of him or her, but still created a framework around his or her life and identity. He or she is an individual without historical tradition and context.

Understood in this way, this individual is also a project which is the antithesis of mediated Orientalism. Where the latter presents an Orient without individuals, the former creates, by means of amputation, an individual without an Orient. Between these two projects, one totalizing and one atomizing, another character makes his or her claims for recognition: the individual who at the intersection between past and present transforms traditions and lives culture. What future this individual goes towards is still an open question.

References

Andersson, Åsa. 1996. Grannar emellan. In Hallerstedt, Gunilla and Johansson, Thomas (eds.), *Främlingskapets anatomi*, 165–181. Stockholm: Carlssons.

Berg, Magnus. 1998. *Hudud: Ett resonemang om populärorientalismens bruksvärde och världsbild*. Stockholm: Carlssons.

Ehn, Billy. 1981. *Arbetets flytande gränser: En fabriksstudie*. Stockholm: Prisma.

Mahmoody, Betty, and Hoffer, William. 1988. *Not Without My Daughter*. New York: St. Martin's. (*Inte utan min dotter*. Stockholm: Bonniers.)

Said, Edward W. 1993. *Orientalism*. Stockholm: Ordfront.

Part 2

Beyond integration:
Transnational connections

Renegades and
the remote-controlled

The Turkish debate on the national allegiance
of the Turkish immigrants in Germany

Mehmet Ümit Necef

"The most serious conflict that has been created by loyalties running both to the United States and to the homeland has been the one experienced by the ethnic group itself in the process of establishing its American identity," writes Mona Harrington (1980: 686) in an illuminating essay discussing the issue of the dual allegiance of immigrants who have come to the United States since the beginning of the 19th century. A similar process can be observed among Turkish immigrants in the European countries, especially Germany, where the largest group of Turkish immigrants and their descendants reside. In their quest for a legitimate place in their new lands, Turkish immigrants experience a deep conflict among themselves about national loyalty. Harrington adds that "[t]he most important link to the homeland has been the need of each ethnic group for a source of pride and self-respect to aid it in establishing a dignified place in American society" (Harrington 1980: 686). Also in this respect, the Turkish immigrants in Europe repeat what their "comrades in destiny" went through in the United States. Different political tendencies among the Turkish immigrants in Europe are striving – in different and sometimes fiercely conflicting ways – to reshape and construct a "Turkey", which would serve their integration into the European societies. Harrington observes furthermore that most immigrants and the vast majority of their descendants formed a primary tie with the United States. She notes that "[i]f they felt loyalty also to the homeland of their parents, it was not because they psychologically

116

had never left it; rather it was because it represented something important to them despite their having left it – or, in the case of many of the American-born immigrants, in spite of their having never seen it" (Harrington 1980: 677). Many Turkish immigrants also feel attached to their country of origin. However, different contents and manifestations of this allegiance are a reason for disputes on the definition of "real" and "authentic" Turkishness.

In this article, I am going to discuss the concepts of nationality, ethnicity and citizenship in relation to the position of immigrant minorities in host societies. I am going to present the fierce debate between two German politicians of Turkish origin and the columnist of *Hürriyet*, the largest and most important Turkish daily newspaper published in Europe. It is a debate between those Turkish immigrants who want to keep their ethnicity, while shifting to German nationality, and those who want to maintain both their Turkish ethnicity and Turkish nationality. It shows that Turkishness is not a well-defined, self-evident and clearly demarcated, but a rather contested identity. It is an arena in which different political, ethnic, religious, generational, social, sexual etc. sections of the Turkish "community" play out their sometimes "hot", and sometimes "cold" disputes.

Nationality and ethnicity

We have to differentiate between nationality and ethnicity of both the majority and the immigrant minorities to be able to discuss the political position of immigrant minorities in a host society meaningfully. Charles Taylor (1992), Will Kymlicka (1989, 1995), Jürgen Habermas (1994 a, 1994 b) and David Miller (1995) offer theoretical frameworks useful in the discussion of nationality and ethnicity. According to them, immigrants do not have to integrate or assimilate into the ethnicity of the host group to be able to qualify to be a part of the host nation. What is expected of them is to take over the nationality of the host nation, without necessarily assimilating into its ethnicity.

Nationality and ethnicity are often confused because, as David Miller (1995) puts it, they are phenomena of the same general type. "Both nations and ethnic groups are bodies of people bound together by common cultural characteristics and mutual recognition; moreover, there is no sharp dividing line between them" (Miller 1995: 19). He somewhat stipulatively defines an ethnic group as "a community formed by common descent and sharing cultural features (language, religion, etc.) that mark it off from neighboring communities" (Miller 1995: 19).

Miller argues that ethnic groups and nations are similar in certain respects, but different in a number of ways. Therefore, in order to understand national identities of various peoples in the world today, we need to examine their ethnic origins. Typically, though not always, a nation emerges from an ethnic community that furnishes it with a distinct identity. His second point is that ethnicity continues to be a possible source of new national identities.

Having stressed their interrelatedness, Miller also insists on their dissimilarities. He points to the fact that even nations that originally had an exclusive ethnic character may come, over time, to embrace a multitude of different ethnicities. The clearest example of this, according to Miller, is the American nation, originally ethnically Anglo-Saxon, but now incorporating Irish-Americans, Italian-Americans, and many other such hyphenated groups (Miller 1995: 20).

This example also reveals the limits of the second point, that is, rethinking ethnicities as possible sources of national identities. We have no reason to believe, observes Miller, that Italian-Americans, an ethnic group, will try to develop a national identity separate from that of other Americans. In other words, it seems perfectly possible for ethnicity and nationality to co-exist, neither threatening to drive out the other. Everything depends on, he stresses, whether the ethnic group feels secure and comfortable with its national identity and the corresponding political institutions.

"To say that the boundary between nationality and ethnicity is a porous one is not to say that the two phenomena should be conflated" (Miller 1995: 19–21). Miller lists five differentiating aspects of nationality vs. ethnicity.

First, national communities are constituted by belief: nations exist when their members recognize one another as compatriots, and believe that they share characteristics of the relevant kind. In contrast to national identity, whose very existence depends upon mutual recognition, ethnic groups are aggregates of people distinguished mostly by their physical or cultural traits.

The second feature of nationality is that it is an identity which embodies historical continuity. (Miller does not comment on this, but historic character might also be seen as common to nationality and ethnicity.)

The third distinguishing aspect of national identity is that it is an active identity. Nations are communities that do things together, make decisions, achieve results, and so forth. Ethnic identities are of more passive character, as long as an ethnic group feels secure and comfortable within the national entity in which it lives. We have indeed seen many examples of how ethnic groups can become active if they do not feel safe in a national state. Here one can point to the fact that the participation of immigrants in the political process of the host country is an important factor in their acquisition of the national identity of that country. (It is no accident that the most outspoken and the most eager advocates of assuming German nationality among Turks in Germany are two German politicians of Turkish origin, one a member of the German Parliament and the other a member of the European Parliament.)

The fourth aspect of national identity is that it connects a group of people to a particular geographical area. Here again, there is a clear contrast to ethnic identities which are based on places of origin, but for which residence in a certain place is not essential. A nation, in contrast, must have a territory, a homeland to live in.

Finally, a national identity requires that the people who share it should have something in common, a set of characteristics that in the past was often referred to as a "national character", but which Miller prefers to describe as "a common public culture". Again there is a contrast between nationality and ethnicity, because the common public culture of a nation can be "learned" and acquired by initial non-nationals, while ethnic characteristics are often of objective character: one is Turkish because one is born to Turkish parents.

Miller tries to guard against the elementary error, i.e., the claim that the shared national characteristics must be based on biological descent, that our fellow nationals must be our "kith and kin", a view that leads directly to racism. "If what matters to nationality is that people should share a common public culture, then this is quite compatible with their belonging to a diversity of ethnic groups... All that matters is that the melting together of different 'races' should have produced a people with distinct and common characteristics of its own" (Miller 1995: 25). Miller observes that it has proved possible in the United States and Australia to regard immigration in itself as a formative experience, calling forth qualities of resourcefulness and mutual aid that then constitute the national character. However, his examples of American and Australian national identities suggest that it may be more difficult for more settled nations, such as the "old" nations and national states of Europe, to naturalize immigrants.

My own distinction between nationality and ethnicity is not similar to the "fashionable" one between German (ethnic) and French (civic) type of citizenship. Civic citizenship defines belonging on the basis of participation through rights and obligations, while ethnic citizenship denotes community-based notions of belonging through particularistic identities. I agree with Yasemin Soysal's (1996) criticism that ethnic identities versus civil rights are not profound differentiating factors across national citizenships and that both are embodied in national citizenship as an ideology and as an institution (Soysal 1996: 17). Nationality, as I use it, is "thicker" than the concepts of rights and obligations that naturalization involves. On top of citizenship, and sometimes independent of it, nationality entails a subjective feeling of national loyalty.

Persons of immigrant origin may feel part of the new nation, but for some reason they may not have acquired the citizenship of their new country. The opposite cases can also be observed: people who have acquired citizenship of the host country for practical reasons, but who do not (yet) identify with the new country's national culture. Another example is the case of a young Turkish man who feels like a member of the host nation, but still bears Turkish nationality, because his father wanted to retain the Turkish nationality of all family members.

The nationalist theory of nation conflates nationality and ethnicity: members of a nation should all belong to the same ethnic group. We can look at immigrants from the position of two kinds of nationalism: nationalism of the host or majority society and nationalism of the nation of origin of an immigrant group.

The nationalism of the majority does not accept that immigrants can gradually become members of the nation, since they are ethnically and culturally different. Therefore they have three choices: either they should get assimilated to the ethnicity of the majority, live like eternal foreigners/strangers, or go back "home", where they "really belong".

According to the nationalism of the immigrants, it is impossible to identify with a new nationality as long as one belongs to an ethnicity different from that of the dominant group. The nationalist conception of nation thus leaves only two alternatives for immigrants: assimilation, which is often presented as national and cultural treason, or eternal exclusion from the host nation. If the ethnic group one belongs to has its own national state, then one has to retain the national identity related to that state.

This concept of nation has consequences for the way Turkish immigrants conceive both the ethnic makeup of their country of origin and their new homelands. What sort of theory of nation informs the immigrants is important pertaining to the country of origin, since Turkey has a large Kurdish minority. How this minority is seen and treated is of great relevance and importance both in Turkey and in Europe. This issue creates tension, as we shall see, not only between Turkish and Kurdish immigrants, but also between the Turks themselves. Furthermore, the ways immigrants define nation and nationalism also influence the ways they conceive their position in the new societies.

The Turkish debate: "Integrationists" vs. "nationalists"

Among the political elite of the Turkish immigrants in Western European countries, especially in Germany, one can discern three fiercely competing discourses on the place of Turkish immigrants in the host societies: the Turkish "nationalist" discourse, the "integrationist" discourse and the Islamist discourse. In accordance with the theoretical framework summarized above, I am going to take the debate between the advocates of the first two discourses. (Not all the terms I use to describe these discourses are used by the people involved. One of them has vehemently and repeatedly denied that he is a "nationalist", since the concept of nationalism has very negative connotations in German political culture. I use the term "nationalist" in a descriptive sense, as the most suitable concept in my own theoretical framework. I could just as well use the term "the official national(ist) Turkish discourse", but that would probably only help to radicalize his protests.)

The "nationalist" discourse is represented most clearly by Ertug Karakullukcu, the editor of the European edition of the Turkish daily *Hürriyet*, which has the largest circulation and is the most influential among the Turkish ethnic press. Besides *Hürriyet*, three more daily newspapers (*Milliyet*, *Sabah*, *Türkiye*) are published in Frankfurt, Germany, and distributed all over Europe, as well as *Özgür Politika*, the semi-official paper of the PKK (The Workers Party of Kurdistan), published predominantly in the Turkish language.

The "integrationist" discourse is best represented by Cem Özdemir, a Green Party member of the German Parliament (*Bundestag*) and Ozan Ceyhun, a Green Party member of the European Parliament.

Since the mid 1990s, issues of ethnic and national identity have very often been debated in the Turkish newspapers mentioned above. The longest and most heated debate still takes place in *Hürriyet*. Ertug Karakullukcu started a campaign against Cem Özdemir in December 1994, the day after Özdemir held his first speech at the *Bundestag* as the first "Turkish" parliamentarian. Karakullukcu gradually began targeting Ozan Ceyhun, too, as his statements became prominent in public debates on immigrant issues, Turkish politics and German foreign policy towards Turkey. In the months preceding the German general elections in September 1998, in which Özdemir was a candidate, Karakullukcu wrote long articles nearly every day, attacking almost every word uttered by Özdemir and Ceyhun on immigrant issues and Turkish politics. Nevertheless, Cem Özdemir was elected to the *Bundestag* once again and became an even more prominent politician (especially after The Greens formed a coalition government with the Social Democratic Party). In 1999, the quarrel took on somewhat bizarre proportions with accusations, counter-accusations and denials of sexual blackmail. Özdemir accused MIT (The Turkish Intelligence Agency) of trying to set him up with a sexual offer (Hufelschulte 1999: 98). This case was extensively reported on in *Hürriyet*.

"Integrationist discourse": Cem Özdemir and Ozan Ceyhun

Cem Özdemir was born to a Turkish immigrant family in 1965 in West Germany. He studied social pedagogy and entered the German

Parliament in 1994 as the first parliamentarian of Turkish origin, to be re-elected in 1998. Furthermore, he was elected as the Greens' spokesman on interior affairs.

As described in his book *Almanya'da Bir Türk* ("A Turk in Germany") (Ceyhun 1995), Ozan Ceyhun has been politically active since arriving in Germany in 1982. Being wanted by the Turkish authorities for alleged extremist left-wing activities, he was given political asylum. Since the late 1990s, he has been a member of the European Parliament representing the German Greens.

According to Özdemir (1995), Germany should be a "conscious multicultural society", "a civil multiethnic society" and a "pluralistic multicultural society". But a common ground is necessary – fundamental human rights, together with basic social rights.

What does Özdemir have to say about his own ethnic and national identity? In his book *Ich bin Inländer: Ein anatolischer Schwabe im Bundestag* (Özdemir 1997) ("I am a Native [*Inländer* is a pun on the German word *Ausländer* used for immigrants]: An Anatolian Swabian in the German Parliament")[1] he describes himself as follows:

> I am a German citizen of Turkish origin. The Swabian is emotionally closer to me than the German, and my Turkish origin is not that simple. My father comes from a Circassian[2] village near Tokat in Anatolia, and my mother is from the metropolis of Istanbul. I myself come from Swabia. Therefore the best description would be an Anatolian Swabian (Özdemir 1997: 6).
>
> When I was elected to the German parliament, the Turkish media celebrated me as "the Turkish parliamentarian". At that time I had to draw the attention of the Turkish community that I was of Turkish origin, no more, no less. If I were a Turkish parliamentarian, then I would live in Ankara, not in Bonn or Ludwigsburg. Everybody had to accept that. Then the next origin problem soon emerged. Since my father stems from a Circassian village in Turkey, the organization of Caucasians in Germany, "The Caucasian Community in Germany" contacted me. "You are a Circassian. Why don't you emphasize this more in public?" See, I do not speak a word of Circassian. ... My mother's grandmother was Greek. She is herself, as it was called in Nazi-German parlance, "a quarter Greek". As can be seen, he who begins ethnicisms of this kind commits hara-kiri (Özdemir 1997: 8).

When describing himself, Özdemir does not use the ethnic term *Türk* (Turk) or *Alman* (German) but the territorial terms, *Türkiyeli* (resident in Turkey) or *Almanyali* (resident in Germany). These terms are neologisms that cannot be found in Turkish dictionaries. Also, when talking about immigrants who stem from Turkey he uses the territorial term *Türkiyeli göcmenler* ("immigrants from Turkey"). He also uses the expression: *Türkiye kökenli* ("Turkey-rooted" or "stemming from Turkey", but not "of Turkish origin") (e.g. Özdemir 1998). This is a source of constant irritation to his opponents, who take every opportunity to mock him in the media (e.g. Karakullukcu often writes: "The Turk, sorry, *Türkiyeli*, Cem Özdemir"). (Already at the beginning of the 1970s, many Turkish leftists began to use the territorial neologism *Türkiyeli* to take a critical attitude to Turkish nationalism, and began to emphasize that not only Turks, but for instance also Kurds, lived in the country. The nationalists have always seen it as yet another sign of the leftists' national treason and support for Kurdish separatism.)

Özdemir's party The Greens used a political slogan in the last elections, which again irritated Turkish nationalists: "Everybody living in Germany, all *Deutschländer* of Turkish, Kurdish, Spanish, Greek, German... origin, should unite for a better life." A nationalist-minded Turkish reader of *Hürriyet* found the expression "*Deutschländer* of German origin" most outrageous. Germans were Germans, and Turks were Turks. Period.

With his understanding of ethnic and national identity, Cem Özdemir defines himself as "a German citizen of Turkish origin" and advocates what he calls "integration policy".

> The Greens advocate that the immigrants should integrate into German society without losing their own identities, and see the Citizens Act and a number of other laws which curtail the rights of immigrants, as the hindrance to this integration. ... We have to maintain our culture, to add our beautiful traditions to the cultural mosaic of the country we live in, but at the same time, we have to participate in the social, political and cultural dynamics of the society we live in... This is the common ground of the new identity we have to create (Özdemir 1998).

It is precisely this emphasis on the search for a "new identity" that infuriates the nationalists. For them, Turkish immigrants already have an identity, which is being Turks.

Özdemir criticizes both what he calls the self-encapsulation of some Turkish immigrants in Germany and the demand for assimilation, which comes from certain German nationalist circles. He believes that the Turkish newspapers in Germany are not really interested in the immigrants' problems, but in spreading Turkish nationalist propaganda.

Rejecting the accusation that he advocates "forceful assimilation", an accusation often directed at him in *Hürriyet*, Özdemir says:

> Both *Hürriyet* and the hawks in Ankara know perfectly well that I advocate a model based on first-class citizenship and non-forced integration. On the other hand they advocate the Ottoman policy in the Balkans in the last century, which can be summarized as establishing a Turkish minority which later could be mobilized by command from the centre. Those who follow Germany only through the Turkish press meet a very distorted picture of Germany. Everything is being assessed through the spectacles of Ankara. The way a person or party looks at Ankara becomes the determining factor. The social problems in Germany fall into the background" (*Hürriyet*, 29 July 1998).

However, Özdemir is not against immigrants' involvement in the politics of the countries of origin:

> It is beyond doubt that our people living in Germany will be interested in the politics of the country they originate from. The sorrows of Turkey are also our sorrows and the happiness of Turkey is also our happiness. It would be surprising if this was different in the age of information and communication. On the other hand, we indeed belong here. We also share the sorrows and happiness of the country we live in. Together with people of many national origins we are on the streets, in the factories, at schools, in kindergartens, political parties, in the parliaments for the welfare and happiness of the country we live in… Germany has become a multicultural, multiethnic, multireligious immigration country (Özdemir 1998).

Özdemir's fellow partisan Ozan Ceyhun openly argues against the idea that Turks in the European countries should establish pro-Turkey lobbies:

> I am against the Turkish state forming a lobby in Germany. I would like to remind that although Turkish immigrants will maybe one day have dual citizenship, they will still be German citizens (Ceyhun 1995: 10–11).
>
> A part, not all, of the Turkish media in Germany, acts like a Turkish lobby and for example thinks that defending torture in Turkey is defending Turkey. These media influence a section of the Turkish community and this section can sometimes be misused in political schemes in the name of "loving Turkey". ... This lobby is racist. Ankara is a foreign centre [for us immigrants in Germany]. ... If the Turks with German citizenship begin to allow themselves to be manipulated and remote-controlled by politicians in Turkey, this will harm the social peace in Germany and will become a problem" (*Hürriyet*, 15 October 1998).

Another aspect of Özdemir's and Ceyhun's political standpoints is their active involvement in German and European policy towards Turkey. They have repeatedly criticized the violation of human rights in Turkey, have visited Turkey in German political missions to investigate the condition of human rights and repeatedly criticized the policies of the Turkish authorities towards the Kurdish minority in the country.

Ceyhun undercommunicates the "differences on Turkey" between his party and many Turkish immigrants:

> We may think differently about Turkey. But in spite of this we should not forget the fact that we live in Germany and are going to live permanently in this country. Germany's home politics and foreign policy pertaining to Turkey are without doubt very different areas. Everybody can be active in both areas without mixing them up (Ceyhun 1995: 77).

The impression should not be created that there is a consensus in the whole Turkish press against Özdemir and Ceyhun. This is not an issue of ethnicity, as nationalists like Karakullukcu attempt to present it, but of political ideology and political line. Newspapers like *Cumhuriyet* and

Milliyet, or individual commentators who are critical of Turkish official rhetoric on a number of issues, especially on the Kurdish issue, take a more positive attitude and reflect Özdemir's and Ceyhun's standpoints relatively objectively. For example, Oral Calislar (1998) from the daily *Cumhuriyet* was appalled at *Hürriyet's* attacks at Özdemir and Ceyhun, whom he described as "young and successful politicians". Calislar observed that the German public opinion followed *Hürriyet's* campaign against Özdemir and Ceyhun with anxiety and irritation.

The accusation of "traitor" hurled at critical politicians, journalists or intellectuals is not specific for Turks, or unique for advocates of certain political tendencies among Turks. Thomas Friedman (1990), the former Beirut correspondent of the *New York Times* and an American Jew himself, was described by a New York Jew as "the most hated man in New York City today". "What had I done to deserve this shame?" asks Friedman and answers: "My crime, it turned out, was that of a messenger. As the *New York Times* bureau chief in Beirut, I had helped to inform the Jews of New York City of the less-than-heroic behavior of the Israeli army in Lebanon, the Sabra and Shatila massacre, and other unsettling stories" (Friedman 1990: 477–8). His explanation for this reaction is probably valid as well for Turks infuriated by Özdemir and Ceyhun's views: "I am convinced that the anger which the American Jewish community, from the leadership down, directed at the news media, and reporters such as myself, was largely the result of the fact that they were deeply disturbed and confused by what Israel was doing in Lebanon" (Friedman 1990: 478). Likewise, the way Turkey is treating its citizens and its minorities does not strengthen the position of Turkish immigrants within their new societies, but tarnishes their image as Turks.

The views of Ertug Karakullukcu

Ertug Karakullukcu is the editor of the European edition of *Hürriyet*. The daily newspaper has a supplement called *Avrupa Gazetesi* ("European Newspaper"), in which he has a column called *Kulak Misafiri* ("One who overhears"). In his articles, appearing nearly every day, he takes up different issues such as the problems of Turkish immigrants in Germany, Turkish politics, German policy towards Turkey etc.

Karakullukcu writes in an easily accessible colloquial style and has a quite sentimental and aggressive tone.

One of Karakullukcu's articles extensively quoted below is of interest for two reasons. First, it was the first signal of a campaign that has been going on continuously for five years. Secondly, the style and the rhetoric are typical of both Karakullukcu and popular Turkish nationalism. The article was printed in *Hürriyet* in December 1994, immediately after Cem Özdemir's first speech at the German Parliament in which he harshly criticized violations of human rights in Turkey and Turkey's policy towards the Kurds, especially the banning of the pro-Kurdish DEP (Democratic Party) and the arrest of its members in front of the Turkish Parliament. Typically, the article is entitled "The Dagger in Our Back":

> What can be more painful than reporting[3] on one's motherland? God forbid! But unfortunately, unfortunately…
>
> Did not Cem Özdemir's heart bleed while informing on our Turkey to the German Parliament? By doing this he must even have shocked Sirri Sakik [the Kurdish member of the Parliament from DEP, who was arrested in 1994 on charges of supporting terrorism], who flatly rejected to speak with French parliamentarians, saying to them "I cannot inform on my country to you".
>
> Özdemir is a Turkish son [*Türk evladi*] who grew up in Germany. We would have liked to applaud him with all our hearts, when he spoke to the parliament for the first time. But what did he do? He took the DEP dagger in his hand and stabbed us in the back. Cem, my brother, this is not fair.
>
> Cem accused Ankara of human rights violations in his speech. And protected … PKK [The Kurdish Workers Party] militants.
>
> And he did not stop there. Cem Özdemir also published a statement together with Ozan Ceyhun, who is also from The Greens.
>
> Here are some "precious" sentences from their statement. Hold tight:
>
> "We, politicians originating from Turkey (Look: They cannot say 'of Turkish origin' –Karakullukcu), want to express our anxiety about the harsh jail sentences given to parliamentarians from the DEP."
>
> "DEP-parliamentarians are punished, not because the judicial system is functioning independently in Turkey, but because some circles, who are in power and who reject a peaceful solution of the

Kurdish question, exerted political pressure on the judicial system" (What about the laws? – Karakullukcu). [...]

"It is sad that our colleagues in the Turkish Parliament are being accused of being terrorists and separatists, just because they spoke Kurdish in the parliament" (The real reason is their relations with the PKK and separatism – Karakullukcu). [...]

"No matter whether those who die in the conflict are Turks (that is Turkish soldiers – Karakullukcu) or Kurds (that is terrorists – Karakullukcu), they are all humans of Anatolia" (That means soldiers and terrorists are the same – Karakullukcu).

Are these the words of a Turkish child [*bir Türk cocugu*]?

Oh, God! How painful and bitter! [...]

Later Cem Özdemir talks about how he is struggling for "dual citizenship" for immigrants in Germany as if he is throwing peanuts at a monkey, as if he is trying to make good again his critique of Turkey.

We do not see any friendly tone in his behaviour.

Özdemir even claims something which nobody dared to claim, that "Kurds" are being treated in a cruel manner in Western Turkey as well.

Can you imagine [the lie], dear readers?

Even [the PKK leader] Abdullah Öcalan could not make such a big lie.

My young brother, Herr Cem...

Most of the Turks in Germany and in Turkey do not think the way you do. You must know this.

If you follow this course, maybe your star will shine even brighter in your party, but you will be estranged in relation to the Turkish community. You will not be able to look anyone in the face. You must also know this.

Our recommendation to you. Look into the mirror and please ask yourself: Cem, Cem, whose spokesman are you?! (*Hürriyet*, 16 December 1994).[4]

According to Karakullukcu, the identity issue of the Turkish immigrants is very simple: they are Turks and should retain both their ethnic and national identities as Turks in foreign countries, even if they were born there. For him "Turk" is a self-evident category, which cannot take different meanings in different contexts. Therefore Karakullukcu often uses the two expressions for the Turkish immigrants in Germany: "Turks living in Germany" and "the Turkish community in Germany". Turks in Germany are a part of the Turkish nation and their duty is to be loyal to the Turkish state and follow its recommendations pertaining to home and foreign policy. Turks should try to get the citizenship of the countries they live in and establish a pro-Turkish lobby to influence European policies towards Turkey in a positive direction. To be able to be influential in Germany, Turks should become "modernized", "civilized" and "westernized". They should live like modern urban Turks and show the Europeans that Turks are a civilized and a modern nation.

As regards Turkey's ethnopolitics, Karakullukcu repeats the official view on the Kurdish question. He seems to have changed his views on the question as to whether Kurds existed in Turkey at all, since he used to put the word Kurds in quotation marks in his earlier articles. Since recently, he has claimed that there is no Kurdish "minority" in Turkey. It is true that there are some citizens of Kurdish origin (*Kürt vatandaslarimiz*), but all of them should ethnically become Turks and in fact they want to become Turks. Every Turkish citizen is equal and enjoys the same rights. Since there are no minorities, it is absurd to talk about minority rights. People who do so aim at splitting Turkey's territorial integrity, i.e., at creating a Kurdistan. People like Özdemir and Ceyhun, who advocate a "political solution" for the Kurdish question, speaking about a "Kurdish minority" in Turkey and their "minority rights", are in fact enemies of Turkey (*Hürriyet*, 25 November 1998).

For Karakullukcu, the most important duty of the Turks abroad is to keep bonds with Turkey:

> For the great majority of Turks living in Germany, "relations with Turkey" are a determining factor. Leave the debate about integration or allegiance to Turkey [*Türkiye'ye baglilik*]. Forget also whatever Cem Özdemir claims. Those two things [integration or allegiance to Turkey] do not contradict each other. The concrete fact is self-evident: our people do not want their motherland to be sneered at, looked down upon, despised, degraded or treated as inferior (*Hürriyet*, 10 October 1998).

Not only the Turkish-born, but also the German-born young Turks should not consider Germany as their motherland: "The real motherland of the young Turks is Turkey" (*Hürriyet*, 13 October 1998). In Karakullukcu's ethnocultural universe people like Özdemir and Ceyhun are false and inauthentic Turks. They have sold their souls to the German authorities and have become renegades:

> Ozan Ceyhun calls himself "A Turk in Germany". No, sir! He is a travesty of Turkishness [*Türk bozuntusu*] … No German politician has harmed the Turkish community in Germany and the image of Turkey in Germany more than he has. He is the gravedigger [*kuyu kazicisi*] of Turks (*Hürriyet*, 17 October 1998).

The concept of kin-state

The claim of Turkish nationalists on the national allegiance of their "kith and kin" in European countries stems from two factors. From a political standpoint, the Turkish state wants to establish pro-Turkish lobbies in a number of European countries and wants *inter alia* to isolate and weaken the political influence of persons of Turkish origin who do not share the official views of the Turkish state. From a historical and ideological standpoint, Turkey still sees itself as the "kin-state" of the Turkish immigrants in Western Europe. This is an extension of the traditional way of thinking about Turkish and even Muslim minorities in other countries.

According to the British historian and Balkan expert Hugh Poulton, Turkey poses an interesting case of "kin-state", defined as "a state composed of and governed by a majority community, for which groups who reside outside the state's sovereign territory maintain a strong affinity as a result of shared ethnicity, culture, religion, language or perceived history" (Poulton 1997: 285). Poulton notes that when working with the concept of kin-state in relation to Turkey, we immediately face the questions of who a Turk is, which groups are regarded by Turkey as their "kin" and which groups view Turkey as their "kin-state".

> The foundation of the Turkish Republic in the 1920s on the ruins of the Ottoman Empire saw large numbers of Turkish speakers who previously had been part of the Ottoman Empire combined with the heritage of the Islamic Caliphate has resulted in many Muslims who are not ethnic Turks from the former empire, especially in the Balkans, looking to Turkey as their kin-state. This is amply reflected

in the huge numbers of non-Turkish speaking Muslims who have immigrated to Turkey (and earlier to the Ottoman Empire) from Russia, the Caucasus and the Balkans (Poulton 1997: 275).[5]

Poulton underlines that despite the strong territorial model for Kemalist nationalism based on common citizenship (as reflected in Article 66 of the current Constitution which states that "everyone bound to the Turkish state through the bond of citizenship is a Turk"), there were from the start also elements of both perceived aliens within, and kin outside. The conscious policy of propagating a cohesive sense of national identity and creating a widespread national consciousness in Turkey saw a great emphasis on the ethnic Turks and their language at the expense of other groups like the Kurds, whose separate identity and language were denied.

Furthermore, the state propagated an affinity with other Turkic peoples in Central Asia, which has led to a retention of the sense of "kin" in Central Asia. Combined with the ethnic factor is the religious factor which has led many Balkans Muslims who are not ethnic Turks to look up to Turkey as a potential kin-state.

Poulton underlines that Turkey sees itself as the kin-state and the possible protector of not only Turkish (or Turkish-speaking), but also Muslim minorities in the Balkans. The Turkish and Muslim minorities in the Balkans, conversely, "look to Turkey as a kin-state".

Regarding Turkish immigrants ("foreign workers" or "guest workers") in various European countries, the Turkish Republic is also constitutionally bound to take an interest in them. They are specifically referred to in the 1982 Constitution (Article 62): "the State shall take the necessary measures to ensure the family unity, the education of the children, the cultural needs, and the social security of Turkish nationals working abroad, and shall take the necessary measures to safeguard their ties with the country, and help them on their return home". In line with this, notes Poulton, the Turkish state pays teachers and imams to work in German schools. Moreover, Turkey is only a couple of hours of a cheap and frequent flight away from any European capital. Four daily newspapers are published simultaneously in Turkey and in Germany. The modern technology of the satellite dish has given access to at least six television channels and a number of radio channels broadcast from Turkey.

Why do some immigrants get involved in "homeland politics"?

The interest of immigrants in the politics of their countries, and in the way their countries are presented in the media of the host country, cannot merely be seen and interpreted as "patriotism", "love of the homeland", "allegiance to the land of memories" and nostalgia. For Max Weber, "[t]he persistent effect of the old ways and of childhood reminiscences continue as a native country sentiment [*Heimatsgefühl*] among emigrants even when they have become so thoroughly adjusted to the new country that return to their homeland would be intolerable (this being the case of most German-Americans, for example)" (Weber 1978: 388). The role of *Heimatsgefühl* should not be rejected, but there is more at stake. It has also more down-to-earth aspects, since the positive or negative symbolic capital of the land of origin has a direct impact on the symbolic capital, i.e. the image and the prestige of the minority in the host society. In other words, the symbolic capital of the homeland becomes a part of "impression management" of the immigrants in relation to the new society (Lyman and Douglass 1973). A "good" image of the homeland would put them in a more positive position *vis-à-vis* the host society and other ethnic groups, and the "spoiled" image of the homeland would be a negative capital, since the individual has to demonstrate that he or she does not share negative characteristics of the homeland such as poverty, ignorance, violence etc.

The concept of impression management is very useful in explaining why the presentation of the homeland becomes such a controversial issue among different sections of the same immigrant group, evoking deep sentiments.

Borrowing the concept of impression management from Erving Goffman, Lyman and Douglass (1973: 344) define it as the strategic and tactical employment of racial and ethnic identities by which groups and individuals work through situations and careers. "At the group level of social organization, ethnic relations usually translate themselves into sets and series of strategic and tactical situations played out over time as contending ethnic groups seek to alter their respective statuses *vis-à-vis* one another" (Lyman and Douglass 1973: 344–345). Strategies adopted by a minority in a pluralistic society may be used, among other aims, for active participation in the public life of the larger society while retaining significant aspects of its own cultural identity or for retaining confederational ties with the larger society while at the same time securing its own territorial and communal control over minority issues. These strategies are likely to be a source of societal disruption and, as such, to be a source of political, social and personal problems as well.

Lyman and Douglass explain the appearance of stereotypes in multicultural societies with reference to official culture, that is, the culture of the dominant ethnic group, and to social contract, that is, a set of rules governing interaction and relationships between members of the groups composing the plural social order. These rules constitute a deeply ingrained understanding transcending the cultural differences which divide groups, while at the same time binding them at the level of a basic social contract.

Lyman and Douglass assert that ethnic minority groups employ different forms of collective impression management to strengthen and improve their position in the pluralistic society.[6] Being aware of the outsiders' stereotypes of them, members of any ethnic group seek to defuse potentially dangerous aspects of these stereotypes. "They attempt to arouse sympathy for their position as a minority, and influence outsiders toward a more appreciative and tolerant attitude" (Lyman and Douglass 1973: 347–8). Collective impression management strategies include a range of attempts, from casting the dominant group into a role which is advantageous for the minority, to restricting public displays of their ethnicity to those aspects which are acceptable to the larger society, e.g., confining public displays of their ethnic culture to "dance, dress, or diet".

Such psychological mechanisms are also at work concerning the Turks. Although Turkey does not strictly belong to the poor Third World, it is not considered to be a rich country. For Turkish immigrants there is, first of all, the stigma of stemming from a country that is relatively poor compared to the host countries of Europe. Secondly, Turkey has for many years been trying to enter the European Union, but has been rejected several times on the grounds of lacking democracy as well as economic strength. These rejections have frustrated the national dignity of many Turks and radicalized anti-European feelings among both the Turkish elite in Turkey and the Turkish immigrants. Thirdly, Turkey is a country where more than 36,000 people have been killed in a conflict (see Dietert-Scheuer 1999: 26), whether one calls it a "civil war", a "fight against terrorism" or a "fight for Kurdish national independence". The frequent critical reports on violations of human rights, shootings, violent demonstrations, burning down of villages, claims of massacres, torture etc. threaten the identity and self-respect of many Turks. Nobody has an interest in being presented as coming from a country where people "butcher, torture or mistreat each other".

Turkish communities throughout Europe employ three strategies to overcome the negative image of their homeland. One strategy presents a glorifying picture of Turkey and denies all the charges of violations of minority or human rights (such charges are called communist, neo-liberal, separatist, treacherous, imperialistic, culturally arrogant, ethnocentric, orientalistic etc.; Karakullukcu's texts offer rich examples of this strategy).

Another strategy is to take a critical position towards different aspects of Turkish culture and the political situation in Turkey. One is not seen as a representative or advocate of the official political line of the homeland state. I will illustrate these two strategies by presenting the attitude of Ozan Ceyhun as manifested in two passages in his book "A Turk in Germany" (1998), and the contrasting attitude of a Turkish television journalist. According to that other attitude, individual members of ethnic and national groups often see themselves as representatives ("ambassadors") of their groups (and are often seen as such by outsiders).

"It is one of my primary duties to struggle against the fact that Turks, living in Germany and in other European countries, are harmed because of the mistakes committed in Turkey and are held responsible for these misdeeds," writes Ceyhun in the essay entitled "The Punishment of Being a Turk" (Ceyhun 1995: 55). He does not explicate how the Turks are harmed and who holds them responsible. He is talking about the "spoiled image" of the Turkish immigrants in the European countries due to human rights violations and political violence in Turkey.

In contrast to that, Reha Erüs, the Rome correspondent of TRT-INT (a Turkish state-owned television channel) takes the line of denying negative aspects of the homeland. Shortly after the arrival of Abdullah Öcalan, chairman of PKK (Workers' Party of Kurdistan), in Rome in September 1998, Erüs was complaining about his Italian neighbors asking him "Why do you Turks treat the Kurds so badly?" He was not bothered by the fact that he was held individually responsible for the alleged mistreatment, but by the fact that Italians claimed that the Kurds were badly treated in Turkey. He apparently did not see himself as a correspondent of a television channel, but as a representative of "the nation". He thus told the viewers how he argued against his neighbours' allegations and how he denied the mistreatment of the Kurds in Turkey.

The third strategy is not getting involved in "Turkish politics" and not taking public positions on "Turkish affairs". It is rather common among intellectuals of Turkish origin living in Europe, who have developed a certain demeaning attitude not only towards people who glorify Turkey, but especially towards those who criticize it. The "silent" Turks dislike people like Özdemir and Ceyhun for taking "modernistic" and "orientalistic" positions, i.e., for what they see as merely reflecting the Western images of "The Orient" and copying the "Western" criticism against it.

In a way, the criticism people like Cem Özdemir and Ozan Ceyhun direct at the Turkish state and society, which can be conceived as their own mode of impression management, spoils the impression management of Turks following the other two strategies. The first strategy, the one that glorifies and kitschifies Turkey, is spoiled because its presentation of Turkey is contradicted not by "outsiders", but by "insider Turks" – a fact which makes the criticism even more credible in the eyes of the German public and therefore more devastating. The third strategy, that of silence on controversial matters pertaining to Turkey, is spoiled because more attention is drawn not only to the controversial matters, but also to the silence itself.

Limits of sovereignty

This Turkish debate on the position of Turks in Germany leads to a debate on the limits to the sovereignty of national states in principle. The Turkish nationalists often use the argument of national sovereignty when countering the critique coming from the West about

the violation of human and minority rights in Turkey. The standard
official Turkish answer on this issue has until recently been: Turkey
is a sovereign state and the way she treats its citizens and its minorities is an internal affair in which foreign states should not intervene.
It is precisely the fact that Cem Özdemir and Ozan Ceyhun as
German politicians regularly criticize Turkey on these issues that
infuriates people like Karakullukcu. However, on the other hand, the
Turkish nationalists see no problem in intervening in German national sovereignty by enciting campaigns against German politicians
and by openly discussing which German party German citizens of
Turkish origin should support.[7]

The untrustworthiness of demanding every possible right for Turkish
minorities in the name of minority and human rights from the European states, but denying exactly the same rights to the Kurds in Turkey,
is easy to see through. Such rhetoric by Karakullukcu and other nationalists serves only to discredit Turkey and the Turkish minorities in the
European countries. In an age in which peoples of the world have the
right and the technological means to be informed instantly and abun-
dantly about each other, and in which the concept of human rights and
not the rights of national citizens constitute the guiding lines, the
rhetoric of Turkish nationalists sounds hollow. Leaving aside their views
on other issues, Özdemir and Ceyhun, demanding certain reforms
concerning the civil rights of ethnic minorities from the German state
while at the same time criticizing the violation of human and minority
rights in Turkey, have created a trustworthy political position.

Notes

1   The famous film director Elia Kazan, who is of Turkish-Greek origin, wrote an
    autobiography entitled *The Anatolian*.
2   A Muslim ethnic minority in Turkey which originates from the Caucasus.
3   Karakullukcu uses the term *jurnal etmek*, which means to denounce, to report,
    and act as an informer, denouncer, delator.
4   In order to reveal the harsh flavour of the debate, here is Ceyhun's (1995) reaction:
    Karakullukcu smears anybody coming his way. He accuses the German press of
    being "immoral" [*ahlaksizlik*]. He incites our [Turkish] citizens living in Germany
    against certain German politicians with the slogan of "Turkey above everything",
    and contributes to the xenophobia which is on the rise in Germany. Recently he
    incited our citizens against the mayor of Hannover Schmalstieg. He published the

private fax and telephone numbers of the mayor and incited his fanatic readers, who act more royal than royalty, to insult him by fax and phone, because the mayor had made a speech in a Kurdish demonstration. But Karakullukcu had not thought it was necessary to investigate and debate either the content or the form of the speech in his articles. But it is without doubt that he contributed greatly either knowingly or unknowingly to the xenophobia and the spoiling of the image of Turks [*Türk imajinin zedelenmesi*] in Germany, because hundreds of "heroes" incited by Karakullukcu told the mayor even in writing that they would "cut off his tongue", "f... his mother", "peel his skin off with torture worse than that in horror movies" and "kill him". Of course, the German newspapers published all the threats page after page. Thus hundreds of thousands of Turks, who in the last thirty years have tried to explain to the Germans that they were as Western as the Germans, were in one instant again stamped as "barbarians" by the German public. The xenophobes, of course, made utmost use of this situation. ... Another destruction, which Karakullukcu has brought on us, has to do with SPD [The German Social Democratic Party]. Because he did not like a number of SPD's positions on Turkey, especially pertaining to the Kurdish question and human rights violations, he tried to incite the Turkish members to resign from the party, and claimed that those who did not resign, would be behaving like "renegades" [*vatan haini*]. This incitement has been really effective and many Turkish citizens or German citizens of Turkish origin have resigned from the party one after the other.

I have written an article in the newspaper *Milliyet* and warned immigrants who were members of the SPD not to resign, since I regarded SPD as very important for us immigrants who have settled in Germany... A Turkish friend who has a high position in the party told me that 10,000 citizens of Turkey were members of the party... Our party The Greens has a similar problem, since a lot of Turks, who are sympathetic towards us due to our politics on questions pertaining to the immigrants, have come to hate us, because of our critical views regarding Turkey... Since we have different views on human rights [in Turkey], many Turkish immigrants living in Germany who are sensitive on the issue of Turkey, see our party as "a party which one as a Turk cannot be a member of" (Ceyhun 1995: 76).

5   Poulton does not mention the Turkic and Muslim Uigurs from East Turkestan, the Sinxiang province of modern China.

6   A Turkish example is the popular Turkish discourse on the "double standards" (*çifte standard*) of the Europeans. A typical accusation one can hear and read in the Turkish media is that while the European countries criticize Turkey for human rights violations, they often violate the same rights of immigrants.

7   Fatih Altayli, columnist in *Hürriyet* and host in a popular political debate programme on a Turkish television channel, who can be described as a nationalist and a person who often follows the official national(ist) line on a number of issues such as minority rights, wrote an unusually open-hearted and self-critical article about Turkish interventions in German politics. In the article entitled "Who would like to have foreign representatives in his own parliament?" Altayli (1999) analysed why German public opinion was against double citizenship, and concluded that the main reason was – justifiably in his own view – the German anxiety that voters and *Bundestag* members of Turkish origin will not primarily have the inter-

ests of Germany in mind, but will be manipulated by Turkish politicians and state. His recommendation to Turkish politicians and commentators was to stop trying to intervene in German politics through politicians and voters of Turkish origin. Professor Faruk Sen, the director of the Institute of Turkish Studies in Essen, Germany, and a frequent commentator on Turkish politics and immigrant issues on German television channels, is openly disturbed by some utterances of a number of Turkish politicians visiting Germany: "One of the greatest obstacles for the Citizenship Act in Germany is the belief that Turkey will continue influencing politically the Turks who will become German citizens". Regarding the possible attitude of the new Germans of Turkish origin, Sen claims that Turkish citizens, after becoming German citizens, should follow their own policies in German parties, not paying much attention to the incapable Turkish politicians.

References

Altayli, Fatih. 1999. Kim parlamentosunda yabanci temsilci ister? ("Who would like to have foreign representatives in his own parliament?"). *Hürriyet,* 10 February 1999.

Anderson, Benedict. 1992. The New World Disorder. *New Left Review* 193: 3–13.

Armstrong, John A. 1976. Mobilized and Proletarian Diaspora. *The American Political Science Review* 70: 393–408.

Brown, Thomas. 1966. *Irish-American Nationalism, 1870–1890.* Philadelphia: Historical Books.

Buk-Swienty, Tom. 1999. I Guds eget land ("In God's Own Land"). *Weekendavisen,* March 5–11, 1999.

Calislar, Oral. 1998. Hürriyet in Avrupa baskisinda ("In the European edition of Hürriyet"). *Cumhuriyet,* 25 September 1998.

Ceyhun, Ozan. 1995. *Almanya'da Bir Türk* ("A Turk in Germany"). Istanbul: Sis cani Yayinlari.

Dietert-Scheuer, Amke. 1999. *Möglichkeiten der Konfliktlösung in der Türkischen Republik, Mitteilungen* 57. Hamburg: Deutsches Orient-Institut.

Friedman, Thomas. 1990. *From Beirut to Jerusalem.* New York: Anchor Books.

Habermas, Jürgen. 1994a. Struggles for Recognition in the Democratic Constitutional State. In Gutman, A. (ed.), *Multiculturalism: Examining the Politics of Recognition,* 107–148. Princeton: Princeton University Press.

Habermas, Jürgen. 1994b. Citizenship and National Identity. In van

Steenberg, B. (ed.), *The Condition of Citizenship*, 20–35. London: Sage Publications.

Harrington, Mona. 1980. Loyalties: "Double and Divided". In *Harvard Encyclopaedia of American Ethnic Groups*, 676–686. Cambridge, Mass.: Harvard University Press.

Hufelschulte, Josef. 1999. Türkische Sexfalle: Wie Ankaras Geheimdienst den prominenten Grünen-Politiker Cem Özdemir erpressen wollte ("Turkish Sex Trap: How Ankara's Secret Service Wanted to Blackmail the Prominent Green Politician Cem Özdemir"). *Focus* 12: 8.

Kymlicka, Will. 1989. *Liberalism, Community, and Culture*. Oxford: Oxford University Press.

Kymlicka, Will. 1995. *Multicultural Citizenship*. Oxford: Oxford University Press.

Lyman, Stanford, and Douglass, William. 1973. Ethnicity: Strategies of Collective and Individual Impression Management. *Social Research* 40(2): 344–365.

Miller, David. 1995. *On Nationality*. Oxford: Clarendon Press.

Özdemir, Cem. 1995. Immigrants and Immigration in Germany. Speech given at Michigan State University on 17 February 17 1995.

Özdemir, Cem. 1997. *Ich bin Inländer: Ein anatolischer Schwabe im Bundestag* ("I am a Native: An Anatolian Swabian in the German Parliament"). München: Dtv premium.

Özdemir, Cem. 1998. *Hürriyet'*e Mektup: Aslini inkar eden haramzadedir ("Open Letter to *Hürriyet:* He who Rejects his Origin is a Thief"). *Hürriyet*, 1 June 1998.

Poulton, Hugh. 1997. *Top Hat, Grey Wolf and Crescent: Turkish Nationalism and the Turkish Republic*. New York: New York University Press.

Sen, Faruk. 1999. Hüsran ("Disappointment"). *Milliyet*, 18 February 1999.

Soysal, Yasemin Nuhoglu. 1996. Changing Citizenship in Europe: Remarks on Postnational Membership and the National State. In Ceserani, D., and Fulbrook, M. (eds.), *Citizenship, Nationality and Migration in Europe*, 17–29. London and New York: Routledge.

Taylor, Charles. 1992. The Politics of Recognition. In Gutman, A. (ed.), *Multiculturalism and "The Politics of Recognition"*, 25–73. Princeton: Princeton University Press.

Weber, Max. 1978. *Economy and Society*. Berkeley: University of California Press.

Low profile diasporas?
Ethnic communities from
the Republic of Macedonia in Copenhagen

Jonathan Schwartz

The specific sites of diaspora are significant for noticing the refractions of ethnic and national identity. The notion of *diaspora*, like its closely related terms *exodus* and *exile*, emerge in the narratives of the collective historical experience of Jewish people (Schwartz 1998). *Diaspora* is probably the summary term for experience that replaces emancipatory exodus and repressive exile over a long duration away from the *homeland*.

Diaspora has won widespread currency in the sociology and anthropology of migration, and the term in this paper will refer to several ethnic communities from the Republic of Macedonia whose first members settled in metro-Copenhagen during the late 1960s as "Yugoslav guestworkers". Whereas the term, "Yugoslav guestworkers", after the war in Bosnia, sounds archaic, the experience of diaspora, upon inquiry, indicates some unexpected aspects of continuity with the classical "golden age" period of labor migration. The "brotherhood and unity" under Tito was manifested under specific circumstances, like National Holiday dances, and soccer matches. But much "identity work" of the guest workers was performed through and within their ethnic and regional affiliations. Ethnic affiliation is particularly salient in contemporary diasporas, which include recent refugees as well as former guest workers. An old Yugoslav joke about "brotherhood and unity" made the ironic comment: "If brothers were so good, God would have had one."

Albanian, Macedonian, and Turkish communities from the Republic of Macedonia share, but most often divide, urban space and place in greater Copenhagen. This process of dividing up diaspora is the topic for this article. I shall avoid, however, putting the divisive matter in the shape of a time-bomb that threatens momentarily to explode. There can be diasporas which keep low profiles as well as distances. If I reject the time-bomb metaphor, I also avoid the metaphor of sugar-coated multiculturalism. With his home base in Montreal, Charles Taylor has articulated the morale for a "politics of recognition" (Taylor 1992) which encompasses a wide range of mutualities for conduct. Neither the time-bomb nor the sugar-sweet metaphor is what multiculturalism is about. Differences between groups, and within groups, are conditions for civil society. They can be talked about in public space, but they can also be protected in privacy.

An essay on the politics of recognition requires an open conversation, playing one's best cards openly on the table. One of my informants gave me a piece of feedback which sets the theme for this article: "You never write behind our backs." I trust that this essay will continue the conversation in that spirit.

The paper will situate these communities in several events of their leisure time, for example, at all-male clubs and at occasional dance parties where families celebrate their ethnic identities. A suburban municipal hall in metro-Copenhagen is a frequent site of diaspora culture where the guest anthropologist can join the dance of several bodies politic. To the question Schierup and Ålund (1987) posed, "Will They Still Be Dancing?", the answer is definitely, "Yes!" – but under dramatically new circumstances; and "Yes!" – we social scientists will still be writing about it.

Fieldwork under fire?

This article was researched and written in the shadows of two infernos in 1998: the systematic burning by Serbian police, army, and para-military forces of Albanian-owned farms and homes in the Yugoslav province of Kosovo, and the sudden, unexpected fire in late October 1998 which swept through the meeting hall of the Macedonian Association in the Swedish town of Gothenburg. Over sixty young people were killed in the flames and smoke, most of them immigrants and refugees in Sweden. It was a group of Kurdish young people who had rented the building from the Macedonian Association.

By the end of 1998, the public authorities in Gothenburg have not ascertained the cause of the fire. Rumours, however, tell that it was arson by Nazi organizations. Another early rumour attributed the arson to Albanian militants, some of whom advocate separation from the Republic of Macedonia and the establishment of a "Great Kossova". That the fire occurred immediately prior to the second and final round of national elections in the Republic of Macedonia probably gave credence to the rumour in some circles.

The recurrence of fires in Kosovo and the single incident in Gothenburg have made the question mark in the title "Low profile diasporas?" more emphatic than was originally intended. Keeping a "low profile" is a form of "impression management", to borrow Erving Goffman's (1959) well-known phrase. Changing situations can turn subdued atmospheric backgrounds into highly contrasting, baroque illuminations.

Members of ethnic diaspora groups in Scandinavia are usually characterized in the dominant discourse of integration, and their actions outside the putative trajectory of integration are not deemed significant by policy-makers and their researchers. Perhaps these non-integratory actions are believed to be exotic and private, but they are not the real stuff out of which relevant, fundworthy research projects are made. Even when researchers do challenge the clarity of the conventional concept of integration (Preis 1998) their projects remain, nevertheless, within the parameters of "integration problems". Anthropologists aim at deconstructing the dominant discourse of integration, and they reproduce it unwittingly. To assert that "integration" is a poorly defined concept apparently does not weaken its rhetorical force in the least. I will attempt to demonstrate that it is worthwhile inquiring into the making of diaspora without the constricting framework of integration.

This present article, therefore, is an attempt to escape the discursive bonds of integration in a recent fieldwork involving ethnic communities from the Republic of Macedonia in greater Copenhagen, Denmark. The fieldwork is a multi-sited effort to, as it were "island hop" like a tourist in the Aegean from the social gatherings of one

ethnic group to another. The effort at establishing a stable inter-
ethnic organization, a Danish-Macedonian Friendship Association
in 1994–6 will be presented as the exception, which proves the rule.
The ethnic communities typically keep their distance from one another
and thereby keep low profiles in the Copenhagen public. The process of making and keeping ethnic boundaries in Copenhagen, with
conflict always imminent, suggests that what is happening for the
time being is the work of "low profile diasporas". No permanence in
the ethnographic present is intended in these fieldnotes.

A recent collection of articles, *Fieldwork under Fire* (Nordstrom et
al., eds. 1995) documents the personal experiences of anthropologists
who research and reflect upon sites of violence. If the normal, or
archetypal, ethnographic field was fairly stable, if not peaceful, ethnographies in our time tend to be in places "under fire". The concept
of fieldwork itself is likewise – though figuratively – "under fire".
Critiques of the "ethnographic present" (Fabian 1983; Schwartz 1998)
as a concept of time are joined to critiques of the static, isolated, and
remote field as a site of culture. *Fieldwork under fire*, then, does not
just refer to ethnographies of violence; it also dispels the very notion
of single time/single space in our research.

To suggest that communities from ex-Yugoslavia in Copenhagen
are "low profile" also contrasts them with more prominently outspoken ethnic communities in other metropoles. In Toronto and Melbourne, for example, Macedonian and Hellenic groups not only
"contest" and "inflect" their social identities, they have occasionally
had fist fights over them, as was the case when Macedonians attempted to place a wreath in front of the statue of Alexander the
Great in Toronto's Greek neighborhood section in 1990. Greek nationalist organizations that donated the statue to the city did not
allow the Macedonians to touch and venerate their historic hero, and
a riot ensued (Danforth 1995; Schwartz 1994; Schwartz 1996).

A similar altercation took place in December 1992, when the
Macedonians raised their flag at a meeting in North York. An angry
Greek man kicked Mayor Mel Lastman, who spoke at the event, in
the shin. The Mayor commented: "What are these people trying to
do? They want to improve their way of life; they wanted to come to
a better country. When it comes to Canada, they've got to leave their

hate at home" (*Toronto Star*, 8 December 1992).[1] When I speak of "low profile diaspora" in this paper it is in contrast to the dramatic assertions and confrontations of national affiliation such as those in Toronto and Melbourne. Kurdish and Turkish diasporas in Germany are not "low profile," but the Copenhagen sites I have visited and revisited still deserve the modifier, "low profile".

I shall now pinpoint several separate moments in a history of ethnic communities and immigrant organizations from the Republic of Macedonia in metro-Copenhagen. The pinpoints are intended as if they formed a constellation. As author and diviner of this little history, I was present at these events and, on occasion, was a primary agent in their occurrence.

The actual field or territory where these events took place can be easily pointed out on a map of Nørrebro reaching north-west to Ballerup. A bus ride along the main artery of Nørrebrogade and its extension Frederikssundsvej to Ballerup takes about a half-hour, so we are traversing a small urban and suburban space. The "inner Nørrebro" and the "outer Nørrebro" have definite marks of otherness. Storefronts with Pakistani and Turkish names are frequent; *kiosks* – itself an "Oriental" word – are managed by members of ethnic minorities. A combination of exotic and slum is striking, with young Danish people's subcultures augmenting the foreignness of the street scene.

As the bus leaves the Nørrebro district, a distinctly non-foreign, that is, Danish, environment comes into view. Newer apartment buildings, shopping malls, industrial parks and playgrounds dominate the landscape by their anonymity. We are away from the foreign and are back in Denmark, as the bus drops us off at the terminal in Ballerup.

Since the 1970s, Ballerup has been one of the "low profile" suburban municipalities with sizeable immigrant populations. Compared to Ishøj, Høje Tåstrup, Albertslund, and Avedøre, or Aarhus' Gjellerup, Ballerup is seldom mentioned for its immigrant problems in the integration debates in the press or on television.

Be that as it may, Macedonian and Albanian "guestworkers" did settle down in Ballerup, in proximity to several of their workplaces, and it is these two communities' distance-keeping that I was interested in following up in recent years. A registry of over 100 voluntary organizations in the municipality includes two Albanian organizations, one Macedonian, one Montenegrin, and one Serbian.

A decade ago I had attended a performance in Ballerup of Macedonian folk dance during the town's summer festival. When there were cultural programs sent from Skopje, Ballerup was chosen as the town for the event to happen. This remains so in this decade as well, after the breakdown of Yugoslavia and the independence of the Macedonian Republic. Ethnic organizations choose the familiar municipal hall in Ballerup, "Tapeten", for their dance parties. ("Tapeten" means "wallpaper" in Danish, because the land had been formerly used for a wallpaper factory). Here now is found a plain, functional party space for a maximum of four hundred people. "Tapeten" has a decent kitchen, and a window adjacent to the kitchen to serve beer and soft drinks. Long tables each set with thirty-two folding chairs flank a large central space for the orchestra and the long lines of dancers in the *ore*, the traditional chain dance. The members and guests arrive, slowly but surely, within two hours after the scheduled start of the evening. Whole and large families sit down at the tables. They come from various, widespread sections of metro-Copenhagen. The parking lot outside the hall is also filling up.

The orchestra sets up its equipment, plays a few numbers and eventually a string of bold young women steps onto the dance floor and begins to dance together. They keep, nevertheless, a low profile. They maintain, one notes, similar and generally simple steps, and their numbers increase when they are joined by those women who were perhaps too shy at first. Men begin to enter the line after two or three dances by the women.

"Tapeten" in Ballerup is the preferred place for large social and cultural functions. A nucleus of Ballerup residents can make arrangements for renting the space. Members of the wider ethnic community hear of the plans and they attend. The "grapevine" for the ethnic communities is well maintained. Club membership is one of the pillars for the ethnic grapevine. Mailings that announce the dance parties are also helpful for spreading the news of a dance.

In 1996, I attended two parties in Ballerup, one held in March by the club "Makedonija" and another in May, held by the Albanian club. In September 1998, I attended a party in Ballerup to celebrate the seventh anniversary of the Macedonian Republic's independence from Belgrade.

These three dance events which connect with the "body politic" (Cowan 1990)[2] of the Republic occupy the centre of attention in this article, but there are other sites in the field. The "Macedonian Association Prespa" has its club quarters in a former factory located in outer Nørrebro. "Prespa" (the name of a large lake in the Balkans with borders on Albania, Greece, and Macedonia) is primarily a club with its membership coming from the Turkish minority in the Republic of Macedonia. Many come from the Lake Prespa region (Schwartz 1985; Schwartz 1989; Schwartz 1996). Finally, Macedonian men, who have no rented space of their own, meet on Sunday afternoons behind the bowling alleys of the huge recreation hall Grøndals Center in outer Nørrebro. With the noise of bowling balls and enthusiastic shouts of Danes who score a strike in the background, the Macedonian men talk and play cards. They bring coffees, beers, and snacks to each other from the cafeteria. These sites of cultural politics, when accounted for, could lead to a modestly affirmative nod to the question in the article's title – indeed, these are low profile diasporas. My cognitive map of ethnic communities allows for separate space and time, so that "cultural collisions", thus far at least, are a rarity among Copenhagen's ex-Yugoslav diasporas.

Will they still be dancing? revisited

In 1987 Carl-Ulrik Schierup and Aleksandra Ålund published what is to date the most detailed comparative study of Yugoslav immigrants' integration in Scandinavian societies. Their book had the provocative title *Will They Still Be Dancing?* The term *integration* in the book's subtitle, however, is one of the clues to the book's promise of success among the Scandinavian readers. In the 1980s, "the problems of integration" pervasively shaped research and policy interests, and the term integration almost had to appear in the project proposal if funds from the state research councils in Sweden or Denmark would arrive.

The question posed in the title alluded to how and why immigrant communities of Vlachs and Macedonians integrated into Danish and Swedish societies respectively. Varying strategies of these two ethnic groups adapted to the receiving welfare states' administrations. The structure of differences between Swedish and Danish municipal governments and local employers precipitated differences in the integration patterns, or lack of them, among Vlach and Macedonian immigrants.

The book thus attempted to show how "two groups become four". Whereas the Vlachs in Sweden remained marginalized, and therefore not integrated, their counterparts in Denmark were well integrated into the local Danish communities. The reverse tendencies were manifested among the two Macedonian communities: in Sweden successful integration was the case; in Denmark the Macedonians were among the marginalized. The reception of immigrants in the Scandinavian welfare-state societies created hierarchical divisions among the arrivals.

As I pointed out in my review of Schierup and Ålund (Schwartz 1990: 49–50), the relative success of the Vlachs in the Danish industrial towns of Northern Sjælland was a consequence of the marked and unwelcome presence of Yugoslav Rom (or Gypsies) in those same towns. The hosts preferred the "hard-working Vlachs" to the "idle Gypsies", who quickly found out how to use the resources of the welfare state (Schwartz 1985; Schwartz 1990). The stigma of the Rom was therefore double. They were "guestworkers" who were soon among the unemployed clients of the natives' welfare system.

In Sweden, the Macedonians were appreciated as hard-workers, and the Vlachs, in comparison, were less able to integrate – or be integrated. They got the stigma of being stubbornly traditional and peasant-like, that is, less modern than the more urbane Macedonians. The integration process, upon closer examination, proved to be built upon practices of stigmatization and predatory assimilation.

Will They Still Be Dancing? then, had to do with the force of tradition and its inflections in new, changing contexts. "Do they dance to keep up tradition?" was a corollary question to that of the title (Schierup and Ålund 1987: 204). One can concur with the authors' comprehensive answer that spans even the violent breaking up of Yugoslavia. For the social scientist, the dance of *ore* is indeed very intriguing, but not because of its exoticism. The *ore* is not just folklore, a dance in which the participants form a long, doubled, and then tripled chain. It is an important part of ongoing social life; a scene for the unfolding of multiplex social life in a migrant community. It is a scene that reflects interests, conflicts, and dilemmas in the total field of migrant existence (Schierup and Ålund 1987: 205).

The key event that gave rise to Schierup and Ålund's question in 1987 was the celebration of the Yugoslav national holiday on November 29. Schierup had taken photographs of Yugoslav *ore* dancing in a city north of Copenhagen in 1981. Tito had died in 1980, so there were still warm memories of his rule among emigrant workers, and the commemoration of Yugoslav "brotherhood and unity" was still to be observed in the guest-worker milieu Schierup visited in Denmark.

Owe Ronström's article "In search of the Yugoslavs: dance, music and ethnicity" (Ronström 1988) is another excellent ethnography of Yugoslav dance groups in Sweden during the 1980s. One could recognize the Yugoslav dancehall in metro-Stockholm by its visual, musical, and olfactory imagery:

> It is a low-ceiling, well-lighted room. The atmosphere is simple and what one might describe as "functional": no tablecloths, no candles, very few decorations and pictures. A cold, white light from an overhead reflecting lamp floods the dance floor; a slightly warmer light shines on the table. At the bar a middle-aged woman sells *Coca-Cola*, *Fanta*, beer, and wine at low prices. There is a powerful aroma of meatballs – they are *ćevapčići* – which are served with raw onions and pommes frites. They are excellent and cheap. Soda and beer are drunk from bottles; there are no glasses. The food, the strong smell of onions, the hot deep-fry oil in the kitchen, blends with the smoke of all the cigarettes, the mild American and the heavier, slightly thicker Yugoslav brands (Ronström 1988: 149; my translation from Swedish).

Ronström also answered the vital question as to who was dancing in that hall:

Everyone in the room spoke Serbo-Croatian, in some form. Many came from the same region in Serbia, and of these many from the same town. Others came from Bosnia and Montenegro. Some Croatians and Macedonians were among them, but Slovenes, Albanians, Vlachs, Slovaks, Hungarians, or people from some of the over twenty ethnic groups in Yugoslavia never came (Ronström 188: 150; my translation from Swedish).

In short, some, but not all, Yugoslavs danced together. There were some who stayed away and perhaps were uninvited. In two of the annual national holidays in the Tito-inspired Yugoslav calendar, November 29 (National Holiday) and March 8 (International Women's Day), official parties were held for all the guestworkers/immigrants from Yugoslavia. But the local, ethnic organizations may have kept separation from one another during the period of "brotherhood and unity".

I refer to the two studies of the late 1980s to indicate both continuity and change. The eruption of war in 1991 took many of us by surprise. We like to think, when we write, that the rear-view mirror is confounded with a crystal ball.

The question in the title of the book by Schierup and Ålund in 1987 did not catch a glimpse of 1990s Bosnia or Kosovo in the crystal ball. The two scholars were interested in the trajectory of Scandinavian integration, not of explosive mortar shells in Mostar.

Their old question, however, remains of haunting relevance, particularly in light of the past few years of war and threat of war. In this article I shall attempt to pose the same question, with the break-up of Yugoslavia and the independence of the Republic of Macedonia in September 1991 as the immediate foreground. "With whom will they be dancing?" is the appropriate question for the present article.

In 1996, my wife and I were invited to attend two separate dances in the same municipal hall of Ballerup, a suburb west of Copenhagen. The local club "Makedonija" held the first dance we attended in March, the second in May by one of two Albanian clubs in that suburb. It is a functional coincidence that two contending ethnic clubs in the same small Danish suburb met to dance to their own music and song. A few words, however, are needed to retrace the recent history of the conflict in diaspora.

150

The chairwoman of "Makedonija" knew me through my active participation in the Danish-Macedonian (*Dan-Mak*) Friendship Association. Together with my wife – a Danish anthropologist – I had helped to start the Friendship Association in February 1995. Nearly a half-year of discussion and planning had taken place before the establishment of the organization.

The use of the phrase "Macedonian" in the hyphened "Danish-Macedonian Friendship" was among the main topics for the planning phases up to the actual establishment of the organization. In order to include all possible ethnic groups, the term "Macedonian" was defined in the association's preamble as "persons of all groups who come from the Republic of Macedonia". This passage in the text insisted on inclusion and opposed exclusion. It intentionally avoided naming the ethnic groups, because of the possibility of omitting and thereby offending one of them.

The Danish-Macedonian Friendship Association was attempting to practice the "politics of recognition" (Taylor 1992) by comprehensive inclusion. In the discussions leading up to the February 1995 foundation meeting participants did include members of the Albanian, Turkish, Rom, and Macedonian communities. The planning committee invited all the clubs with memerberships from the Republic of Macedonia to a meeting at the Grøndals Center in Bronshøj. About 65 persons attended the foundation of *Dan-Mak* on a Sunday afternoon in 1995. A group of fifteen Albanians (from Tetovo) came to the meeting and soon protested at the use of the term "Macedonian" in the *Dan-Mak* name.

I explained the way the term was meant, pointing out that the phrase "Macedonian" was inclusive, not exclusive. The Albanian spokesmen asked for a delay of the start of the organization, because not all of their community had been informed of the meeting. When the proposal for delay was voted down by the nearly fifty other persons, the Albanians walked out of the meeting room. An Albanian from the Prespa Lake region who was involved in the planning of the Friendship Association remained in the room and was elected to the steering committee. The Danish-Macedonian Friendship Association was active for nearly a year, but has been suspended throughout 1997–8. My wife and I were invited to the

"Makedonija" club party in early 1996 in appreciation of our effort in the Association.

The occasion for the Albanian dance in May 1996 was the opening of a local clubhouse in Ballerup. The membership had purchased a dilapidated two-storey residence and made repairs and alterations, so it could serve their organization "Cenel Hasani", named after an Albanian national patriot. It was a Danish acquaintance that passed on the information that the Albanian organization was having an open house followed by a large party in "Tapeten".

At the opening ceremony inside the new clubhouse, the town Mayor of Ballerup praised the Albanians for their initiative and their voluntary efforts to build something on their own. The Municipality, he emphasized in his talk, had not financed the purchase of the building and its remodelling. In this respect he was praising the Albanians for indeed being integrated into Danish society, because they were following the typical Danish model of voluntary organizational life *(frivilligt foreningsliv)*. They were not dependent clients, but self-sufficient co-citizens *(medborgere)*. Following the official reception in the clubhouse, we were driven to the large municipal hall, where there was ample space for just over four hundred members and guests.

Having attended dances of Yugoslav organizations in Denmark since the 1970's, many like those described and analysed by Schierup and Ålund, I could perceive many strands of continuity in the 1996 versions. Both "Makedonija" and "Cenel Hasani" filled the hall with their music, tables, and dance. Perhaps the Albanian party was more crowded than the Macedonian. The styles were slightly different, but clearly both were in the same tradition of what might be called "Balkan diaspora in the metropoles".

Yes, they will still be dancing in 1996, I could affirm. However, they won't be dancing together, but only in their own ethnic groups. The procedures and ingredients for the large dance parties will be almost the same. There will be a large band, playing folk-derived melodies, powerfully amplified. There will be well-known singers flown in to lead the music and dancing. There will be roasted meat, bread, and salad for sale and lots of soda pop, beer, and wine. There will be three hours of dancing; some of the dances will go on for nearly a half hour, and most of the people will join in the *ore*. Old and young, men and women, perform the same simple steps and repeat them with few variations until the music ends. After several such dances, there is a raffle with lucky numbers being drawn and called out in the organization's mother tongue. Prizes are usually bottles of wine, cameras, and round-trip plane tickets, Copenhagen–Skopje.

One should emphasize that it is not just the neighbors from the same suburb, for the dances bring together a large proportion of the ethnic community in greater Copenhagen, many of whom are members of their own local ethnic clubs and organizations. Studying ethnic communities in greater Copenhagen, and perhaps in any large metropole, requires the identification of dispersed segments – literally diasporas – as the familiar urban neighborhood approach is rendered increasingly obsolete (Harney 1998). The dance events in Ballerup are keen markers in the making of diasporas, for they speak vividly, as well as conventionally, to the practices of the "body politic" in diverse, neighboring ethnic communities. The dance events, as institutions, can also show clear traces of continuity from the nation-state that once was Yugoslavia.

Keep the home fires burning: Some polemics in diaspora

Ballerup is a municipality with a large variety of cultural organizations, numbering more than 100, and, as noted, the registry from the town's Cultural Commission includes several clubs from ex-Yugoslavia. Both Albanian clubs' members emigrated primarily from the Tetovo region of the Republic of Macedonia.

In July 1998, I requested an interview with the Albanian steering committee to catch up on the past two years since the clubhouse opening. I was representing a NGO (non-governmental organization) as well as the anthropological profession. This state of affairs is increasingly common for fieldwork that might be termed "NGOgraphy". The classical method of participant-observation is being practised with the new variant, which is a hybrid of civil society and social research. The intensification of the conflict in Kosovo was a topic for discussion, but my explicit reason for the conversation was to find out if the Albanian club "Cenel Hasani" would participate in a coming activity, co-sponsored by the Danish-Macedonian Friendship Association to celebrate, on September 5, the seventh anniversary of independence from Belgrade's rule.

The first statement made by one of the men at the table was: "We are in deep sorrow." He was referring to the ethnic cleansing of Kosovo Albanians. The Serbian offensive was accelerating in violence. The men in the club stated unequivocally that they had no interest in meeting with the Macedonians, who were, in their view "from the same Slavic stock as the Serbs." One of the men in the office had been at the initial meeting of the Friendship Association in 1995. He was among those who walked out in protest after demanding a delay in the establishment of the Association. He thought of me as a supporter of the Macedonians, not the Albanians. The club's officers agreed with one of their spokesmen who commented that "the Prespa Mafia" was in charge of the Independence Day celebration. Here he was attacking a putative regional hierarchy, with "Prespa" at the top. By virtue of its successful soccer team, "Prespa" club has considerable prestige in metro-Copenhagen. He said, moreover, that the policies of the Macedonians were just like those of the Serbians. His evidence was the attempted repression of the Albanian University in Tetovo, as well as the Albanian Mayor of Gostivar whom the police arrested in July 1997 for flying the Albanian flag outside the City Hall. The Albanian organization in Ballerup devoted much of its energy to raising funds to support the Tetovo University.

If the Macedonians were to change their policies in the Republic, one man said, the Albanians would consider meeting with them here in Copenhagen. It was evident to the Ballerup Albanians that their politics ought to mirror as perfectly as possible the militant Albanian activists in the Republic. To advocate a more moderate, conciliatory position would be nothing short of traitorous. Diaspora politics and polemics, then, tend to magnify the opposing ends of the homeland's political spectrum, that is, the infrared and the ultra-violet bands. The moderate colors of the spectrum are invisible. When I speak of "low profile diasporas", I am by no means implying that the mobilizers of diasporas voice moderation. Their organizations of the civil society in the metropole promote *cultural rights*, but most often they are *national rights*. The line between "cultural" and "national" is perhaps just as ambiguous as the cartography of the various Balkan nation-states. In the multicultural diasporas, however, cultural rights and national aspirations are made to feel congruent as they seldom are in the multicultural homelands.

On the subject of Macedonian national identity, there was agreement among the Albanian men in Ballerup that "the Greeks are right; there are no such people as the Macedonians. They are Bulgarians, like the Greeks say."

Here we have what might be an inflection of "Macedonia", where congruence between three otherwise different and often antagonistic national loyalties constitute a consensus in their opposition to the self-identification of Macedonians. Congruence, however, does not mean shared consciousness. One shares a polemic position *vis à vis* another "common other". The different national spokesmen namely agree on their derogatory opinions toward one another, whose existence they deny. These polemical opinions are kept within the community as a partially kept secret of the type Michael Herzfeld (1997) calls "cultural intimacy". There are few secrets that are really kept. Members of opposing ethnic groups know very well how and what the other groups think of them. Stereotypes by their very character are not secrets, but common knowledge. One might wish, with the Mayor of North York, Toronto, that contending communities in free, modern urban space "leave their hate at home". Perhaps the most one can hope for is that the groups keep low profiles and let the people at home work – unhampered by diaspora militants – at solving their problems.[3]

The plans for the September 5 celebration of Macedonian Independence were laid in August, and the choice of the feast and party was the same municipal hall in Ballerup. In my role as chairman of the almost forgotten Friendship Association, I received an invitation to attend the dinner dance.

In "Tapeten", the wall behind the orchestra was decorated by adjacent Danish and Macedonian flags, with a logo of two folk dancers and inscribed with "Danish-Macedonian Friendship". Also above the bandstand, there hung a portrait of Goce Delćev, who inspired the abortive independence movement against Ottoman Turkish rule in August 1903. The band of five players, called "Grom"

("Lightning") had driven in from Gothenburg, and the well-known singer, Blagoja Gruevski, had flown in from Skopje.

My colleague from the Friendship Association said that the turn-out for the party was pitifully small: "a catastrophe" he called it. To be sure, there were about two hundred people attending the party, about half the size of the two parties that I had attended in the same room in 1996. From my observations, the scale of the party was reduced, but it was by no means a catastrophe. My Macedonian friend was disappointed that the Turkish, the Rom, and the Albanians did not come to celebrate the Republic's independence from Belgrade. His spirits picked up during the dancing, but he felt disappointment that the other ethnic groups in diaspora seemed indifferent to their common citizenship in the newly established Republic. I knew from my interview earlier that summer that the Albanian community in metro-Copenhagen was more concerned with the current movement for Kosovo Albanian independence.

In 1998, the Ambassador of the Republic of Macedonia to Denmark was an ethnic Albanian. Together with his wife and a few staff members, he attended the September 5 anniversary party in Ballerup. They sat at the guest of honor table facing the entry and close to the orchestra. The Ambassador gave a short speech, thanking the organization for the invitation and wishing the people an enjoyable evening. He and his wife did not join the dancing. They remained at the table for two hours after which time they got up and left. After their departure, I noticed that the dancing and songs became more animated. My friend also began to join in the dancing, and he exclaimed to me: "This is Macedonian!" The repertoire of the orchestra included most of the loving songs for Macedonia, where mother, village, and nation were fused in the dance.

Here there should be a flashback to an earlier event. In early May 1996, I arranged a cultural event for *Dan-Mak* to celebrate Green George's Day. My friend in *Dan-Mak*, mentioned above, was agreeable. It was also his name day. During my fieldwork in Macedonia in 1995, I noticed that George's Day was not only a Christian Saint's holiday, but it was celebrated by Muslims, and especially by Rom Muslims, to mark the joyful coming of Spring. Throughout the Balkans, fresh willow sprigs are hung in all the doors and windows

(Stoianovich 1967). Lambs are slaughtered, roasted, and served in honor of Green George. I thought that George's Day would be a good occasion for *Dan-Mak*'s multiethnic intentions. I invited a colleague from the University, a Leftist intellectual and NGOer, to give a talk at the evening social event attended by some thirty people.

The university teacher chose to give a talk supporting the Albanian university in Tetovo, and as this topic was, and still is, a thorn in the Republic of Macedonia's body politic, the evening ended in a sharp exchange of polemics. As moderator and chairman of *Dan-Mak*, I felt obliged to be hospitable to the guest speaker and colleague. The fragile unity of *Dan-Mak*, nevertheless, was broken on Green George's Night. Subsequent attempts to call the steering committee together failed, so in effect *Dan-Mak* no longer exists. A Turkish member of the steering committee much later told me that it had been a bad mistake to invite the guest speaker, who tactlessly defended the Albanian university against Macedonian repression.

The Macedonians mistrusted me for being "pro-Albanian", and this meant the rupture of the friendship league. Moreover, being suspected of "pro-Macedonian" opinion by the Albanians was the other side of this tarnished coin. It might be that the mixing of civil society goals with research projects is itself the problem of NGOgraphy. One ought to learn from one's mistakes in the field. Reflection on such mistakes may be the proper path to ethnographic understanding. Dancing in various diasporas in not enough, but it is a first step in perceiving the opposing communities.

"Neighbors to war": Macedonia revisited (October 1998)

October 1998 was the month of the first round of national elections in the Republic of Macedonia, and I had three overlapping topics on my research agenda while doing fieldwork there: civil society, ethnic relations, and citizenship. To give the research project legitimacy and urgency, I gave it a title with an infectious and typical "time-bomb" rhetoric: "Neighbors to War".

What was I to expect? Violent confrontations between Albanians and Macedonian police? They were not unheard of. Democratic, free elections sometimes precipitate street fights and burning buildings.

There were seventeen lists on the election ballot for the first round, and there were coalitions of several party lists promised in the campaigns. Even some of the lists were themselves coalitions. A new party Democratic Alternative (DA) – which actually won an impressive number of seats – included members of all the ethnic groups. DA was, I think, adopted from the Democratic Party practice in the U.S., which in urban areas had as many ethnics on the Party as possible. The leader of the Democratic Alternative is a professor of Political Science in Skopje, and he has taught several years at a university in the United States. This gave him and his new party considerable symbolic and electoral capital.

My favorite multi-ethnic coalition was one of the smallest and most plural. It included two Rom political parties, the socialist party, and the Turkish Democratic Party (TDP). In Resen, the municipal center of the Prespa Lake region (Schwartz 1996), I stayed at the home of an active young member of the TDP, so I know that the small party was also in coalition with the Social Democratic party. One of the strangest expressions of this quasi-mosaic came from visiting the office of the TDP in Resen, which turned out to be one room in the house that was the main office of the Social Democratic Party. The room was filled with men, all speaking Turkish, and in the rooms next door were the Social Democratic regulars speaking Macedonian. I say "strange" or "uncanny", but on recalling my own ethnic history in Detroit and Boston, there are "elective affinities" (Goethe's phrase) in democratic elections, where ethnic identity and political loyalty merge and diverge in unexpected patterns.

"Taboo University" in Tetovo

Compared to the easy ambience of inter-ethnic, political relations in Resen, the outlawed Albanian university seemed to many Macedonians to be a militant confrontation, a threat to the social order.

In one of my first interviews in the office of an NGO, I asked about the Tetovo University. "It is a taboo university", the staff member said bluntly. "You can't mention it." This statement proved to be an exaggeration.

When I visited the illegal university in Tetovo, I sensed a more relaxed atmosphere and a more communicative position than the images of animosity I met among Copenhagen's Macedonian and Albanian diasporas. True enough, most Macedonians in the Republic are opposed to the Albanian university in Tetovo, but they are also willing to tolerate its continued existence and growth, if only to keep the civil peace. According to a Professor whom I interviewed in Tetovo, the university has now 6,000 students, 2,000 of them just starting their studies in 1998. Several municipalities in the Republic with Albanian populations and city councils help finance students' fees with stipends. There is, then, some public recognition of the university, legitimacy that is backed up by several NGOs in the metropoles. There are, too, some militant students at the university whose large supplies of weapons have been found by the police. Support for the UCK (Kosova Liberation Army) is evident, but most of the students I saw were enjoying the many cafes that had sprung up in between the houses. The university has now thirty of these large homes, some only half-built. Their owners in Switzerland and Germany have loaned them to the university for use as classrooms and administrative offices.

In diaspora, the university in Tetovo represents the promise of national emancipation to the Albanians and the threat of violent secession to the Macedonians. There is a tendency to view the university as "purely political" and to minimize its curricular program. Most muted are the voices of moderation. Although the Tetovo University is still provisional, it has, nevertheless, achieved that status where "the politics of recognition" (Taylor 1992) become imperative and where taboos must drop away. One might hope that the communities in diaspora would engage in a politics of mutual recognition, instead of mistrust. At least one might urge that the mutuality, which is practised in the homeland, would inspire the diasporas. In my observations of citizenship in a frail nation-state that is a neighbor to war, I heard members of different ethnic groups complain about each other. The election campaign allowed some of these complaints to be aired publically; the complaints thereby took on a tone of civil decency that summoned hope rather than despair. This process of negotiating diversity will spell the future of the Republic of Macedonia.

Conclusion to the chronicle

Upon returning to Copenhagen from Macedonia in late October 1998, it seemed appropriate to revisit the sites of diaspora. I knew that Macedonian men met at Grøndals Center on Sunday afternoons. Moreover, I had often heard that the Macedonian men did not have their own clubhouses, and they expressed some envy for the Albanian and the Turkish men who did have their own quarters. The Macedonian men explained this by stating that there were so many more Muslims, and that they were well organized.

A rough, demographic estimate of the three ethnic groups (Albanian, Macedonian, and Turkish) in metro Copenhagen would indicate 3,000 Albanian, 2,000 Macedonian, and 3,000 Turkish members. This proportion of Muslim to Orthodox members is the inverse of the population in the Republic of Macedonia. Put succinctly, the two minorities in the homeland become the definite majority in Copenhagen's diaspora. There are many Albanian clubs, but to my knowledge, the Turkish men from Macedonia are consolidated in the "Prespa" club, which is primarily a soccer team.

Three tables behind the bowling alleys in Grøndals Center served as the clubhouse for the Macedonian men. As I walked towards the table, a man whom I knew from the September 5 dance yelled: "There's the guy who likes Muslims." It didn't take me long to answer:

"Look, when I am with the Albanians, they say I like the Macedonians. When I am with the Macedonians, they say I love the Albanians." The man accepted my reply, and the topic rested for the time being.

I asked him what he thought was the cause of the fire in Gothenburg. "I have just come back from visiting some friends in Malmö", he said. "They know that the fire was set, and the police know it too, but they won't say so." He made a solemn gesture with the palms of his two hands, as if they were cymbals, twice meeting each other. This gesture meant, "the job was quickly finished." He looked at me straight in the eye and said: "You are a journalist who never writes behind our backs." This compliment healed some of the hard feelings of his first remark. One could refrain from quoting nasty opinions which members of ethnic groups say about the others. Or, one could frame these nasty remarks in such a way as to reveal the symmetry and reciprocity of mistrust. There is a risk always at being candid, but there is also a risk involved in not being candid. Forcing dialogue between two hostile communities (e.g. praising the "Taboo" Tetovo University on Green George's Day in 1996) is not the way we social scientists can keep the peace. But writing about such situations several years later may help keep the proverbial evil eye at a distance. *Machallah*!

The last site of fieldwork for this article was reached by a bike ride to the "Makedoniensk Forening Prespa 1974" in Nørrebro. It was a rainy Sunday afternoon in November.

The club was located on the second floor of a former factory in outer Nørrebro. On the first floor of the building was a fitness center. It is amazing how many former workplaces have turned into places for leisure culture! Since the 1980s, "Prespa" increasingly has a Turkish membership from the Prespa Lake region of the Republic. It is important to point out that "Prespa" keeps the name "Macedonian" and the year of formation in its official title to mark its duly respectful age, but the incorrect spelling of "Macedonian" (*Makedoniensk*) may indicate that the words means "from Macedonia" and does not denote the national affiliation, "Macedonian" (see Mehmet Ümit Necef's contribution to this volume on the distinction between "Turks" and "those from Turkey"). "Prespa" is one of Denmark's first foreign workers' soccer teams and associations. Its biggest base in the 1970s was Vognmandsmarken, a slum and a ghetto that provided immediate housing for newly arrived guestworkers from Yugoslavia, Turkey, Pakistan, and Morocco. "Prespa" in the early days included Albanian, Macedonian, and Turkish members, most of whom came from the Prespa Lake region.

The continuity of "Prespa" is concurrent with its becoming more and more a Turkish minority association. There is a "Prespa" club in Malmö as well as in Copenhagen, and the ethnic composition in the Swedish city is likewise Turkish. "Prespa" was one of the associations that supported the formation of *Dan-Mak* in 1994–5. The Turkish community is in some respects an intermediary between the Albanian and Macedonian communities, but it can also denote its difference to the two dominant groups in the Republic of Macedonia.

Diaspora in Copenhagen mirrors some of the reality in the homeland. A Turkish member of "Prespa" explained to me in 1992 the difference between "Prespa" and the other ethnic groups in Copenhagen: "The Albanians and the Macedonians have political organizations. Ours is a social organization" (Schwartz 1994).

In the Prespa region, moreover, all three ethnic groups share a history of emigration and apple growing. To observe and participate in the intensive apple harvest of October, you find yourself in a time when ethnic and religious differences undergo a moratorium. Tractors, driven by men, ridden by women, head for the orchards every morning with empty wooden crates and return in the darkness loaded with apples. The whole town roars with the sound of tractor engines and is scented by the fresh apples.

The meeting room of "Prespa" in Nørrebro was filled with men and boys; there were about thirty boys (aged 12–16) and fifty men (aged 18–68). Many were playing cards. The tables were filled, so we stood at the bar drinking coffee or beer. We spoke Danish together. The main language of conversation in the room was Turkish, and when the Sunday Bingo started, the numbers were called first in Turkish and then in Danish. A refugee from Bosnia came up to the bar. The language shifted to Serbo-Croatian so he could participate. "Prespa" in Nørrebro was the closest club I could find among Copenhagen's diasporas to a transnational association of men.

On the way out, two notices at the club bulletin board immediately struck my attention. First, there was a call for a collection of "humanitarian aid to the people of Kosovo". Second, there was a photo and name list of the soccer team, "Bratstvo" ("Brotherhood") in Resen. When, in October, I saw a game in Resen where "Bratstvo" was playing, I commented to my friend that the team's blue uniforms were really nice. "They were given to us by 'Prespa' in Copenhagen". This was an unexpected pearl from the field! There is a second division team in Resen called "Prespa", but "Bratstvo" is a third division team with mostly ethnic Turkish players. The name "Bratstvo" is Macedonian, and the ethnic brother team in Copenhagen sends them uniforms. One might have thought that "Prespa" in Resen could get uniforms from "Prespa" in Copenhagen. But the ethnic community and its segments are more resilient than the same name "Prespa".

The Sunday visit to the club room of "Prespa" in Nørrebro indicated the fragmentation process since the days of "guestworkers", but
there were also traces of the past on the bulletin board with an appeal
to help those whose homes were destroyed during a war in Kosovo.
Surveying the past thirty years of guest workers, foreign workers,
immigrants, and refugees in Copenhagen from Yugoslavia ought to
reveal continuities as well as ruptures. Prespa, the name of a lake and
not a nation, with borders on Albania, Greece, and Macedonia, gives
a clue to the blend of histories.

My goal in this article has been to put together several pieces of
evidence found in diverse, separate sites. Observations and conversations over the last two decades are primary sources. A form of social
scientific validity ought to emerge by virtue of the time span. Former
impressions are either reinforced or they give way to new impressions. Research in diaspora is not only multi-sited: it is best when of
long duration.

For the present, I propose that we carry into public attention the
good news and the bad news from the field. We know too that there
is nothing new about the news. That conflicts exist is well known,
especially by the actors themselves. Albanians, Macedonians, Rom,
and Turks know what the others think and say. An ethnographer in
diaspora has no secrets to keep. The problem is how to tell the stories
in a different way than they are usually told. The ways we write about
the fragmentation – or so-called Balkanization – of diaspora communities can affect the outcome of the conflicts, maybe even for the
better.

Notes

1   Thanks to Nicholas Narney, anthropologist at York University, who sent me a
    copy of the newsclip from the *Toronto Star*.
2   Jane Cowan (1990) reveals a plurality of milieu and events for presenting "the
    body politic" where gender is the central field of contest (*champ* in Bourdieu's
    sense). The northern Greek and Macedonian town, Soros, in Cowan's mono-
    graph is filled out and dressed up with dance events. The small town, or large
    village, is the scene for an anthropological fieldwork that invites sustained par-
    ticipant observation. Cowan's focus on dancing forms the groundwork for a com-
    munity study. Community here must not be taken as a holistic, all-coherent unit.
    In both Schierup and Ålund (1987) and in my present account, the topic for study

is the celebration of a contested national holiday. The presence of diaspora is punctuated with celebratory events, many of which are judged as failures, because they do not bring the imagined community together as was desired.

3   This in fact may be what is taking place in early 1999. The new government of the Republic of Macedonia, which was formed after the defeat of the Social Democratic-led coalition in November 1998, is composed of ministers from the nationalist Macedonian, the Democratic Alternative, and the nationalist Albanian parties. The former extremists thereby join in a mosaic-like government. Whether the ethnic diasporas follow this example from the homeland is not yet clear.

References

Cowan, Jane. 1990. *Dance and the Body Politic in Northern Greece.* Princeton: Princeton University Press.

Danforth, Loring. 1995. *The Macedonian Conflict: Ethnic Nationalism in a Transnational World.* Princeton: Princeton University Press.

Fabian, Johannes. 1983. *Time and the Other: How Anthropology Makes its Object.* New York: Columbia University Press.

Goffman, Erving. 1959. *The Presentation of Self in Everyday Life.* New York: Doubleday.

Harney, Nicholas. 1998. *Eh, Paesan!: Being Italian in Toronto.* Toronto: University of Toronto Press.

Herzfeld, Michael 1997. *Cultural Intimacy: Social Poetics in the Nation-State.* London: Routledge.

Nordstrom, Carolyn, and Robben, Antonius C. G. M. (eds.) 1995. *Fieldwork under Fire: Contemporary Studies of Violence and Survival.* Berkeley, Los Angeles and London: University of California Press.

Preis, Ann-Belinda. 1998. *Kan vi leve sammen?: Integration mellem politik og praksis.* København: Munksgaard.

Ronström, Owe. 1988. På jakt efter jugoslaverne: Dans, musik och etnicitet. In Daun, Å. and Ehn, B. (eds.), *Bländ-Sverige. Kulturskillnade och kulturmöter.* Stockholm: Carlsons.

Schierup, Carl-Ulrik, and Ålund, Aleksandra. 1987. *Will They Still Be Dancing? Integration and Ethnic Transformation among Yugoslav Immigrants in Scandinavia.* Göteborg: Almqvist and Wiksell.

Schwartz, Jonathan. 1985. *Reluctant Hosts: Denmark's Reception of Guest Workers.* Copenhagen: Akademisk.

Schwartz, Jonathan. 1989. *In Defence of Homesickness: Nine Essays on Identity and Locality.* Copenhagen: Akademisk.

Schwartz, Jonathan. 1990. On the Representation of Immigrants in Denmark. In Røgilds, F. (ed.), *Every Cloud has a Silver Lining: Lectures on Everyday Life, Cultural Production, and Race.* Copenhagen: Akademisk.

Schwartz, Jonathan. 1994. Cracks in the Ethnic Mosaic: "Macedonia" in Toronto. In Hjarnø J. (ed.), *Multiculturalism in the Nordic Societies.* Copenhagen: Nordic Council.

Schwartz, Jonathan. 1996. *Pieces of Mosaic: An Essay on the Making of Makedonija.* Højbjerg: Intervention Press.

Schwartz, Jonathan. 1998. Visions of Diaspora in Contemporary Social Science. In Haxen, U., Trautner-Kromann, H. and Goldschmidt Salamon K.L. (eds.), *Jewish Studies in a New Europe,* 757–769. Copenhagen: C.A. Reitzel.

Stoianovich, Traian. 1967. *A Study in Balkan Civilization.* New York: Knopf.

Taylor, Charles. 1992. *The Politics of Recognition.* Princeton: Princeton University Press.

Construction of identities in diaspora and exile
Croats in Sweden in the 1990s

Maja Povrzanović Frykman

The purpose of this article is to present a current research project on Croatian diaspora and refugees in Sweden.[1] It is an ethnological project assessing narration on war as creating symbolic spaces and collective images of belonging which are salient to the historical memory of the wars which divided, confronted and victimized people on the basis of their ethnic affiliation. It questions some aspects of the common "ethnic conflict" explanation of the wars in the former Yugoslavia, namely the generalized notion of ideological (nationalist) homogenization along ethnic lines. It aims to show how the homogenization in post-Yugoslav countries caused by the war is counterpointed by manifold divisions among the people of the same ethnic affiliation living in Sweden. The central hypothesis concerns their radically different war experiences as the reason for differences in strategies of imagining home, homeland and nation.[2]

What matters politically is who deploys nationality or trans-nationality, authenticity or hybridity against whom, and with what relative power (cf. Clifford 1997). When applied to the war-related differences between Croatian diaspora and Croatian refugees in Sweden, this general claim can be translated into many relevant research questions. How are home, community, solidarity, enemy, ethnicity and nation constructed in the narratives on war and war-related issues, and in what ways do different – diasporic and exile – experiences of living away from homeland affect these constructions? Referring to the work in progress, I am going to present preliminary answers to some of these questions, and contextualize them in more general insights into the important social features of Croatian diasporas and their political concerns.

This text is based on preliminary field insights from the Malmö area in 1998 and 1999 among Croatian *refugees* from Bosnia-Herzegovina and Croatia who came to Sweden in the 1990s and *immigrant workers* who have lived in Sweden since the 1960s. Here, the latter are called *diaspora* in James Clifford's (1997: 256) sense of being a part of an ongoing transnational network that includes the homeland not as something left behind, but as a crucial place of attachment which affects their strategies of identification (see the extensive discussion of the notions of diaspora and transnationalism in my introduction to this volume).

There are six Croatian clubs in Malmö.[3] The active members meet in the clubs regularly, and engage in sporting activities, folk dancing for women and children, or in organizing festive gatherings and dance evenings. They have been friends since their arrival in Sweden. They form the core of the Croatian community in Malmö, and take care of the "Croatian Home" – a hall with several side-rooms, a bar and a kitchen, into which five of the six clubs, formerly in different locations, moved in 1999. The sixth club, which also belongs to the Association of Croatian Clubs but has remained separate, has always had a reputation of being "pro-Yugoslav". Unlike any other Croatian club in Malmö, that one has been taking part in cultural events organized by the Yugoslav embassy in Stockholm and has received support (e.g. in the form of children's books and soundtracks) from the Yugoslav institutions dealing with "workers temporarily working abroad".

The Croatian ethnic community in Malmö in a wider sense consists of all people who visit the clubs on a weekly basis, or on festive occasions such as celebrations of national or Catholic holidays (with dancing and a performance by some pop singer invited from Croatia as a central event). They listen to the weekly local radio programme in the Croatian language (supported by the Association of Croatian Clubs and sponsored by a private bus company specializing in weekly trips between Sweden and Croatia), and read the "Croatian Messenger" (*Hrvatski glasnik*), published quarterly and distributed to all 6,000 members of the 33 Croatian clubs in Sweden.

Several Swedish scholars have been doing research among the communities of immigrants coming from Yugoslavia in the late 1960s and during the 1970s (Ehn 1975, Magnusson 1989, Ronström 1992, Schierup and Ålund 1987). Recently, considerable scholarly attention has been devoted to the legal positions, problems of adaptation, and the possibilities of return of refugees coming from post-Yugoslav countries, mostly from Bosnia-Herzegovina (Gustavsson and Svanberg 1995, Magnusson et al. 1996). Theoretical frames and empirical results of these studies offer a welcome possibility of considering some results of this research in a comparative perspective, or to contextualize them in sociological terms (Slavnić 2000). There has so far been no research focusing on diaspora Croats in Sweden after the decay of Yugoslavia in the early 1990s. However, valuable insights have been published on disapora Croats' attitudes and cultural practices in Australia and Canada (cf. Kolar Panov 1996, Kolar Panov 1997, Skrbiš 1995, Skrbiš 1997, Skrbiš 1998, Winland 1995).

As noted in the part of the introduction to this volume concerned with methodology, it is difficult to assess the construction of identities by or of people in diaspora and exile without taking into consideration – as a starting-point or as a constant point of reference – the transnational, homeland-oriented aspect of their daily lives, their emotional links and their political concerns. The wars in Croatia and Bosnia-Herzegovina will for decades ahead have consequences for the everyday lives of people in post-Yugoslav countries, and as such they will continue to affect people from those countries living in Sweden, too. Therefore, a well-informed insight into the ongoing identity formation processes comprising both Swedish and homeland experiences is crucial. Some layers of meaning could hardly be uncovered by a researcher not familiar with the world to which the people presented here are constantly referring.

It is thus important to stress that – in accordance with its title – this article does not take into consideration the political changes in Croatia that followed the parliamentary elections of 3 January 2000, when the party that was running Croatia for a decade suffered a remarkable loss of support. These changes have had severe repercussions for the current relations between diaspora Croats and the Croatian state. Generally speaking, a civil-territorial model of the nation that has been promoted in Croatia since the elections in 2000 has raised ambivalent, and often very negative, feelings among the Croats in the diaspora. These changes seem to be giving impetus to new processes of re-defining the local diasporic identities. It is yet to be seen whether they will provide for a new "enemy" against which the diaspora groups might solidarize, and whether they will make diaspora Croats lose interest in current Croatian politics, since they might feel that they cannot affect it any more. According to the official activities and public statements of the Association of Croatian Clubs in Sweden, the latter is very likely to be the case. Yet, according to my field insights among diaspora Croats in Sweden, the former process is also going on. For many of them, the new Croatian government and the new president (elected also in early 2000, after the first president died) embody "the old communists" – the Croatian diaspora's historical enemy which has now regained power. If the fuel for meaningful political engagement was lost for Croatian diasporic groups in Sweden, whose goal of freeing Croatia from Yugoslavia and communism was completed in 1992 (when Croatia was internationally recognized as an independent state), there is a potential of refuelling the diasporic group conciousness in the presence of the new/old ideological enemy. Among diaspora Croats in Sweden, this tendency is not discernable in an institutionalized form, but only in personal contacts with people. Many of the people I know tend – at least at the level of narration concerning nationality, identity, and historical memory (cf. Gilroy 1992) – to side with the right-wing political forces within Croatia.

Croatian diasporas past and present

The refugee flux from the disintegrating Yugoslavia in the early 1990s is only the latest mass migration of the Croats. They have a long and varied history of migration. According to the figures from *The Croatian Statistics Yearbook* for 1995, 53.39% of the Croats live in Croatia, and 10.88% in the neighbouring Bosnia-Herzegovina (where they are considered to be "autochthonous population"). Some 11.86% live in

Western European countries (6.43% in Germany) and the rest in other continents. According to that source, 0.43% of the Croats, which means some 30,000 people, live in Sweden.

While Croats in other former Yugoslav republics, Hungary, Slovakia, Romania, Italy and in Austria are predominantly historical diasporas living there for centuries, those in the USA and Latin American countries came with the first major economic migration at the beginning of this century, followed by the steady migration to Western European countries in the inter-war period (see Cohen 1995 for details on migrations from the Austro-Hungarian empire and the former Yugoslavia). After the Second World War, a new diaspora of between 200,000 and 300,000 people was produced due to the collective guilt ascribed to the Croats for the crimes of the *ustasha*-based state of Ante Pavelić (more about that can be read in Paul Stubbs's contribution to this volume). *Ustasha* sympathizers formed radicalized diaspora communities in several countries, most importantly in the USA, Canada, Australia, Chile and Argentina.

During the 1960s and the 1970s, the former Yugoslavia was one of the most important sending societies of the international migratory system (Schierup 1995: 285). The German world *Gastarbeiter* became a part of Croatian language (in the form *gastarbajter*), as a term for "workers temporarily working abroad" (*radnici na privemenom radu u inozemstvu*), while the terms "emigrants" (*emigranti*) and "emigration" (*emigracija*) were highly politicized, meaning "nationalist enemies of the Yugoslav state". In the official discourse of Croatia since the 1990s, the term "diaspora" (*dijaspora*) as a unifying concept is supplanting both. It seems that people to whom it applies adopted it with great satisfaction. It unifies all people who live away from the homeland – no matter whether it is actual or inherited, visited or imagined, and regardless of the reason for living away and its political implications. The former Yugoslav differentiation depoliticized the reasons for mass labour migration by semantically presenting the migrants as only "temporarily abroad". It stigmatized Croatian political exiles as enemies of the state. (Most of them could not enter the country at all, and sometimes the relatives they met in the neighbouring countries were called in for "conversations" with the Yugoslav secret police.) In contrast to that, and very much according

to the logics of the new Croatian state's understanding of ethnicity as kinship at large, such differentiations could not matter after Croatia gained independence. In the popular media presentation, political exiles – many of whom visited their native place in Croatia for the first time in thirty years – were rather seen as heroes, and the labour migrants as true representatives of the hard-working and God-fearing Croatian people, victimized by the Yugoslav regime that was forcing them to live "in foreign lands" (*u tuđini*).

Most of the Croatian labour migrants never permanently returned to Croatia, but formed economically efficient transnational communities, which were later on accompanied – and politicized – by political emigrants. The opponents of Tito's regime were escaping without a passport, especially after the suppression of the "Croatian Spring", a mass populist-democratic movement, in 1971. So, during the 1970s and the 1980s, Croatian diaspora communities in Europe, but also overseas, were given new and very strong political impulses. Their local histories reveal what people refer to as "the fight for Croatia". In different ways, they were trying not only to support their political cause in the homeland, but also to make the public in their respective countries understand their quest for an independent Croatian state.

As one of the consequences of the wars in Croatia and Bosnia-Herzegovina in the 1990s, new ethnic communities in exile emerged. Between 1991 and 1993 more than 5 million citizens of the former Yugoslavia became refugees or displaced persons; 700,000 of them went to Western Europe (Fassmann and Münz 1995: 476). Some 74,000 people came to Sweden, Bosnian Croats among them (as well as a smaller number of Croats from Croatia). Most were granted Swedish citizenship after having spent five years in the country.[4]

This overview should help readers understand that there is no unified "Croatian Diaspora", for the range of different homeland experiences and different positions in the countries of residence. It is also obvious that people of different age are involved in Croatian diasporic discourses and politics today, including people of Croatian heritage who do not speak Croatian and have never visited the country, and those who were forced to start living abroad in adult age. However, an umbrella organization of diaspora Croats called the Croatian World Congress was initiated in 1994 by the by then leading Croatian nationalist party *HDZ* (*Hrvatska demokratska zajednica* – Croatian Democratic Union). In 1999, it was the first Croatian non-governmental organization assigned a counselling role within the United Nations.

The establishment of the Croatian state and the subsequent war made the relationships between Croatia and Croatian diaspora(s) livelier than ever. It is widely believed that the economically most potent and the politically most radical overseas diaspora groups' financial support was decisive in *HDZ*'s winning the first democratic elections in 1990. In return, particular kinds of inclusion of diaspora Croats in the homeland politics and economy have been launched by the Croatian state. A weekly supplement *Dom i svijet* ("Home and the World") to a widely read daily newspaper is printed in Frankfurt, Germany. Satellite television programmes selected to suit diaspora Croats' interests and at the same time confirm their political attitudes have been transmitted since 1991. In 1998, a digital system was introduced which allows worldwide direct reception of all Croatian television programmes. A Croatian Information Centre was established in the 1990s. It has websites in Croatian, English and Spanish and sends Croatian newspaper articles into diaspora Croats' e-mail boxes on a daily basis, free of charge. "Croatian Task Force" organizes and financially supports summer programmes for all interested young Croatian people living abroad. The Ministry of Return and Exiles has been established. Most importantly, in the elections in 1995, twelve seats were reserved for diaspora representatives in the Croatian parliament (approximately 398,000 Croatian citizens not residing in Croatia have the right to vote, which is equivalent to around ten percent of Croatia's total voting population). Since all of them come from the *HDZ* party branches worldwide, they have in fact been adding votes to *HDZ* (out of 121 such branches abroad, three are in Sweden). That is why the opposition (successfully) demanded changes in the electoral law in 1999, not to exclude diaspora Croats completely, but to lessen their pro-*HDZ* political influence (for more details on these matters see Stubbs in this volume).

The 1990s war: different perceptions

It is a common insight based on research into diasporas and transnationalism that the stronger the belief in or the experience of foreign – in this case Yugoslav, i.e., Serbian – suppression and injustice in the homeland, the more likely the reactions in migrant communities will be emotional and active (cf. Skrbiš 1997). Political organizing and lobbying in the countries of residence, and sending financial and other aid to the homeland are the most common responses.

The revitalization and reinvention of Croatian diasporic discourses and the intensification of transnational links as consequences of the international recognition of Croatian independence in early 1992 and of the war called The Homeland War (*Domovinski rat*) have been documented in Australia (Kolar-Panov 1996, Kolar-Panov 1997, Skrbiš 1995, Skrbiš 1997) and Canada (Winland 1995). Even the communities historically keeping a low profile, like the one in Canada, began to assert their ethnic pride primarily by identifying with the political cause of their kin in the former Yugoslavia (Winland 1995).

Such revitalization and intensification have been remarkably evident in Sweden as well, where the dominant part of the community consists of the so-called first generation of immigrants who often have belongings and close relatives in Croatia. It goes without saying that the reports on war destruction and sufferings in Croatia watched via the satellite programme of the Croatian Television in Croatian clubs, thus among groups of co-ethnics, raised strong emotions and intensified the identification of the Croats in Sweden with their homeland, in opposition to the Yugoslav communist state, defined as the enemy.

Throughout the world, the Homeland War has affected the second and the third generations of Croats in diaspora: some even came to fight in Croatia, and were given considerable media attention in the country. The mobilization of all kinds of resources among the Croats was characteristic of literally all Croatian communities. So was the abundant exposure and celebration of national symbols, too.[5]

For diaspora Croats in Sweden, the sense of a very strong and active Croatian community during the war was shared by many, especially in 1991–92. Even for many Croats who never participated in any of the clubs' activities, it went without saying that they should help in collecting all kinds of aid, as well as lots of private money for their country at war. A firm consensus on the rightfulness of the Croatian plight was reconfirmed during the Homeland War. It raised strong emotions – fears, worries and sorrow, but also hope and national pride. The Croats from Malmö region held regular weekly demonstrations supporting Croatian independence for several months in 1991 in one of the Malmö's biggest squares. They attracted not only the active community members mentioned above, but also the Croats who did otherwise not take part in the community's activities. A woman in her thirties, born in Sweden, told me that she met and made friends with more Croats during those demonstrations than during her entire life in Sweden. Some people wrote letters to the editors of different Swedish newspapers, reacting to what they perceived as unjust reports on and analyses of the war in Croatia.

Money and medical aid were sent or personally driven to Croatia in 1991–92, but very much also to the Croats in Herzegovina in 1993–94. I was shown numerous letters of thanks from the receiving institutions. (This kind of engagment continues: in the late 1990s, the Association of Croatian Clubs initiated fund-raising for the rebuilding of Vukovar, the Croatian town that was almost totally destroyed by the Yugoslav Army attacks in 1991.)

Regardless of the many differences between Croatian diasporas noted above, and regardless of the differences within particular diasporic communities due to date and cause of migration, social status, education or region of origin, the primary focus of most Croatian expatriate organizations and publications was the overthrow of the communist Yugoslav state (cf. Winland 1995). Therefore, generally speaking, the war was interpreted by diaspora Croats as an utterly unjust, but logical continuation of what is seen as the Serbs' long-lasting political and economic oppression of Croats in former Yugoslavia. From the diasporic point of view, the war in the 1990s was the peak of Croatia's demand for independence: a hard, but necessary transitory period towards the accomplishment of the historical goal; the most difficult, but decisive step towards a wished-for freedom. The exultant exclamations "We have Croatia!" at home and "We have been given Croatia!" in the diaspora since January 1992, can be interpreted as implying *the end of history* of the Croatian struggle for independence.

The impacts of the wars in Croatia and Bosnia-Herzegovina for people living there and eventually becoming refugees, were of a different quality. Both internal and international refugees lost their concrete physical homes. For them, the war has first and foremost been their personal tragedy: rupture, loss and displacement.

The refugees' narratives on war and exile collected in Croatia (cf. Prica and Povrzanović 1996) and in Sweden reveal a striking need for self-explanation and the re-narration of recent history, i.e., the over-lapping of the war as a historical turning point with the turning points of their lives. Although these narratives are easily appropriated by the overriding "master narrative" related more to the interests of political groups in power than to people's lived experience (cf. Povrzanović and Jambrešić Kirin 1996), they reveal a multiplicity, diversity and complexity of experience that often challenges the "prescribed" uniqueness of the national narrative (Prica and Povrzanović 1996).

So, while a man living in Sweden for thirty years talks about "living his whole life for Croatia and her ideals", a female Croatian refugee from Bosnia-Herzegovina talks about having lost fifteen kilos in the first three weeks after arrival in Sweden, about suffering hours-long outbursts of crying, and about feeling "deaf" for never being able to express herself in Swedish the ways she would like to. While a political exile talks about the religious-like experience of standing in the Zagreb central square after thirty years of absence, a refugee chooses to tell me about revisiting his former apartment in Sarajevo as one of the crucial moments of his refugee experience. While the former has a kind of private shrine with a consecrated building stone of the Zagreb cathedral, the latter tells about some of the books which he misses most, left and lost in the war.

Generally speaking, the refugees talk about the lived experiences of fearing, suffering, leaving, losing and longing, while diaspora Croats talk about the fulfilment of their dreams and efforts. They establish a narrative continuity of Croatian political history as a continuous – finally completed – struggle for freedom, and of Croat-hood as a fixed identity marker, implying love for the Homeland and sharing Catholic values. In contrast to that, most refugees I met instead hesitate with regard to any general statements about ethnic and national belonging. They narrate about the war and exile as its consequence from a personal point of view. While the public presence of the Croatian diaspora community in Sweden entails some aspects of "long-distance nationalism" (Anderson 1983), the refugees from Bosnia-Herzegovina (but also those I met from Croatia) tend to link their perceptions of ethnic affiliations and national identifications primarily to their personal experience of war and exile. Only secondarily (and not necessarily) do they slip from the domain of personal life history into a wider field of collective history (cf. Malkki 1990).

Meetings in Sweden: relational quality of ethnicity

Some war-related attitudes of diaspora people towards the refugees from all post-Yugoslav countries – people of their own ethnic affiliation included – also speak clearly about their different positions. Although some enthusiastic contacts and friendships have been developed, it is possible to generalize the dominant trends in these attitudes. They range from lack of interest ("they were taken care of by the Swedish authorities"), silent disapproval (reflected in unwillingness to help), antipathy (creating new stereotypes) and envy (for the refugees' "easy" access to the benefits of welfare state on the one hand, and "ruining" the old immigrants' social status in Sweden on the other), to open and direct reproaches for not staying behind and "fighting for the homeland". A few people from Malmö who wanted to join the Croatian Army were turned away for being too old. Some younger Croats from Sweden did fight on the battlefield, but they should be regarded as exceptions; I heard of only eight such people from Malmö. Since that is a very sensitive topic, it is not discussed openly. The moment it is judged from within life in Sweden, with its common-sense life-in-peace understandings of moral obligations and individual choices, the *difference* of diaspora people's concerns and reasoning comes out in a striking manner. This, I believe, explains people's ambivalence about the topic. Still, offering one's own life "for the Homeland" has been seen by many diaspora people (as well as by those living in Croatia) as the ultimate proof of love for and loyalty to Croatia – a proof surpassing any other. Although Croats living abroad are by no means obliged to answer a call-up in Croatia, this explains the tacit feeling of guilt among some people, or at least some kind of double standards applied to the men living in and out of the homeland enmeshed in war. I read it between the lines of diaspora Croats' comments about the refugees who chose not to fight, but escaped the war and came to enjoy comparative economic benefits of life in Sweden.

"No one hates us like our people," a young Bosnian refugee woman told me. The refugees themselves interpret antipathy and envy by the fact that the social and educational background of a considerable number of them (as well as their age) is beneficial when it comes to using the possibilities of social and economic promotion in Sweden by means of education (cf. Daun 1993). Regarding the reproach for not staying behind in order to fight, the refugees' angry counter-reproach is based on pointing to their right to give priority to their individual, and not "national" interest: "We should be dying, and they would send us socks to the battlefield!" They are "so detached from concrete experiences," commented a Croat refugee from Bosnia, *concrete* meaning bodily real, experiential. He was "very, very disappointed", and thus demotivated for any kind of involvement in diaspora Croats' activities.

A diaspora Croat from Gothenburg who was fighting in the battle-field in Croatia was the only one to respond to my plea published in the 1998 summer issue of the Croatian newsletter in Sweden: I was asking people to write about how they themselves perceived and dealt with the war in Croatia while living in Sweden. It confirms my hypothesis on the primary importance *of the lived experiences of war* as an impetus not only for the story that should be narrated for the researcher, but also for formulating self-presentation in other con-texts.

Another woman, a refugee from Croatia, said: "How can he [a diaspora Croat she met shortly after arriving in Sweden] tell me I am not a good Croat [because she came to Sweden with her family]? How can anyone judge how I love Croatia? Why doesn't he go and live there? My sons are on unemployment benefit, he says, so they can't leave and go to fight... It's ridiculous!"

A Croat from Sarajevo insisted that "no one can prove he is more a Croat" than himself. However, this statement should be related to another statement he made as a kind of personal introduction at our first meeting: he told me that he is a Croat "only so much that it doesn't bother other people". By pointing that out, he made it clear that his ethnic belonging is highly relevant for him, but that he shares the tolerant attitude once characteristic of the multi-ethnic setting of Sarajevo. This could also be interpreted as an understanding of the relative, context-bound quality of ethnic belonging, which is different from the rhetorical "ethnic absolutism" typical of diaspora Croats.

Although the divisions are manifold and presented as important by some people, there are many Bosnian Croat refugees who do take part in the clubs' activities and develop friendly relations with diaspora Croats in Sweden. This might be related to Zoran Slavnić's (2000) insights into the strategies of group identification "in need" among Bosnian refugees of different ethnic affiliations. For example, the mass presence of Bosnian Croat youth at the celebration of the Croatian national holiday in Malmö in 1998 made many diaspora Croats feel "not at home". These young people were asking the singer invited from Croatia to perform songs diaspora people were not familiar with, which belong to the Yugoslav rock generation of the late 1970s and early 1980s. The young Bosnian Croats engaged in a combination of disco and "oriental" dancing (with both hands stretched up), seen as "Bosnians" by the diaspora Croats who use to dance pair dances, waltzes, polkas and tangos on similar occasions. Finally, as I was told, there never was so much spilled beer on the floor as after that evening: "Bosnians" do not know how to behave.[6] On the other hand, the clubs in Malmö organize dances – most recently exclusively disco evenings with performers currently popular in Croatia – that attract mostly young Bosnian Croats. The entrance fee brings modest financial gains which the organizers can use for their own purposes, e.g., for the clubs' maintenance and activities or for gifts to Croatian towns destroyed in the war.

The president of a Croatian club from another Swedish town told me that Bosnian Croats "belong to a different cultural circle, but we [diaspora Croats] are not supposed to state that aloud". A certain "self-censorship" among diaspora Croats in Sweden can be noticed on numerous occasions, based on the ideological imputation of national unity, intesified by the war. The Croats should be united at all levels, regardless of where they live today or have lived in the past – and regardless of how they "behave". (Croatia, as mentioned in note 4, granted citizenship to people of Croatian ethnic affiliation regardless of their actual residence.) This might explain the conscious effort by some Croatian refugees and some Croatian diaspora people, to reach and include the other, while the perception of otherness depends on the situation experienced, or on the narrative context.

Some people, on the other hand, are not interested in contacts with other Croats in Sweden at all. A refugee family of Croats from Croatia became friends with their neighbours, a Serbian family from Bosnia. "We have the same problems, the same interests," I was told when meeting them together. They also share active efforts (through participating in the Swedish educational system) to become integrated into Swedish society and allow themselves a lifestyle they were used to in their home countries. Becoming eligible for good jobs is their priority. This Croatian family's main concerns and practices are not understandable from an ethnic paradigm, but from the cluster of questions on the processes of refugees' and immigrants' adaptation and social promotion. Yet, the ethnic moment is not insignificant in this family's daily life. Croatian television programmes are watched at home on a regular basis, and entertainment shows presenting the recent Croatian pop and folk-pop music production are recorded for the teenage children in the family.

Yugoslav criss-crossing

Does "being a Croat in Sweden" mean anything at all, if we at the same time do not know when and why the person came to Sweden, where from, at what age and with what social and educational background? What is the relevance the Croats themselves ascribe to their ethnic and national belonging, and does it vary in different contexts? Are yesterday's refugees who nowadays hold Swedish passports aware of the newly acquired possibilities of identity-creating practices they or their children might choose to explore as EU citizens? These questions could be intriguing not only for theoretically concerned research on identities, but also in the framework of European ethnology exercised in an age of European integrations that unite and divide people(s) in new ways. They are, however, beyond the scope of this paper. In this context, an almost obvious question seems to be more important – the one concerning old and new relations between people of different ethnic affiliations from the former Yugoslavia living in Sweden.[7]

While ethnic awareness and national struggle for independence are central to the narrative construction of Croathood in diaspora, a Croat refugee from a small village in Bosnia stated that "they didn't even know they were Croats before the war". By this she implied that ethnic affiliation acquired extreme importance only after it became the basis of victimization in the war. An educated man from Sarajevo told me that he was a Croat before the war since he stems from an "ethnically aware" family, but that it was normal for him and for everyone he knew to have close friends of different ethnic affiliation.

The Croats who settled in Sweden in the 1960s and 1970s were listed as "Yugoslavs" in the Swedish statistics, which did not reveal their ethnic affiliation. Yet, it is of great importance within my research that the labour migrants came with regular Yugoslav passports and thus could travel home and visit their families, while the political exiles could do the same for the first time only after Croatia gained independence, i.e. after several decades of life "in the foreign country", as they often call it in spite of holding Swedish passports. The implication of having a Yugoslav passport was that the person recognizes the existence of Yugoslavia – a stance highly disputable in the ethnic community politically sensitized by the political exiles in the early 1970s. It is well depicted by the following example. When the father of a girl attending Croatian mother-tongue classes in a small Swedish town found out that the new teacher came to Sweden with a Yugoslav passport, he called him in anger, forbidding him to approach his daughter ever again. That was an extreme case, but more generally, "people were very cautious about who the teacher was", I was told. So, many Croatian children in fact did not use the possibility of free mother-tongue teaching offered by the Swedish state, either because the teacher was not a Croat, or because the language was called Serbo-Croatian.

In the 1990s, it is often the case that the same mother-tongue teacher is teaching Bosnian, Serbian *and* Croatian language, as they are now officially distinguished in Sweden and in Bosnia-Herzegovina (*BKS* in Swedish school catalogues today stands for *bosniska/ kroatiska/serbiska*). Several Bosnian refugees – Croats, Muslims and Serbs – have become BKS mother-tongue teachers; they teach also Croatian diaspora children of the second and the third generation.

The well-known metaphor of Croatia's current otherness/westernness/betterness in relation to Serbia, namely the metaphor of *Europe* as opposed to the *Balkans*, has been explained in note 6. It became especially relevant during the 1990s war, and was charged with heated political meaning. On the one hand, there is a widely shared "knowledge" about "what the Serbs are like" (see note 7 in Paul Stubbs's contribution to this volume). They should not be trusted, to say the least. On the other hand, I witness friendly relations between some diaspora Croats and Serbs (as well as between Croats and Macedonians, Montenegrins and Slovenes), as well as their regular daily contacts at some workplaces. The narrative dimension of identity contruction seems to be a strong "given" with which people comply, although at the same time they might not behave in accordance with it.

It must be stated at this point, however, that many diaspora Croats literally never meet the Serbs (and possibly no other ex-Yugoslav people) in Sweden, are not interested in their public activities and do not make spontaneous statements about them when encountered by the researcher. They simply do not feel connected and do not care – in contrast to all the legal and scholarly insights into "Yugoslavs" as a *group*. When it comes to Serbian and Croatian diasporas in Sweden, a picture could be presented of parallel existence with no formal, and certainly no public communication. In 1998, a letter signed by a group of women from all over the former Yugoslavia now residing in Sweden, was sent to one of the Croatian clubs in Malmö, asking for collaboration in some humanitarian activities. It was received with amazement by the club's officials. They saved the letter in the archives, but did not even consider sending an (obviously negative) answer. Such collaboration was not only hard to imagine, but totally out of the question.

Among the ex-Yugoslav refugees in Sweden, some avoid telling exactly where they come from, but say they come from "those parts", referring to the former Yugoslavia. Inasmuch as my field insights allow generalizations, these are Serbian people who may not feel like encountering the collective guilt ascribed to them, or who for some reason may suffer guilt feelings themselves.

Regarding the construction of identities in exile, the relevance of ethnicity is relative. Zoran Slavnić (2000) has written about the recent refugees to Sweden from Bosnia-Herzegovina, who came from a war in which the Serbs were first attacking Croats and Muslims, later on the Croats attacked Muslims, and finally Muslims engaged in attacking Croats, while both latter groups at the same time fought back against the Serbs. It is thus not surprising that, living as refugees in Sweden, they (like diaspora Croats) repeat pre-existent, home-land-made and war-made rhetorical stereotypes about "what they (Serbs or Muslims or Croats) are like". But, Slavnić shows how they at the same time form an efficient network based on mutual help with information about illegal jobs. The refugees from Bosnia-Herzegovina whom he interviewed think that it is more "normal" to help "one of our own" – in such a case meaning "coming from Bosnia, with no regard to ethnicity"– than, e.g., someone from Poland.

Although ethnic identity for many refugees from Bosnia-Herzegovina was the very reason for victimization, its gains different relevance in another context. It seems to be of secondary importance in the realms of an underprivileged everyday life in Sweden, where people who speak the same or a very similar language and who are in the same social position are easily recognized as closer (regardless of "ethnic conflict" aspects of the war that turned them all into refugees). Open conflicts are minimal and mutual help may often be considerable. Within the ethnically mixed group of refugees from Bosnia in Leksand, people (even) state that their relations are "as they were before", at home, in peace.

These insights point to the fact that ethnicity-based mistrust and violence were the result and not the reason for the wars in Croatia and Bosnia-Herzegovina (cf. Povrzanović 2000). However, personal war experiences should not be dismissed as the crucial moment in the construction of identities in exile. For Muslims who fled from Serbs it might be much easier to contact the Croats than the Serbs in

Sweden. For people who fled before the worst war events in their region, it might be easier to meet and trust any people on a personal basis, than for those who came to Sweden heavily traumatized.

A woman working as an interpreter for the refugees coming to Sweden in the early 1990s met some poeple who first did not want her to translate for them because she was a (diaspora) Croat, but later were ashamed and apologized to her. On the one hand, she was surprised and angry for such an ethnification in a situation in which she acted as a professional, hired by the Swedish state. On the other hand, the same person remembers a Muslim man from Bosnia who also asked for another intepreter. "I understood that the Croats really did something awful to him," she said.

The "Yugoslav" criss-crossing of imposed and chosen identifications in diaspora and exile in Sweden may be concluded by mentioning a less charged example. A Croatian guest lecturer met a young Muslim woman from Bosnia in a small group of Swedish students attending her lecture, given in English. In a conversation following the lecture, the young Bosnian Muslim woman was eager to tell the Croatian teacher how *proud* she was of her fluency in English, "so that they [the Swedish students] see how well *we* can speak English". The *usness* perceived by the young woman was an instance of satisfaction or even momentary superiority because the Croatian person was the teacher and the Swedes in the classroom were the students, because her own English was worse than that of her Swedish peers, and because she had to cope with the entire education in Swedish – the language she started to learn only a few years earlier. Her spontaneous identification had little to do with ethnicity and nationality (hers was Swedish, by the way), but very much with her own (post)refugee frustrations in Sweden. And, of course, with the quality of the *personal* encounter with the Croatian-speaking person, which was obviously perceived as positive.

Culture and tradition: contrasting examples

"Tradition" – site of a thousand essentialisms, exclaimed James Clifford (1997: 268) voicing the ambivalence of many an ethnologist. During the past two decades, scholars of different background have

been attentive to the "invention" of cultures and traditions, particularly as this process is associated with nationalist and ethnic politics. In an important essay assessing the usefulness of the notion of
identity, Richard Handler (1994) states that one result of this scholarship is that analysts are increasingly wary of employing reifying
conceptions of nation, ethnic group, culture, and tradition. Cultures and social groups, taken at local, regional, national, or transnational level of analysis, are now – as in this article – conceptualized
in terms of ongoing processes of "construction" and "negotiation"
(Handler 1994: 27).

Yet, Handler warns against the epistemological problem of reifica-
tion that pervades the scientific rhetorical and conceptual apparatus.
Recently, suspicious terms like "tradition" and "ethnic group" have
been – again as in this article – replaced by "identity". Handler
argues that it is peculiar to the modern Western world and therefore
should not be used cross-culturally as a neutral notion. More important in this context is Handler's presentation of the current scholarly
analyses of collective identities, since there is a tension between the
notion of identity as essential, fundamental, unitary and unchanging, and the notion that identities are constructed and reconstructed
through historical action. Current insights into the "construction"
of culture present a predicament, for

> the very idea of culture has been elaborated in terms of bounded-
> ness, homogeneity, and the idea of immutable natural essence. We
> speak more readily of culture as a noun – "a" culture, "this"
> culture, "our" culture – than as a verb indicating process, inter-
> communication, and the ongoing construction and reconstruc-
> tion of boundaries that are symbolic and not naturally given.
> Furthermore, this tension in culture theory is found in common-
> sense and nationalist discourse as well as in the work of scholars.
> Nationalists believe profoundly in the uniqueness of their cultural
> identity. They also believe that the boundaries they construct to
> define that identity are naturally given and *not* a symbolic con-
> struction of their own devising (Handler 1994: 29).

Thus, identity is conceived as unchanging even in changing cultural
contexts. Imbued with modern notions of progress and linear

temporality, nationalists also see the nation as a project of becoming. However, it is in the sense of restoring or recapturing a lost identity, "as if a definitive collective identity existed in the past and can be recovered through correct historical scholarship and political action" (Handler 1994: 30).

These thoughts lead us into the midst of the *19th Festival of Croatian Culture in Sweden* organized by the Association of Croatian Clubs on 7 November 1998 in Malmö Concert Hall. (The festival is held once a year, alternating between Malmö and Gothenburg.) The core of the 1998 *Festival of Croatian Culture* programme consisted – as every year – of the stylized folk dances performed by altogether thirty women of different generations, and some twenty schoolchildren, accompanied by live *tamburica* (string instrument) music performed by eight young men. Regardless of the uneven quality of performances, that part of the programme was a true replica of what, today in Croatia, is considered to be a proper way of presenting folkdances on stage. That genre has been well defined by applied folkloristics in Croatia.

The reactions of the audience were also similar to the ones I witnessed in Croatia on numerous occasions of that kind. Malmö Concert Hall was rather full, and the atmosphere was one of celebration. It was a family occasion marked by the presence of even the youngest children. Some children from Gothenburg recited, sang and danced – dressed in the Croatian football team colours. Concluding their performance by dancing to the playback of football fans' hymn "Croatia is the champion of the world" – thus evoking the national pride over bronze medal for Croatia in the World cup the same year. They made the audience highly amused.

The programme, however, did not consist of dance and music only. It was framed by the Croatian and Swedish national anthems, and speeches given by the secretary of the Association of Croatian Clubs in Sweden and by another "professional Croat" in Sweden, namely the Croatian ambassador – a medical doctor who has formerly been living in Denmark and thus shares some diasporic experiences with his compatriots in Sweden.

While the ambassador's message was that "we as a nation, as well as a minority in Sweden, need *cultured* Croats", the secretary of the

Association (a young woman born in Sweden), said that "the Festival is supposed to present our culture, but more importantly, our togetherness – today, when we are blessed by the greatest gift of our Homeland". With these words, she was referring to Croatian independence: Croatia was internationally recognized in early 1992. She also expressed joy and pride for the fact that the Croats in Sweden "never divided themselves on the basis of regional belonging" (which means regional background in Croatia). "The young people who are performing today are a proof of this upbringing", she said, and pointed out the praiseworthy fact that the "young third-generation of Croats is today dancing under the leadership of the second generation".

Along with the speeches, clear messages about the current identity issues relevant for Croats were easily recognized and readily approved of by applause. They were sent through the lyrics of two older patriotic poems recited by a middle-aged woman. The Gothenburg children in Croatian football-team colours – all born and living in Sweden – were reciting that it is "difficult to be a stranger in a foreign land". The church choir from Malmö sang: "Oh, Croatia, you sacred land / crucified for centuries! / The dawn is rising in your skies / and waking the Croats from the dream!" Four young women from Malmö sang a song about Vukovar, the town that suffered a three-month siege under heavy attack, with many civilian victims, thereby gaining the status of the key symbol of Croatian resistance and martyrdom in 1991.

A small exhibition accompanied the Festival of Croatian Culture in Malmö Concert Hall. It consisted of the objects possessed by the club "Croatian Woman": a few coffee-table books on the ecclesiastical history of Croatia and on Croatian cultural heritage (art and architecture) were exposed. The rest of the exhibition consisted of some tools from the domain of peasant female textile production and predominantly of parts of folk costumes. These bits and pieces – exhibited because they were "ours", "old", and "Croatian" – created an almost surreal background for the crowds of people eager to meet friends. According to the subsequent article in "Croatian Messenger", the Croatian quarterly in Sweden, *narodno blago* (the German *Volksschatz* is the most accurate translation) was presented in a "high-quality and true way", to the delight of "faithful adorers of Croatian folk tradition" (in the singular).

The image of Croatia celebrated by diaspora Croats in Sweden is reduced to the symbols of "old traditions". That image is coherent with the mainstream folklorization of culture, which is a long-lasting trend easily traced in the former Yugoslavia, but also in Croatia in the 1990s. While it is not related to any Swedish contexts in terms of diaspora Croats' legal and economic status, such a celebration of their ethnic and – since 1992 – national identity is proof of the existence of a strong Croatian community in Sweden, directed towards the Croats themselves. It is meant to confirm and reinforce the ties among people who formed the enthusiastic audience and shared the happy emotions on 7 November 1998 in Malmö. They have safe standard images of *Croatian culture* and discourses of Croatia to relate to and to perpetuate, which are invested with love, pride and nostalgia. In the context of the festival, they can be considered as coming out of a common sense conception of national belonging. It is, however, possible to see them as straightforwardly nationalist, too. Richard Handler's "diagnosis" of the de-historicizing effort to recapture a unique cultural identity into which all the Croats are born, is very much to the point here.

Although assessing the symbols and discourses used in the public activities of an ethnic community is necessary for understanding identity-formation processes, it can never encompass their complexity. On the one hand, public presentations of a group's identity are necessarily reduced to some core images and discursive models. On the other hand, it is a tiny minority of the most active people in the clubs that shapes these representations and voices them through ethnic media. More passive community members would maybe agree with somewhat different representations, too, if they were offered to them. One of my insights so far is that there is a surprising chance or casuality in, e.g., designing the local Croatian clubs' symbols, as well as in the history of the symbol of the Croatian cultural festival. The latter, consisting of the Croatian coat of arms (cf. Senjković 1993, Senjković 1995) and a *tamburica*, the "national instrument", was designed by one of the clubs' active members at his computer at work. No one bothered to draw an alternative version;

it was simply accepted as it was. This, of course, might not mean that people do not care, but – on the contrary – that the consensus might be so high that it is "obvious" for the group of club members, as well as for the wider diasporic audience, that symbols should look exactly as they do. The same goes for the entire interior decoration of the Croatian Home in Malmö, including a number of historical pictures, tourist posters, and portraits of important persons on the walls. Stjepan Radić, Franjo Tuđman and Pope John Paul II, who visited Croatia twice, have a prominent position (for a brief survey of Croatian history, see Goldstein 1999).

In contrast, Croats from Bosnia-Herzegovina who came to Sweden as refugees lack public cultural representation, especially such a safe and self-assured one. A club of Bosnian Croats has recently been established as the seventh Croatian club in Malmö. Future research will unveil the presumably different trends of activities and codes of representation, to be formulated in the course of their own shaping of their public identity in Sweden. It will indeed be interesting to see how the politically delicate and culturally complex fact of belonging to the same ethnicity, but sharing traditions and experiences of a life in Bosnian social and cultural settings, will be expressed. "Continuous promotion of Croatian culture and identity" intended by the club will be interesting to compare with the diaspora Croats' festival.

The Bosnian Croats' club has *not* been accepted into the Association of Croatian Clubs. The Croatian home in Malmö is open to any individual visitor, but it remained closed for the Bosnian Croats' club activities that would institutionalize and "legalize" the difference within. Some people from Bosnia-Herzegovina are active both in this Bosnian and some older, diaspora Croats' club, but the situation of the formal non-acceptance is a principal issue. The Bosnian club is a branch of the Croatian cultural society "Progress" (*Napredak*) situated in Sarajevo (and not in Zagreb – "the metropolis of all Croats", as dubbed in some Croatian newspapers). The fact that *Napredak* has a century-long tradition of supporting Croatian social and cultural concerns in Bosnia and elsewhere (with more than a fifty branches all over the world in the 1990s), makes the Bosnian Croats' club in Malmö belong to some other frames of reference and incorporate meanings foreign to the local diasporic community.

When asked how they feel about the seventh Croatian club in town, some diaspora Croats from Malmö thought that "if they really were interested in sports and culture, they could very well have done it in the existing clubs". Others responded that it is expected and normal, because Bosnian Croats have other problems and interests than the Croats who have lived in Sweden for decades. Some were tolerant on one occasion, and fiercely against it on the other. In the interview in *The Croatian Messenger* (no. 1, 1999), the chairman of the Association of Croatian Clubs in Sweden accused the Bosnian Croats of "splitting" the ethnic community in Malmö on the basis of regional(!) belonging (the notion of "region" is politically charged inasmuch as it dismisses Bosnia-Herzegovina as a separate state). The Bosnian Croats' answer, published in the first issue of the club's bulletin *Progress*, started in November 1999, hints at the vanity of some prominent dispora Croats who do not want to lose control over the local diasporic scene. More importantly, the published answer also reveals anger and disappointment about the Bosnian Croats' "patriotism and Croathood" being questioned, and points to these people's direct engagement and sufferings in the recent war.

Postscript

What does it mean to be a Croat in Sweden? This question becomes especially intriguing when the researcher is supposed to give a personal answer. I have so far been met by diaspora Croats in Sweden as a *persona grata* for the very fact of coming from Croatia (in 1998). On the one hand, one of my interviewees took a day off from work in order to talk to me for four hours, saying that she wants to do "everything for Croatia". On the other hand, many refugees – Croatian and Muslim – meet me in their Swedish homes as a newly acquired friend to whom they spontaneously confide thoughts that would never be uttered if the tape-recorder was introduced. I often feel it would be wrong – not only in relation to those people, but also to the quality of my research – to try to redefine the situation by insisting on the researcher-informant relation. As in most ethnological research, much highly relevant information is acquired through participant observation, when the distance between the researcher and "the researched" is blurred by the informality of contacts. Östen Wahlbeck's justification of "methodological pragmatism" (Wahlbeck 1999: 192) mentioned in the introduction to this volume comes to mind here as well.

My complex "native" and emergent diasporic position can at the same time be an advantage and a predicament, but it will certainly be crucial for the outcome of this research. After a period of ambivalence, I see it as an advantage. It provides for "experimental" situations of mutually testing perceptions and definitions of Croathood against the background of the others' experiences and understandings. Besides, my *true-Croatian-living-in-Croatia* aura seems to have faded since 1998. When introducing me to a Croatian embassy representative in late 2000, a diaspora acquaintance presented me, to my surprise, simply as someone who had "not lived here long". In that situation, the diasporic community (or the diasporic experience he shares with the others) was the frame of reference, and not the Croatia proper that the representative comes from. I was seen as a member of the local diasporic community, although not an equal one. What used to be an instance of prestige some years ago, nowadays might be seen as a sort of shortcoming: I was not here when Croathood in Sweden was defined in the context of political struggle against Yugoslavia. Levitating in between positions might prove to be a difficult, yet worthwhile effort towards the understanding of why, when and how identities in diaspora are negotiated, by whom, against whom, and with what relative power.

Notes

1   The project entitled "Seeds of war: Narrative Construction of Identities in Diaspora and Exile" is financed by the Swedish Council for Research in the Humanities and Social Sciences (HSFR) in 2000 and 2001.

2   This article is based on the paper "Narrative Construction of Identities in Diaspora and Exile: Croats in Sweden in the 1990s" presented at the conference "Identity Formations in Diaspora and Exile" (Lund University, 4–5 December 1998), and on the paper "Homeland Lost and Gained: Croatian Diaspora and Refugees in Sweden", presented at the conference "New Approaches to Migration: Transnational Communities and the Transformation of Home" (University of Sussex, 21–22 September 1999).

3   In the early 1990s, before the war started in Croatia and Bosnia-Herzegovina, some 11,000 immigrants from all the former Yugoslav republics were living in the city of Malmö. The majority of them were Serbs, but Malmö, together with Gothenburg, is the town in Sweden with the highest concentration of ethnic Croats. Together with other labour immigrants, they came to Sweden in the 1960s and 1970s. Today, 20% (out of 230,000) of Malmö inhabitants are immigrants or of immigrant origin, 15,000 of them from the former Yugoslavia (cf. Slavnić 2000).

4   Around 50,000 people from Bosnia-Herzegovina who arrived in Sweden before June 1993 were granted a permanent residence permit. Another 5,000 people came from Bosnia-Herzegovina after June 1993, although a visa was required for Bosnian people to enter Sweden. Most of them entered the country with Croatian passports, and then sought asylum as Bosnian refugees (for more details see Slavnić 2000). Croatia granted citizenship to people of Croatian ethnic affiliation regardless of their actual residence, so Bosnian Croats could acquire Croatian passports. In spring 1995, some 3,500 of them received temporary residence permits, while 1,500 left for third countries or were returned to Croatia. In November 1997, after a long period of uncertainty and political negotiations, families with children who had spent more than three years in Sweden were granted permanent residence permits. That applied to some 1,500 Bosnian Croats.

5   The emotional significance of the free celebration of national symbols for many Croats who gather in their clubs in Sweden lies in the fact that many people of the first migrant generation, and especially the ones who fled in the 1970s, were threatened by prison for exposing them in public under the communist regime. In 1971, numerous students ended up in prison for taking part in the "Croatian Spring" demonstrations and for exposing, e.g., the Croatian red-and-white "chequerboard" (coat of arms) on their jackets. This enjoyment of the free exposure of national symbols has been prominent in Croatia since 1990, too. The Croatian national belonging has been overcommunicated in public rituals, official media discourse and images, as well as in everyday practices – in contrast to the time as part of Yugoslavia, when it was forcefully undercommunicated (cf. Senjković 1993, Senjković 1995).

6   Underlying this use of the notion of "Bosnians" is a complex cluster of meanings and understandings that, on the one hand, can be directly related to the everyday Orientalism that Magnus Berg writes about in this volume, and, on the other, to the Croatian obsession with "belonging to Europe" that I have discussed elsewhere (Povrzanović Frykman 2001). There is a basic, widely shared agreement among diaspora Croats in Sweden that Croats should be recognized as a distinct people sharing Western European cultural traditions (in architecture, literature and the use of Latin) since medieval times. People coming from Bosnia-Herzegovina can be – and often are – perceived by the Croats from Croatia as "coming from the Balkans". The ending of all formal relations with other former Yugoslav peoples in early 1992, with whom they have been sharing two states since 1918, was perceived by the Croats – and here a general statement is accurate – as a welcome ending of all their connections with the Balkans. The notion of the Balkans – regardless of the variety of its possible meanings – is most often reduced to the

opposition of Europe in a dichotomy in which *Europe* stands for high culture, wealth and freedom. Europe is urban, middle-class, Western and modern, while *the Balkans* is the negative opposite: it means primitivism, poverty and wars. It is rural, peasant, wild, oriental and backward. "Bosnians" who "do not know how to behave" in the example mentioned were not called "Balkan people", but the same negative stereotype was implied. A young (second-generation) diaspora Croat told me that the behaviour of his relatives – refugees from Bosnia – "made him see the difference between the West and the Balkans".

7   In the framework of the project presented in this article, I am interviewing not only Croats (immigrants and refugees from Croatia and Bosnia-Herzegovina) in the Malmö area, but also Muslim and Serbian refugees from Bosnia-Herzegovina. I consider this neccessary for putting my research in the perspective of the manifold interrelatedness of almost all war-related processes not only in Croatia and Bosnia-Herzegovina, but in all post-Yugoslav countries.

References

Anderson, Benedict. 1983. *Imagined Communities: Reflections on the Origin and Spread of Nationalism.* London: Verso.

Clifford, James. 1997. *Routes: Travel and Translation in the Late Twentieth Century.* Cambridge, MA and London: Harvard University Press.

Cohen, Robin (ed.). 1995. *The Cambridge Survey of World Migration.* Cambridge: Cambridge University Press.

Daun, Åke. 1993. Nationalism and Internationalism in Sweden: Toward a New Class Society? *Ethnologia Scandinavica* 23: 3–11.

Ehn, Billy. 1975. *Sötebrödet.* Stockholm: Tidens Forlag.

Fassmann, Heinz and Münz, Rainer. 1995. European East-West Migration, 1945–1992. In Cohen, R. (ed.), *The Cambridge Survey of World Migration,* 470–480. Cambridge: Cambridge University Press.

Gilroy, Paul. 1992. Cultural Studies and Ethnic Absolutism. In Grossberg, L., Nelson, C. and Treichler, P. (eds.), *Cultural Studies,* 187–199. New York: Routledge.

Goldstein, Ivo. 1999. *Croatia: A History.* London: Hurst & Company.

Gustavsson, Sven, and Svenberg, Ingvar (eds.). 1995. *Bosnier: En flyktinggrupp i Sverige och dess bakgrund.* Uppsala: Centrum för multietnisk forskning.

Handler, Richard. 1994. Is "identity" a useful cross-cultural concept? In Gillis J. R. (ed.), *Commemorations: The Politics of National Identity,* 27–40. Princeton, New Jersey: Princeton University Press.

Kolar-Panov, Dona. 1996. Video and the Diasporic Imagination of Selfhood: A Case Study of the Croatians in Australia. *Cultural Studies* 10(2): 288–314.

Kolar-Panov, Dona. 1997. *Video, War and the Diasporic Imagination.* London: Routledge.

Magnusson, Kjell. 1988. Kroater. In *Det mångkulturella Sverige: En handbok om etniska grupper och minoriteter*, 229–234. Stockholm: Centrum för multietnisk forskning and Gidlunds Bokförlag.

Magnusson, Kjell. 1989. *Jugoslaver i Sverige: Invandrare och identitet i ett kultursociologiskt perspektiv.* Uppsala: Centrum för multietnisk forskning.

Magnusson, Kjell, Medić, Midhat, and Runblom, Harald (eds.). 1996. *Krig, exil, återvändande.* Uppsala: Centrum för multietnisk forskning.

Malkki, Liisa H. 1990. Context and Consciousness: Local Conditions for the Production of Historical and National Thought among Hutu Refugees in Tanzania. In Fox, R. (ed.), *Nationalist Ideologies and the Production of National Cultures*, 32–62. Washington: American Anthropological Association.

Povrzanović, Maja. 2000. The Imposed and the Imagined as Encountered by Croatian War Ethnographers. *Current Anthropology* 41(2): 151–162.

Povrzanović, Maja, and Jambrešić Kirin, Renata. 1996. Negotiating Identities? The Voices of Refugees between Experience and Representation. In Jambrešić Kirin, R. and Povrzanović, M. (eds.), *War, Exile, Everyday Life. Cultural Perspectives*, 3–19. Zagreb: Institute for Ethnology and Folklore Research.

Povrzanović Frykman, Maja. 2001. När våldet tar plats. In Hansen, K. and Salomonsson, K. (eds.), *Europa – platser och identiteter.* Lund: Studentlitteratur (forthcoming).

Prica, Ines, and Povrzanović, Maja. 1996. Narratives of Refugee Children as the Ethnography of Maturing. In Jambrešić Kirin, R. and Povrzanović, M. (eds.), *War, Exile, Everyday Life. Cultural Perspectives*, 83–113. Zagreb: Institute for Ethnology and Folklore Research.

Ronström, Owe. 1992. *Att gestalta ett ursprung: En musiketnologisk studie av dansande och musicerande bland jugoslaver i Stockholm.* Stockholm: Akademitryck.

Schierup, Carl-Ulrik. 1995. Former Yugoslavia: Long Waves of International Migration. In Cohen, R. (ed.), *The Cambridge Survey of World Migration*, 285–288. Cambridge: Cambridge University Press.

Schierup, Carl-Ulrik, and Ålund, Aleksandra. 1987. *Will They Still Be Dancing? Integration and Ethnic Transformation among Yugoslav Immigrants in Scandinavia*. Göteborg: Almqvist and Wiksell.

Senjković, Reana. 1993. In the Beginning There Were a Coat of Arms, a Flag and a "Pleter" In Čale Feldman, L., Prica, I. and Senjković, R. (eds.), *Fear, Death and Resistance. An Ethnography of War: Croatia 1991–1992*, 24–43. Zagreb: Institute of Ethnology and Folklore Research, Matrix Croatica, X-Press.

Senjković, Reana. 1995. The Use, Interpretation and Symbolization of the National. *Ethnologia Europaea* 25(1): 69–80.

Skrbiš, Zlatko. 1995. Long Distance Nationalism?: Second Generation Croatians and Slovenians in Australia. In Pavković, A. (ed.), *Nationalism and Postcommunism*, 159–173. Dartmouth: Dartmouth Press.

Skrbiš, Zlatko. 1997. Homeland – Diaspora Relations: From Passive to Active Interactions. *Asian and Pacific Migration Journal* 6 (3–4): 439–455.

Skrbiš, Zlatko. 1998. Making It Tradeable: Videotapes, Cultural Technologies and Diasporas. *Cultural Studies* 12(1): 265–274.

Slavnić, Zoran. 2000. *Existens och temporalitet: Om det samtida flyktingskapets komplexitet*. Umeå: Akademiska avhandlingar vid Sociologiska institutionen Umeå universitet, no. 19.

Wahlbeck, Östen. 1999. *Kurdish Diasporas: A Comparative Study of Kurdish Refugee Communities*. London: Macmillan.

Winland, Daphne N. 1995. "We Are Now an Actual Nation": The Impact of National Independence on the Croatian Diaspora in Canada. *Diaspora* 4(1): 3–30.

Imagining Croatia?
Exploring computer-mediated diasporic public spheres

Paul Stubbs

Introduction

Migration and media

The recent concern within anthropology, ethnology, cultural stud-ies and sociology, amongst other disciplines, particularly in their post-colonial variants, with the vexed question of identities, has involved an attempt to develop and promote "a theory of rupture that takes media and migration as its two major, and interconnected, diacritics and explores their joint effect on the *work of the imagination* as a constitutive feature of modern subjectivity" (Appadurai 1996: 3; emphasis in original). This chapter seeks to elaborate upon Appa-durai's concern, through a specific focus on the conjunction of one aspect of migration, or rather post-migration, namely the construc-tion of particular kinds of *diasporic affinities*, together with the rapid growth of *computer-mediated communication* (CMC), as one aspect of modern media, primarily in terms of the construction of new public spheres through the use of Internet and computer-mediated news-groups.

Going beyond theoretical abstractions, in which particular 'cases' are manipulated beyond 'local' recognition to fit as 'evidence', the text concentrates on contemporary aspects of the imagining of Croatia as a national form emerging into independence through war, post-socialist transition, mass forced migration, and a politicised interpo-lation of 'homeland' across geographical boundaries. The existence of *computer-mediated diasporic public spheres* [1], axiomatic to this chapter, deepens the understanding of what have been termed transnational and postnational imaginings since, as complex discursive and historical fields, they represent particular constructions of the national space from diverse global sites, which become, effectively and in effect, a unified imagined place or homeland.

The chapter focuses on Croatia, a country where I have lived since 1993 and which has been the base for my involvement in a range of projects including academic research, activism, work with refugees, and a range of initiatives in terms of social policy. Above all, it is relevant to note that my engagement with globalisation, and the complex linkages between the local, the national and the global (Löfgren, 1996), began from Croatia rather than from Western academia (Deacon, Hulse and Stubbs 1997, ch. 7; Stubbs, 1997). In addition, from late 1994 onwards, I have used e-mail and, later, Internet, as key sites of academic and activist discourse, being a member of the *zamir* ("for peace" in Croatian) network originally conceived as linking individuals and groups working for peace and human rights in the post-Yugoslav countries (Stubbs 1998: 3.1). Hence, my sociological concern with CMC derives not only from my oft-stated concern to link theory and practice, but from a recent lived engagement with mediated theory and activism in, about, and from, Croatia.

The new Croatian ethnography

The chapter is influenced also by my engagement with what might best be termed the 'new Croatian ethnography', associated mainly with the work of a group of young Croatian ethnologists based in the Institute of Ethnology and Folklore Research in Zagreb. Part of this work addressed *War, Exile, Everyday Life* (Jambrešić Kirin and Povrzanović, eds. 1996) through the development of cultural perspectives on "concepts of identity in the context of a cluster of refugee problems" (Povrzanović and Jambrešić Kirin 1996: 8). This became part of a wider analysis of identities in war (Povrzanović 1997) which now extends to a study of Croatian diaspora and refugees in Sweden (see Povrzanović Frykman in this volume).

Space precludes anything more than a crude summary of the relevant core themes of this body of work for the ideas presented here.

Firstly, there is a critique of the inadequacy of prior, absolutist forms of knowing, applied as much to notions of 'anti-nationalist' as to 'nationalist' discourses. The attempt to construct what has been termed a "multivoiced ethnography of war" (Jambrešić Kirin 1999: 20) does not, however, degenerate into a stance of moral relativism. Rather, and secondly, there is a clear statement of the validity, indeed the impossibility of avoiding, a combination of "critical abilities together with emotional commitment in providing proper scholarly responses to everyday situations of (post)war time" and thereby creating the possibility of accepting "ethnography as a form of critique of the misuse of cultural heritage in political discourse" (Jambrešić Kirin 1996: 65).

Thirdly, the new Croatian ethnography is suspicious of all attempts to essentialise the experiences of forced migrants or to assume any kind of instant correspondence between those experiences and similar experiences. In the axiomatic statement that "(I)dentity does not exist prior to social practices and cultural patterns which negotiate and regulate it" (Povrzanović and Jambrešić Kirin 1996: 9), a profound historical, social and cultural specificity is being presented, which distrusts reductionist explanations which seek to 'read off' everyday life as an expression of broader political motifs.

Ethnicity and primordialism

In some ways, this approach finds echoes in Appadurai's critique of primordialist conceptions of 'irrational' ethnic violence, preferring to see ethnicity as "a historically constituted form of social classification that is regularly misrecognized and naturalized as a prime mover in social life" (Appadurai 1996: 140). The idea that "styles of identity politics" can be consciously worked out strategies of "irony and satire", rather more than being "a knee-jerk symbol of buried and semiconscious ideologies" (Appadurai 1996: 145), to which could be added *even* in war time, and *even* in diasporic public spheres, is explored further in this chapter.

Unfortunately, in the search for "an equally general perspective" with which to move beyond the primordialist thesis, Appadurai's approach to understanding "ethnic implosions" through notions of betrayal and treachery as "large-scale identities forcibly enter the local imagination and become dominant voice-overs in the traffic of ordinary life" (Appadurai 1996: 154–5), can only take us so far in understanding the specificities of the wars in Croatia and Bosnia-Herzegovina since 1991. Indeed, in conjuring up notions of competing decontextualised 'ethnic' rages, it may be no less primordialist than the argument it seeks to supersede.

In terms of the context and antecedents of the war in Croatia, it is important to reject any kind of one-dimensional explanations, which appear to 'know' the causes. Indeed, just this slippage from the general theory to the particular case is that which occurs all too often in post-modernist texts on 'new ethnicities'. The assertion of a 'new Croatian ethnicity', if such there was in any unilinear form, which I doubt, came *after* Serbian President Slobodan Milošević's knitting together of nationalism, conservatism, religious fervour, and anti-bureaucratic populism, as well as appealing to the interests of the Yugoslav Army, which should, in my view, be seen as the main contributor to the wars and huge population displacement from 1991. Nationalist forms inside and outside Croatia must be examined in this context and not seen as equal and opposite ideologies. Within this, the significance of diaspora identifications should be emphasised but, as I shall note in the next section, even this is far more complex and contested than primordialist explanations, including post-modernist variants, seem to be able to allow for.

I continue to argue in this chapter against any notion of a unitary 'Croatian experience', whilst recognising at times of crisis that this may *appear* to be the case, and instead write of 'Croatian experiences' and, indeed, 'imaginings', which include all those who live in or have lived in the space of Croatia; those whose ethnicised identifications are Croatian who live elsewhere (including, but not reducible to, the diaspora); and those affected by any kind of 'Croatian interpolation'. In other words, the recent past can be seen to have produced transformations of, and new choices and restrictions on the choice between, different identities and identifications (Stubbs 1996) which have to be analysed carefully and not simply treated as crude examples proving elaborate theoretical points.

Diaspora, CMC and the construction of ethnoscapes

New diaspora theory

One of the most sophisticated overviews of 'new diaspora theory' is provided by James Clifford who summarises a wide range of anthropological and sociological material. In cautioning against elisions between "invocations of diaspora theories, diasporic discourses, and distinct historical experiences of diaspora" (Clifford 1997: 244), Clifford sees 'diaspora' as one of a number of interpretative terms used to characterise "the contact zones of nations, cultures, and regions" (Clifford 1997: 245). Arguing against defining 'diaspora' by recourse to an 'ideal type', through which groups become identified, according to some predefined features as 'more or less diasporic', he prefers to frame discussion in terms of the borders of the concept of diaspora, or what the term is defined against. Thus, the approach emphasises the ways that diaspora groupings "maintain important allegiances and practical connections to a homeland or a dispersed community located elsewhere" (Clifford 1997: 250). This construction is based on Paul Gilroy's (1987) notion of diaspora discourses constructing "alternate public spheres" or "forms of consciousness and solidarity that maintain identifications outside the national time/space" (Clifford 1997: 251), so that "(s)eparate places become effectively a single community" (Clifford 1997: 246).

The significance and achievement of this approach may well be the way that it moves away from "exclusivist paradigms" (Clifford 1997: 247) in which only some diasporas are really diasporas; in which migrant forms are assigned to bounded categories such as 'immigrant', 'guest worker', or 'refugee'; and in which strategies are labelled as either truly 'diasporic', 'hybrid', 'creolized', or 'transcultural'; in favour of far more fluid, non-exclusive, patternings which can only be grasped, as it were, fleetingly, contextually, and within complex discursive and historical fields. Axiomatic to the approach, however, seems to be the increased opportunities of border relations made possible by "modern technologies of transport, communication, and labour migration" (Clifford 1997: 247), involving the "transformation of everyday subjectivities", so that the diasporic public spheres so created "are no longer small, marginal or exceptional" (Appadurai 1996: 10). Providing they are treated as useful tools rather than predefined realities, Appadurai's distinctions between *diasporas of hope, diasporas of terror,* and *diasporas of despair;* and, by extension, between *cold* and *hot* diasporas, in terms of their implosive aspects; and between diaspora in itself and diaspora for itself, capable of moving beyond shared imagination to collective action (Appadurai 1996: 8), are all of use in understanding the *multiplication* or *pluralisation* of diasporic possibilities, or of ways in which "the idea of the nation flourishes transnationally" (Appadurai 1996: 172).

The caricature of the 'long-distance nationalist'

The relationship of diasporas to forms of nationalism is complex, however. Certainly, it has become axiomatic to state that "the emergent nationalisms of many parts of the world may be founded on patriotisms that are not either exclusively or fundamentally territorial" (Appadurai 1996: 21). However, Clifford's assertion that "(w)hatever their ideologies of purity, diasporic cultural forms can never, in practice, be exclusively nationalist" (Clifford 1997: 251), provides a necessary corrective. In two highly influential texts, Benedict Anderson whose brilliant *Imagined Communities* (Anderson 1983) is, of course, the starting point for any understanding of nations as imagined, sketches the phenomenon of "the long-distance nationalist" which he sees as a new type of nationalism precisely formed at the junction of modern mass migration and mass communication. The caricature is worth quoting in full:

> (W)hile technically a citizen of the state in which he comfortably lives, but to which he may feel little attachment, he finds it tempting to play identity politics by participating (via propaganda, money, weapons, any way but voting) in the conflicts of his imagined Heimat – now only fax time away. But this citizenless participation is inevitably non-responsible – our hero will not have to answer for, or pay the price of, the long-distance politics he undertakes. He is also easy prey for shrewd political manipulators in his Heimat (Anderson 1992: 13).

Two years later, Anderson describes today's long-distance national-ism "as a probably menacing portent for the future" (Anderson 1994: 327), creating a serious but radically unaccountable politics often of an extremist kind, of which he gives some examples including:

> ... the malign role of Croats not only in Germany but also in Australia and North America in financing and arming Franco (sic) Tudjman's breakaway state and pushing Germany and Austria into a fateful, premature recognition (Anderson 1994: 327).

The specific parody or travesty of this example should lead to a rather more serious questioning of the basis of Anderson's arguments here. The complexities of positions taken by persons in the diaspora, and the range of callings from the homeland, are collapsed into this supposed sinister new trend behind which Anderson smuggles in his prejudiced analysis of the geo-politics of the post-Yugoslav space, inaccurate not only in terms of the first name of the Croatian pres-ident. The existence of a hot Croatian diaspora, and the galvanising of this within a particular political project, needs to be proved and not simply asserted as in this caricature. Furthermore, the complex-ities of diasporic identifications need to be addressed given the im-possibility of total closure. In addition, whilst modern forms of communication are noted, their effects are seen as somehow all per-vasive and, again, unilinear, although it is hard to imagine the fax machine, for example, ever having played the crucial role in a new identity politics which the first quote appears to imply.

Computer-mediated communication (CMC) and the problem of community

Whilst the fax machine hardly generated a huge sociological interest, this has certainly occurred with CMC, as e-mail and later Internet, themselves, of course, having a huge base in academia, have been the subject of a large numbers of essays, books and, increasingly, research projects. Whilst there have been very innovative attempts to develop, and to propagate on-line, both 'cybersociology' (<http://www.-cybersoc.com/>)[2] and a more cultural studies-oriented 'cybertheory'

(<http://www.ctheory.com/>), much of the print-published socio-logical literature remains somewhat narrowly focused on whether CMC users constitute a 'community'. One source for this comes from Howard Rheingold's seminal text, which contains within it a number of assumptions, which merit further exploration:

> Virtual communities are social aggregations that emerge from the Net when enough people carry on ... public discussions long enough, with sufficient human feeling, to form webs of personal relationships in cyberspace (Rheingold 1993: 5).

This argument, in fact, suggests that some CMC interactions can be seen as forming a community and others not – hence the need to talk, in the plural, of 'virtual communities', even though his book popu-larised the singular, and unhelpful, concept of 'the virtual commu-nity'. The problems of how to operationalise some of the concepts in this quote in any kind of meaningful social science are legion, begging not only the question of how many is 'enough', but also the vastly more taxing issue of what is to constitute 'sufficient human feeling'? In addition, all of the theorising about whether CMC users constitute a 'community' stemming from this kind of approach rests upon a kind of bi-polar view of a 'real' off-line world and a 'virtual' on-line one. Elsewhere (Stubbs 1998: 2.8), I have sought to reframe the question of whether groups of CMC users are, or are not, a community, in terms of the complex identities which users present on-line and off-line, and the ways in which CMC satisfies some of their needs, some of the time.

In order to analyse the significance of CMC in terms of social, cultural and political change, particularly in relation to diasporic public spheres, different kinds of approaches and frameworks may well be needed. Whilst it is certainly possible to overstate the impact and, indeed, the 'newness' of the 'new' information technologies, their potential in terms of 'networking', itself a term which embraces both technological and political possibilities, are legion. Whilst some CMC uses, notably private e-mails, resemble the one-to-one com-munication of the telephone, and others, notably non-interactive web pages, are very much like the centralised and hierarchical products of broadcast media, although with a vastly greater choice, still others, including e-mail discussion groups, newsgroups, interactive web pages, chat rooms, and so on, may involve highly decentralised forms which "permit a many-to-many dialogic practice to be instituted in a global environment of exchange" (Poster 1998: 190).

In any case, the ways in which different media use may reinforce each other, and in which what are supposedly passive media are used actively in certain ways, through the reposting on an newsgroup, with a commentary or ironic remark, a transcript from a radio or tv programme, for example, are all relevant here. Whilst it is not the case that for dispersed diaspora communities, "the electronic space is the only common space that they can occupy" (Mitra 1997: 70), it certainly affords new possibilities for the polytextual production of images and self-imaginings of particular nations and peoples, both in and for themselves, and in relation to equally stylised, but also radically unfinished, 'Others'.

For this reason, a traditional rationalist anthropological-sociological study of 'the use of technology w' by 'community x' as 'migrants in country y' in relation to events in 'homeland z' is singularly inadequate for the task in hand. Whilst such studies can be of use and, indeed, some are noted below, the development of what Appadurai has termed a 'transnational anthropology' or 'macroethnography' will always be greater than the sum of such national anthropologies or microethnographies. The attempt "to capture the impact of deterritorialization on the imaginative resources of lived, local experiences" (Appadurai 1996: 52), incorporating "the complexities of expressive representation" not as "technical adjuncts" but as "primary material" (Appadurai 1996: 64) is a central element of this. Within a new anthropology less oriented to 'fieldwork', at least in one locale, than to scattered multi-locales and to the study of 'spatial practices', there will be much more attention to CMC, in a kind of 'netnography'. This would assert the scientific value of, for example, monitoring diaspora e-mail and Internet newsgroups in which particular groups can be observed 'worrying together', akin to other kinds of 'intensive listening' in more traditional ethnographies (cf. Clifford 1997: 57–58, referring to Edwards 1994).

New ethnoscapes?

An additional theoretical refinement is provided by Appadurai's discussion of the relationship between five dimensions of global cultural flows: ethnoscapes; mediascapes; technoscapes; financescapes; and ideoscapes, which he sees as "deeply perspectival constructs, inflected by the historical, linguistic, and political situatedness of different sorts of actors" and which, together, form the building blocks of "imagined worlds" (Appadurai 1996: 33). In Appadurai's terms, ethnoscapes refer to "the landscape of persons who constitute the shifting world in which we live" (Appadurai 1996: 33), although there is nothing in his approach which would question a widening of this concept to include a much wider range of "identity-producing activities" (Appadurai 1996: 183) about nation-states.

Ethnoscapes are continuously constructed, practically and discursively, in complex ways which question bounded notions of 'the local' and 'the global' and point to new relationships between the two. These include what have been termed "multiple diasporization" and "pluralistic readings of national identity that are constantly and openly contested" (Alleyne-Dettmars 1997: 165). This is similar to Poster's notion of 'virtual ethnicity' in which virtuality involves "the articulation of new figures of ethnicity, nationhood, community and global interaction" (Poster 1998: 194). In this frame, the focus is very much on the ways in which electronic encoding and decoding "disrupts and reconfigures" ethnicity (Poster 1998: 195), so that a crucial research question becomes the ways in which "specific figures of ethnicity" are constructed, altered and, even deconstructed, "by their electronic constitution in virtual spaces" (Poster 1998: 200).

Aspects of the Croatian ethnoscape

Delineating Croatian diasporas

In seeking to understand aspects of the Croatian ethnoscape, it is important, following Poster, to be aware of their "underdetermined nature" (Poster 1998: 201) in terms of a relative unpredictability or logic of associations. However, "while we can make our identities, we cannot do so exactly as we please" (Appadurai 1996: 170) and, indeed, even more starkly, "(o)ne man's (sic) imagined community is another man's political prison" (Appadurai 1996: 32). In this vein, it is important to make some preliminary, and provisional, remarks about the specificities of diaspora and CMC in the Croatian ethnoscape.

The exact number of Croats living abroad and forming, therefore, some kind of diaspora is unclear. The Croatian World Congress, which presents itself as "the authentic voice of the Croatian Diaspora" (<http://hsk.hic.hr/index-en.htm>) suggests that 4.5 million "Croats and people of Croatian heritage live outside the Republics of Croatia and Bosnia-Herzegovina" (ibid.). Indeed, this itself presents the largest Croatian diaspora community, those living in the neighbouring state of Bosnia-Herzegovina, which may number up to 740,000, as within the Croatian 'homeland', an apparent support for the parastate of 'Herceg-Bosna' which, despite a number of international agreements, still retains a large measure of functional integration with Croatia itself.

In a press conference in December 1995, and following military actions to liberate Croatian territories held by 'rebels' which led to the exodus of up to 250,000 ethnic Serbs from Croatia, the Croatian President Dr. Franjo Tuđman made one of his many statements that "we must do everything possible to bring back as many as possible of the 3.5 million Croats dispersed throughout the world", therefore suggesting a lower figure than that by the Croatian World Congress (<http://www.predsjednik.hr/pc120195.htm>). He pointed out that, of course, there were now many 'deserted' and 'depopulated' areas in Croatia which would make perfect homes for diaspora returnees. In many ways, as with all 'ethnoscapes', the true number is much less important than the complex ways in which the diaspora is here being invoked in a unified construction of "the Croatian Homeland and its Diaspora" (The Croatian World Congress, <http://hsk.hic.hr/index-en.htm>; capitals in original) and in which the idea of the Nation as a "political symbol" (Verdery 1996: 103) involves the exclusion of some groups, 'non-Croats within', from parts of the National discourse, and the inclusion of others, 'Croats abroad', who need not necessarily be so constituted within a territorially-bounded notion of the national space.[3]

When 'Croats and those of Croatian heritage living abroad' is deconstructed somewhat and broken down into its constituent parts, what is most apparent is the diversity and range of identity formations rather than any unified Diaspora. Such a breakdown would include, as the largest diaspora group, those living in neighbouring Bosnia-Herzegovina, including both the contiguous diaspora in Herzegovina, as well as Central Bosnian Croats with, in many ways, a very different religious, social and political profile (cf. Peirce and Stubbs 1999). In addition, significant numbers of Croats live in other former Yugoslav Republics, notably in the Vojvodina area of Serbia which, like Kosova, had its status as an autonomous province revoked by Milošević in 1989 where, at the time of the 1981 census, some 109,000 declared themselves as Croat, and in the republic of Slovenia where the same census recorded some 57,000 Croats (Magaš 1993: 18).

A different group, although with some similarities to many of those in Slovenia, are the 'guest workers' who, from the 1960s onwards, in a climate of more open borders but also because of limited economic opportunities at home, took advantage of the demand for skilled and semi-skilled labour abroad, and worked in a number of countries, particularly in Western Europe, notably Germany, Austria, Switzerland and Sweden. Again, this is also a very diverse group, including those who went alone and whose remittances formed a key family income and investment 'at home', through to those who took dual citizenship or actually emigrated, often as family or extended kinship groups. Mesić records that, by 1991, over a million people from the Federal Republic of Yugoslavia were working abroad, the majority of whom were from Croatia and Slovenia (Mesić 1992: 180).

In many ways the most interesting diaspora groups are those who left, or were expelled, from Croatia at the end of the Second World War. The traces of the civil war in Yugoslavia which involved the victory of communist Partisans, led by Tito, over "anti-communist nationalists" (Pettan 1998: 10), both the Croatian *ustaše* (Ustasha) and the Serbian *četnici* (Chetniks), continues to have huge resonance in the narrative of the Croatian and Serbian ethnoscapes regarding the conflict from 1991. In particular, different constructions of the nature of the *Nezavisna Država Hrvatska* (*NDH*, or the Independent State of Croatia), the Ustasha-based Nazi-puppet state led by Ante

Pavelić, which held a kind of sovereignty over most of Croatia and parts of Bosnia-Herzegovina from 1941 until the end of the war, and which was marked by the systematic killing of Serbs, Jews, Roma, and Croat oppositionalists (cf. Magaš 1993: 314–5), can be seen as an example of the way different groups "remember the past in different ways" (Ramet 1996: 41).

For our purposes here, the events immediately following the Partisan victory, and in particular the mass expulsions of 1948, which could be described as based on a kind of 'collective guilt' for Ustasha crimes, produced a new diaspora of between 200,000 and 300,000 people (Mesić 1992). Whether all these Croatians "took with them the spirit of pre-war nationalism" (McAdams 1978) is debatable, but the fact that leading Ustasha, including Pavelić himself, who fled to Argentina, and their many sympathisers, formed radicalised Croatian diaspora communities in a number of countries, including the United States, Canada, Australia, Chile, and Argentina, is not unimportant.

Another wave of emigration occurred in the aftermath of the suppression of the 'Croatian Spring', a complex mass populist-democratic movement, in 1971, following which the 1970s was a period of increased political activity by sections of the Croatian diaspora. In many cities in the United States, Canada and Australia, where newer migrants mixed with long-standing Croatian émigré communities, some of which had been established in the nineteenth century, 'hot diasporas' were formed, as evidenced by a range of activities. Often, these interpenetrated with cultural and sporting activities, such as the formation of Croatian diaspora football clubs, for example, which oriented the narrative to the Croatian homeland and, in some cases led to a negative stereotyping of Croatians in the 'host community'. Indeed, this was so much the case in Australia, for example, that Vietnamese refugees were even dubbed as "yellow Croatians" (Skrbiš 1995: 161). These diaspora communities existed in complex relations to other Yugoslav groups, particularly Serb communities, and to official emphases from Yugoslav embassies which, themselves, changed considerably over time (Kolar-Panov 1997, ch. 1).

Finally, the mass forced migration from Croatia, Bosnia-Herzegovina and, now Kosova, consequent upon the wars from 1991, created new communities 'in exile', often alongside existing diaspora communities (see Povrzanović Frykman in this volume). Whilst the extent of the new Croatian diaspora formed in this way is small, certainly in relation to the Bosnian Muslim or Bošnjak diaspora, the impact within particular communities may well have been significant. Even more importantly, the refugee crisis consequent upon the wars has, more broadly, affected the status (both formal and informal) of existing diaspora groupings in many Western European and North American countries, particularly Germany where the mainstream political consensus, in response to right-wing violence, is that refugees have to be repatriated as soon as possible, and the rights of guest workers curtailed.

HDZ and the mobilisation of diaspora: bringing it all back home?

Overall, whilst I would suggest that it is analytically flawed to speak of 'the Croatian Diaspora' as a unified phenomenon, outside of a wide range of structures, histories, and logics, which combine to create differences, some of which I have noted above, I would also concur with Kolar-Panov that war 'reconfigured' many relationships within the diaspora and, in particular, "prioritized the homeland-diaspora relationship" (Kolar-Panov 1996: 289). At such a time, perhaps, the 'underdetermined' nature of 'ethnoscapes' may come to be more 'overdetermined' and, in particular, for heightened awareness and sensibility in diaspora communities about events 'at home' to coincide with, and be reinforced by, political projects which seek to 'speak to and with' the diaspora, through specific kinds of interpolations which seek to produce particular kinds of unity and action. However, and this is crucial, there is nothing in either of these forces, nor in their coincidence and mutual reinforment, which is inevitable or a result of frozen diasporic nationalisms just waiting to be taken out of the freezer and popped into the microwave ready to be served afresh.

A crucial role in this active process was, and continues to be, played by the *Hrvatska demokratska zajednica* (*HDZ*, or the Croatian Democratic Union) a political party which was formed ahead of the first democratic elections in Croatia in 1990, which it won, consolidating power in four subsequent elections. Its leader, Dr. Franjo Tuđman, became the first President of newly-independent Croatia. Jailed by the regime for periods in the 1960s and 1970s, because of his revisionist national history and views regarding the extent of killing in the *NDH*, Tudman had begun, in his later years in the formal political wilderness, to cultivate connections with sections of the Croatian diaspora. In the year before being allowed to function legally, *HDZ* had built a powerful network of offices not only in Croatia but also in parts of Bosnia-Herzegovina and Vojvodina, and within Croatian communities abroad, notably the United States.

It has been argued that funding for *HDZ* from the diaspora gave it a distinct advantage over its rivals (Cohen 1993: 95). Whilst *HDZ* voters, in the first elections, were quite specific in terms of their traditionalism and pronounced religious identity (Grdešić et al. 1991: 241), it is perhaps more useful to conceive of *HDZ* as a popular or populist social movement attaining hegemony, in part at least due to the acute war circumstances in Croatia from 1991 onwards. In this vein, the articulation of Homeland and Diaspora in the affirmation of Croatian identity and sovereignty, particularly when threatened by horrific aggression, and which mobilised music, art, culture, and historical symbolism in the service of a new 'common sense', was immensely important.

One of the most important figures in the *HDZ* was Gojko Šušak, born in 1945 in the Herzegovinan town of Široki Brijeg, a town renamed Lištica by the regime in 1951 because of its strong association as a base of support for the Ustasha. Šušak migrated to Canada in 1969 and became a very successful businessman owning a chain of pizza restaurants in Ottawa. Throughout the 1980s, Šušak played a leading role in the Canadian Croatian community and met Tudman on his first visit to Canada in 1987 (Interview in *Hrvatsko Slovo* of 27 December 1996, available in English translation at (<http://www.cdsp.neu.edu/info/students/marko/hrslovo/hrslovo7.html>). Šušak returned to Croatia in 1989, playing an important, and controversial, role in the new Croatian politics including, allegedly, firing missiles into the village of Borovo Selo in the Eastern Slavonia area of Croatia, which was populated by Serbs (Silber and Little 1995: 153), and later becoming Croatian Minister of Defence, holding the post until his death on 3 May 1998.

The significance of Šušak's role is complex partly because he sought to suggest that, amongst diaspora returnees, he was unusual if not unique, and that many others "can't find their bearings ... and expected that Croatia simply had to accept their offer (to serve) and appoint them to a position where they need not do any work" (*Hrvatsko Slovo* interview, as above), even though six such returnees attained the rank of General in the Croatian Army. Šušak formed a vital link between the Croatian regime and what became known as 'the Herzegovinan lobby', many of whom became leading politicians and businessmen in Zagreb, and which advocated for a 'Greater Croatia' politics to include wide areas of Bosnia-Herzegovina.

After the military actions in 1995 which returned three of the four occupied areas to Croatian Government control, snap elections were held which, for the first time, and partly through Šušak's lobbying, set aside twelve seats, almost 10% of the total, in the House of Representatives for a 'Diaspora list'. In fact, most of the votes cast in this way were by Croats in Bosnia-Herzegovina but it included Croats in other countries whose votes were organised through Croatian associations or, *de facto*, *HDZ* clubs. Perhaps not surprisingly, all of the seats returned *HDZ* representatives. Also, perhaps not surprisingly, the coalition of six opposition parties formed in 1998, campaigned for a new election law which would revise the role of the diaspora, not excluding them completely but abolishing separate seats and thus diluting the impact in terms of total support for *HDZ*. The original diaspora voting law that was introduced involved a merging of the broader diaspora question, and the importance of the contribution of the diaspora during the Homeland war, with the question of the relationship between Croatia proper and Croats in Bosnia-Herzegovina which are a contiguous diaspora. This shows, in fact, the complex ways in which diaspora interpolations formed a part of *HDZ*'s attempt to secure hegemony. Even here, there is huge complexity as one part of an oppositional 'common sense', more reflected in everyday jokes than in formal opposition politics, is scathing of the contribution of the 'Herzegovinans' and, to a lesser extent, the diaspora returnees, often labelling them as 'uncivilised' or 'uncultured' and as unjust winners from the privatisation process occurring in Croatia.

A more nuanced understanding of the diverse role of the diaspora in the 1990s is beyond the scope of this chapter. It would have to address the wide range of roles taken by people from the diaspora as soldiers, humanitarian workers, lobbyists, journalists, and so much more, as well as the complex and varied identities which were produced in this lived encounter with what, for many, had been a, more or less, distant Homeland.

War, CMC and the Croatian technoscape

This is lost on the influential commentator Mary Kaldor, a key figure in Western European 'civil politics', who has suggested that 'a new divide' is opening up between 'cosmopolitanism' and 'nationalism' with diaspora groups playing a much more important role in the new nationalism "because of the speed of communications" (Kaldor 1996: 53).[4] This is, in my view, a very crude argument which also leads to a problematic politics precisely because it pits 'cosmopolitanism', hardly likely to be supported by large parts of a society at war, as the only meaningful opposition to 'nationalism', itself rendered monolithic. In addition, the argument suggests something of a technological determinism that fails to address the diversity of forms and ways in which global communications have impacts and effects.

I have argued that war is something of a limit case in terms of CMC and, by extension, other forms of global communication, representing a particular form of global amplification and restructuring and the extended reproduction and assimilation of the conflicts into various kinds of transnational discourse (Stubbs 1998: 2.20). There have been very few studies of this phenomenon with one of the most extensive, Kolar-Panov's pioneering and valuable study of the innovative use of video technology by Croats in Australia (Kolar-Panov 1996; Kolar-Panov 1997), criticised by Skrbiš for failing to make "a more concerted effort to reconcile empirical evidence with fashionable modes of theoretical discursivity" (Skrbiš 1998: 272).

A more nuanced understanding can only come from examining the complex links between CMC, satellite television, the telephone, videos, films, music, and so on, in a context mediated by family, kinship, and community relations and by travel and various kinds of lived encounters with the homeland. Distinctions between various forms of encoding and decoding, and the complex processes involved in negotiating and renegotiating particular narratives, would also have to be central to this analysis, as would the often complex relation between 'official', 'unofficial' and 'everyday' discourses. I state this here simply because of the fact that whilst studies of diaspora communities, even during periods of conflict 'at home', tend to show that CMC is utilised by a tiny minority, although more passive satellite television or short-wave radio broadcast viewing and listening may increase, this does not mean that CMC is without impact.

An unsystematic search for Internet sites about Croatia yields, of course, a very large number and diversity of 'hits'. Some of these are, essentially, official or quasi-official sites, and many originate in or are aimed at, the diaspora. One often finds sites exclusively in the English language, or with both English and Croatian language versions. In addition, print and broadcast media have their own Internet sites, including *Dom i svijet* (Home and the World) which is an eight-page insert included every Monday in the international edition of the popular Croatian newspaper *Vecernji list* (Evening News) and which "aims to inform the Diaspora about issues and events occurring both in Croatia and abroad" (<http://www.hic.hr/dom/>). Like many other sites, it is hosted by the Croatian Information Centre (<http://www.hic.hr/index_en.htm>), whose main site itself contains links to a wide number of sites including Croatianet (<http://www.croatia.net/>), a site for and about the 545,000 Croats which, it claims, live in the USA. Other sites which are interesting are the web page of *HOP* (The Croatian Liberation Movement) whose origins probably lie with Ante Pavelić in Argentina in the 1950s, but which now originates from a server computer in Croatia (<http://www.hop.hr>), and the intriguing, if somewhat shadowy, 'Ustasa net' site (<http:ustasa.net>) which, upon first accessing, presents a picture of Ante Pavelić and an Ustasha symbol above links to the real audio version of the Croatian national anthem as well as to a number of other sites.

In many ways, these different home pages, whilst interesting, are not designed for, nor seeking, any kind of interactive use or development of new forms of transnational narrative about Croatia. My earlier text on e-mail and the wars (Stubbs 1998) sought to compare and contrast three e-mail networks or discussion groups: *zamir*; APC/Yugo/Anti-war; and Soc/Culture/Croatia, drawing the conclusion that the political role of *zamir* derived, precisely, from its position as part of a "localised repertoire of counter hegemonic meanings" (Stubbs 1998: 6.1) but doubting whether, even here, there was any engagement in real dialogue or encounter with everyday lived realities. In none of the newsgroups I studied was there any "place for the profane, the dubious, the doubting, or the simply confused" (Stubbs 1998: 6.3). Nevertheless, I would continue to suggest, in the context of the theoretical analysis presented here, that there remains much to be understood about discourses in newsgroups and, in particular, the relationship between forms of creative national imaginings and the emergence of "(news)group-specific forms of expression, identities, relationships, and normative conventions" (Baym 1998: 38).

The lives and people of Croatia?
Re-reading Soc/Culture/Croatia

The contours of Usenet newsgroups

For this reason, I look again at the Soc/Culture/Croatia newsgroup from Usenet which I discussed briefly in the earlier article (Stubbs 1998: 5.1–5.7). Usenet, one of the first CMC interactive systems, operates as an open forum for specific interest communities through over 13,000 'newsgroups' organised hierarchically (Baym 1998: 39) so that there are 26 different 'Society' or 'Soc/...', newsgroups; 87 current 'Soc/Culture/...' newsgroups from 'Soc/Culture/Afghanistan' to 'Soc/Culture/Yugoslavia', including a 'Soc/Culture/Croatia' newsgroup gathering together people ostensibly with an interest in 'the lives and people of Croatia'. Baym quotes figures suggesting that, by September 1997, Usenet carried a daily average of 682,144 messages (Baym 1998: 39), with Soc/Culture/Croatia, according to the latest figures, having a daily average of 102 messages and being accessed, not necessarily the same as being read, by an average of 12,000 people per day (<http://metalab.unc.edu/usenet-i/groups-html/soc.culture.croatia.html>).

Usenet newsgroups can be accessed, read, and written to in a variety
of different ways so that messages may appear amongst one's private
e-mail, called 'subscribing'; via 'newsreaders' specifically designed to
organise such newsgroups; or through Internet access and browsing.
It is possible to write to the newsgroup without reading it and to
'cross-post', where a user can post the same message, simultaneously,
not only to a number of different Usenet newsgroups but also to
other newsgroups and, even, elsewhere on the Internet. The 'Soc/
Culture/…' newsgroups, typically, have a high degree of cross-posting
and 'Soc/Culture/Croatia' is no exception, with 45% of its messages
cross-posted to at least one other group.

In a similar study of 'Soc/Culture/Indian' and related Usenet newsgroups, Ananda Mitra (1997) has suggested that, by concentrating
on "the textuality of the system of messages that are exchanged"
(Mitra 1997: 74), it is possible "to identify how the discussions proceed through a discursive process in which authors interact with each
other, contributing opinions about issues, and collectively producing a portrait of the virtual community" (Mitra 1997: 62). His method of monitoring the newsgroups is similar to my own although the
fact that the 'Soc/Culture/Indian' newsgroup has some ten times the
volume of messages of 'Soc/Culture/Croatia' sets certain limits for
Mitra. For my earlier article, I resubscribed to 'Soc/Culture/Croatia'
for a brief period in May 1998, at the time of the death of Gojko Šušak.
Subsequently, I have monitored the newsgroup periodically, particularly at the time of Croatia's success in achieving third place in the
football World Cup in June-July 1998, and have systematically collected information on all 554 messages posted, at an average of 55 per
day, in the ten day period between Friday 24 September and Sunday
5 October 1998 (currently these are available as headers, although
not necessarily the full text at <http://mineral.umd.edu/usenet/
soc.culture.croatia>) which, apart from coinciding with the Pope's
second visit to Zagreb, can be seen as a fairly 'normal' and 'typical'
period.

Monitoring Soc/Culture/Croatia

From the messages over this period, it is possible to make some general observations about the formation of this on-line group and its broad contours, codes, and norms. As far as I can judge, 285 of the 554 messages (51%) were in English, the remainder in Croatian and other languages of the post-Yugoslav countries[5], except for two written in German and four in Italian. There is a large measure of cross-posting and, whilst about half the messages are actually 'replied to' in some way, by quoting the message title and, in some cases, parts of the message, there are very few long 'threads' of messages on the same topic. Most of the postings assert some position, sometimes backed up by some item of news, a photograph, or some such, but more usually consisting of statements and counterstatements about Croat and Serb crimes, including those from the Second World War, essential character traits, and prognoses for the future. Most cross-postings occur with the 'Soc/Culture/Yugoslavia' newsgroup. Very few seek to be informative and even fewer seek information – a message headed "Any Croats in Raleigh, NC or nearby?" is, indeed, the only one of its kind, illustrating the virtually total absence of forms of associationality or 'community-building' from the newsgroup.

A small number of frequent posters dominate, including 'Barry S. Marjanovitch' (91 postings); 'peterpan'[6] (44 postings); 'Tony Juricic' (33 postings), and 'Stjepan Balog' (17 postings) who, together, account for one third of all messages posted in this period. Headings with titles such as "Was God mad at us when he created Serbs?"; "A Serb is a Serb is a Serb (they are all alike)"; "Servs are evil" (spelling as in original); "Serbs are no different now than they were in 1912", and "*Hrvati su arogantan narod seljaka*" ("Croats are an arrogant peasant people"), are a major part of the newsgroup, although there are also more specific references to war crimes, to Slobodan Milošević (always referred to by Barry S. Marjanovitch as "Satan Slovo"), and to the current Serb offensive in Kosova, amongst other items.

From the archives it is impossible to state where most of those who post messages live and, indeed, therefore, how far this is predominantly a newsgroup of the Croatian diaspora. There are certainly many posters from North America, particularly the United States and Canada, often with apparently Croatian surnames, and very few posters with e-mail addresses which originate inside Croatia. Barry S. Marjanovitch, by far the most frequent poster, is part of the Croatian diaspora in North America. Marjanovitch's postings, accounting for almost one sixth of all messages in the period surveyed, and much more than this when the average size of each message is taken into account, are of quite a specific nature. He rarely replies to postings directly, preferring to repost news reports, from Associated Press and other agencies which can be received over the Internet, which are about Croatian achievements in sport, current events in Croatia, or any negative news reports about Serbs. In this way, he could be seen as producing a kind of on-line scrapbook which is of interest, primarily, in terms of what he chooses to include and the headings he provides.

In a typical instance, he reproduces an obscure news report, on 27 September 1998, from the San Jose Mercury, about a Serbian national who pleaded guilty to passport violations in connection with a long-standing child custody case, and heads this "Servian culture is cheating, threatening, lying, stealing, ask their neigbors" (spelling in original). This seems, on first reading, quite a long way away from 'the lives and people of Croatia', the ostensible focus of the newsgroup on which it was posted. Yet, in terms of the way in which national communities are defined in relation to 'the Other', in this case, the Serbs or, as he would have it, Servs, the posting, and others like it, becomes central to the presentation of Croatian identity. In addition, by generalising from a rather unremarkable, specific, instance in the United States, to a whole culture, a crude kind of racist discourse is being, quite deliberately, generated, again symptomatic of many other postings[7]. The key to the posting may well be when Marjanovitch suggests we "ask their neighbours" – as no neighbours are mentioned at all in the news report, we can assume that, in this case, the narrative is pointing to, and thus imagining as it were, the territory and people of Croatia and the need for continued vigilance against the neighbour as enemy.

The Soc/Culture/Croatia habitus

In terms of understanding 'Soc/Culture/Croatia', it is worth pausing for a moment to consider some elements which are, on the whole, *not* present. First of all, there are almost no postings which, in his study of 'Soc/Culture/Indian' (or 'sci' as he terms it), Mitra describes as "introduction" or "looking for" messages:

> ... in which a user announces his or her presence on the network, or uses the network to try to find someone who they expect is also a member of the community. Although these messages do not address specific issues, they affirm the communal assumptions that implicate the way in which sci has evolved. ... This signifies that the community produced by, and around, sci is a representation of the allegiances that existed before the diasporic experience occurred (Mitra 1997: 63).

In addition, there is very little comment on the processes of the newsgroup itself and very rarely any expression of dissatisfaction with the nature, form, and content of the postings. It is as if what Bourdieu (1977) would term a 'habitus' of taken-for-granted codes has been formed which appears to meet the needs of a relatively small number of frequent posters in spite of, or perhaps because of, their antagonism to one another's point of view. This habitus seems rather more stable and much less improvised and unfinished which Appadurai (1996: 55–56) suggests is more likely in contemporary diasporic public spheres.

Of course, without triangulation of research methods which begins to interrogate those who continue to read, post, and reply to messages in groups such as 'Soc/Culture/Croatia', it would be wrong to speculate overmuch on the crucial question of how such activity satisfies certain needs and in what ways it relates to other aspects of identity. As Baym has rightly pointed out (Baym 1998: 45), innovations in software technology, particularly ever more sophisticated filters in newsreaders, do allow many more options than the need to read all messages in a newsgroup. This may well have facilitated more selective encoding and decoding of texts and, certainly, "allows users to avoid topics or messages from particular individuals" (Baym 1998: 45), but has also meant that such newsgroups are not, at all, dialogues or arenas for debate but more like a propaganda wall of unlimited dimensions on which different kinds of notes can be pinned.

Innovative currents

Nevertheless, within this bounded habitus, particular kinds of innovation are ongoing. For example, the longest 'thread' in the period I studied, a series of 40 messages headed *"Zbogom lijepi Zagrebe"* ("Farewell beautiful Zagreb"), all in Croatian, begins with a reposting of a news item from the Newsletter Independent Weekly by 'etc', which is an account by a Croatian Canadian of his day in Zagreb which cost, all told, 550 Canadian dollars. Many people reply to this, including the most frequent posters to the newsgroup, and a series of interesting debates ensue about the cost in relation to average salaries and pensions in Croatia; whether cheaper alternatives could have been found; and what these costs may signify regarding Zagreb as a 'European city'. One very interesting strand looks at the potential disappointment of 'homeland nostalgia', and even the way in which those brought up in Canada may have become so used to their 'Anglo Saxon' surroundings that they can no longer appreciate the beauty of 'Middle European' cities.

A complex discourse merging realities, images, and narratives of travel and everyday life is constructed which is quite exceptional in the period in which I have monitored the newsgroup. Perhaps recognising this, Barry S. Marjanovitch seems to take exception to all this concern with prices and mocks it as some kind of wish for a return to communism, factory kitchens, and power to the people. Others, notably Tony Juricic, appear in these interactions in far broader perspective than is usual within their normal postings. Whether this offers an insight into a different, post-war, range of postings, is unclear and only time will tell. It does indicate, however, that whatever their apparent stability, computer-based newsgroups can and do fluctuate in terms of their themes and their capacity for interaction.

Šušak's death

The reactions to the death of Gojko Šušak, which I noted in my earlier article (Stubbs 1998: 5.5), remain much more typical of any interactions which are related to the war, and are worth re-examining, briefly, here:

> The death of the Republic of Croatia's Minister of Defence, Gojko Susak, and his vital role in Croatia's fight for independence should be remembered by future generations of Croatians as the United States today still remembers and honors the memory of its Revolutionary War Generals, Nathaniel Greene and Henry Knox ... ('Susak Like U.S. Revolutionary War Generals', posting by badurinapr@aol.com, 5 May 1998).
>
> The Nazi War Criminal Gojko Susak is dead and burning in Hell. The man who helped resurrect Croatia's Nazi Ustasha past never got to stand trial for war crimes against humanity at the Hague. He now stands before a higher judge.
>
> Susak will be remembered in the press and in history as the racist, neo-Nazi leader who helped exterminate Croatia's minority Serb community. A born Ustasha, Susak openly praised Croatia's horrific Nazi past when in WWII the country was one of Hitler's greatest allies ('War Criminal Susak Dead', posting by nt@sentex.net, 5 May 1998).
>
> So miracles do happen after all. More than 30,000 dead Serbs, and still they are marching back to Ustasha state of Croatia. What urges them to go back? Were they born Ustashe as Gojko Susak too ('Re: War Criminal Susak Dead', posting by jurcicp@cadvision.com, 5 May 1998).
>
> It's quite simple. We do not live in 1941, so today's Croatian Ustase do not have freedom to commit such genocide as they were. Secondly, some people like their homes that much that they can't live without them and because of that, they would accept living in a nasty racist state (Re: War Criminal Susak Dead, posting by aleksandar@myna.com, 6 May 1998).

The closed nature of these narratives, notwithstanding comparisons with the American Civil War, and the mutually antagonistic and certain tone, all of which I noted in the earlier article, remain striking. Moreover, as Mitra has noted in his study, in these moments of extreme emotion, "the arguments begin to lose any rational basis and the debate is often reduced to a series of harangues and name-calling that express deep antagonisms" (Mitra 1997: 66). His idea that 'cross-posting' is a crucial part of the production of national images, both in terms of defining 'the Other' and in marking virtual transgressions, as people go where they 'do not belong', is also crucial in understanding this exchange. What is apparent, however, is that there are no references to Šušak's own diaspora experience, perhaps indicative of the fact that the newsgroup is not particularly oriented to a diaspora thematic.

Concluding thoughts

In this chapter, I hope to have shown that the work of collective imagining which may be found within diasporic public spheres, including newsgroups, cannot simply be juxtaposed to notions of 'cosmopolitan', anti-nationalist identities which, by implication at least, are always and everywhere superior and, somehow, non-contingent. Its inventory of dominant meanings, images, and themes, as history becomes the present and supports particular visions of the future, exist as narrative forms which rely on, but are never wholly reducible to, the available 'stock' of such themes. Nor should the themes themselves be conceived as obtainable from some kind of bargain basement warehouse of cheap, unfashionable, national sentiments, past their sell-by date, and available at reduced prices for bulk purchase. The work of creation, as such it undoubtedly is, from this inventory takes particular forms in the realm of computer-mediated communication, all of which merit further study and a refinement of the 'netnographic' approach which I have advocated here.

The possibility of challenging particular kinds of National narratives within these diasporic public spheres is likely to take very different forms when these spheres are conceived in this way. This is far less likely to come from really existing "postnational movements, organizations and spaces" (Appadurai 1996: 177) than from the minutiae of understandings of, and consciously articulated disruptions to, the slippage from politically oriented National discourses to the sphere of everyday life. These disruptions are more likely if diaspora identities are seen as complex, contingent and fluid and, in and of themselves, worthy of study.

Acknowledgements

Detailed comments on a first draft of this chapter by Renata Jambrešić Kirin and Maja Povrzanović Frykman were of immense value in the process of revision.

Notes

1   The more usual term 'Diaspora' is replaced in this text by terms such as 'diaspora', 'diasporas', and 'diasporic', in order to signify the textual variety of uses of the term and the inadequacies of an absolutist conception of 'Diaspora'.
2   References to web pages and sites are given in the body of the text itself, unless the page is individually authored and resembles a print-based academic text which is then cited under the author's name and listed in the bibliography together with the web address. The problem is, as already noted elsewhere (Stubbs 1998: 1.6), that such Internet links, whilst operational at the time of writing, March 1999, may subsequently change or disappear.
3   "Dragi Hrvati i Hrvatice i građani Hrvatske" ("Dear Croats (male and female) and citizens of Croatia") was, for a long period, the opening remark of Croatian President Dr. Franjo Tuđman in any public address. Of course, the complexities of 'nation' and 'nationality' which this draws upon were not invented by Tuđman but are a product, amongst other things, of the uniquely Yugoslav "socialist federated states" nationalities' policy (Bringa 1995: 25). The call to the people outside the borders of the Homeland has also, of course, been made by other postcommunist states such as Hungary and Romania (cf. Verdery 1996).
4   Indeed, elsewhere in an article written with Radha Kumar, also of the Helsinki Citizens Assembly, the suggestion is that "(m)ercenaries, criminals, the unemployed, unscrupulous politicians, romantic expatriates, and twisted intellectuals are all pulled together under the umbrella of identity politics" (Kaldor and Kumar 1993: 21).
5   Of course, differences between Croatian and Serbian are, in any case, limited, especially as the norms of computer newsgroups means that the Roman, rather than the Cyrillic, script is used.
6   There is no convention on Usenet that 'real names', i.e. those specified within one's own e-mail software package, have to be real names in the off-line sense, so that many posters to 'Soc/Culture/Croatia' are virtually anonymous, with on-line 'real names' such as 'etc', 'AussiCro', 'The Foreigner', 'Agressor', and 'Man in the moo-moo'.
7   The best example of this are the postings of Stjepan Balog as in his posting headed "Never Forgive-Never Forget": "It is in Serbia psyche (sic) to kill, conquer and expand ... Behaving in a civilised and forgiving manner towards the Serbs only

encourages them to plan for more" (Soc/Culture/Croatia, 27 September 1998). Even here there is a complex narrative being constructed in his following argument that "The only thing the Serbs understand is an "OLUJA" (liberation of Krajina, 1995) type comment", explicitly seeing military action as a form of discourse. Moreover, the posting ends with a quote from Mark Twain on lies and malice with a note that states "even Mark Twain knew about the Serbs".

References

Alleyne-Dettmars, P. 1997. "Tribal Arts": A Case Study of Global Compression in the Notting Hill Carnival. In Eade, J. (ed.) *Living the Global City: Globalization as Local Process*, 163–180. London: Routledge.

Anderson, B. 1983. *Imagined Communities: Reflections on the Origin and Spread of Nationalism*. London: Verso.

Anderson, B. 1992. The New World Disorder. *New Left Review* 193: 3–13.

Anderson, B. 1994. Exodus. *Critical Inquiry* 20: 314–327.

Appadurai, A. 1996. *Modernity at Large: Cultural Dimensions of Globalization*. Minneapolis: University of Minnesota Press.

Baym, N. 1998. The Emergence of On-Line Community. In Jones, S. (ed.), *Cybersociety 2.0.*, 35–68. London: Sage.

Bourdieu, P. 1977. *Outline of a Theory of Practice*. Cambridge: Cambridge University Press.

Bringa, T. 1995. *Being Muslim the Bosnian Way: Identity and Community in a Central Bosnian Village*. Princeton: Princeton University Press.

Cohen, L. 1993. *Broken Bonds: The Disintegration of Yugoslavia*. Boulder: Westview.

Clifford, J. 1997. *Routes: Travel and Translation in the Late Twentieth Century*. Cambridge, MA and London: Harvard University Press.

Deacon, B., Hulse, M., and Stubbs, P. 1997. *Global Social Policy: International Organizations and the Future of Welfare*. London: Sage.

Edwards, D. 1994. Afghanistan, Ethnography and the New World Order. *Cultural Anthropology* 9(3): 345–360.

Gilroy, P. 1987. *There Ain't No Black in the Union Jack*. London: Hutchinson.

Grdešić, I. et al. 1991. *Hrvatska u izborima '90* ("The 1990 Elections in Croatia"). Zagreb: Naprijed.

Jambrešić Kirin, R. and Povrzanovic, M. (eds.) 1996. *War, Exile, Everyday Life: Cultural Perspectives.* Zagreb: Institute of Ethnology and Folklore Research.

Jambrešić Kirin, R. 1996. Narrating War and Exile Experiences. In Jambrešić Kirin, R. and Povrzanović, M. (eds.), *War, Exile, Everyday Life: Cultural Perspectives*, 63–82. Zagreb: Institute of Ethnology and Folklore Research.

Jambrešić Kirin, R. 1999. Personal Narratives on War: A Challenge to Women's Essays and Ethnography in Croatia. *Estudos de literatura oral* 5: 73–98.

Kaldor, M. 1996. Cosmopolitanism Versus Nationalism: The New Divide?. In Caplan, R. and Feffer, T. (eds.), *Europe's New Nationalism: States and Minorities in Conflict*, 42–58. Oxford: Oxford University Press.

Kaldor, M. and Kumar, R. 1993. New Forms of Conflict. In *Helsinki Citizens' Assembly Conflicts in Europe: Towards a New Political Approach*, 12–34. Prague: HCA.

Kolar-Panov, D. 1996. Video and the Diasporic Imagination of Selfhood: A Case Study of the Croatians in Australia. *Cultural Studies* 10(2): 288–314.

Kolar-Panov, D. 1997. *Video, War and the Diasporic Imagination.* London: Routledge.

Löfgren, O. 1996. Linking the Local, the National and the Global. *Ethnologia Europaea* 26 (2): 157–168.

McAdams, M. 1978. "An Overview of Croatian Nationalism to the End of the Croatian Spring in 1971". Croatian Information Service, (<http://mcadams.cronet.com/croatian_nationalism1.htm>).

Magaš, B. 1993. *The Destruction of Yugoslavia: Tracking the Break-up 1980–92.* London: Verso.

Mesić, M. 1992. External Migration in the Context of the Post-War Development of Yugoslavia. In Allcock, J. et al. (eds.), *Yugoslavia in Transition: Essays in Honor of Fred Singleton.* New York: Berg.

Mitra, A. 1997. Virtual Commonality: Looking for India on the Internet. In Jones, S. (ed.), *Virtual Culture: Identity and Communication in Cybersociety*, 55–79. London: Sage.

Peirce, P. and Stubbs, P. 1999. Peace Building, Hegemony and Integrated Social Development: UNDP in Travnik. In Pugh, M. (ed.), *The Regeneration of War-torn Societies*. London: Macmillan.

Pettan, S. 1998. Music, Politics and War in Croatia in the 1990s: An Introduction. In Pettan, S. (ed.), *Music, Politics and War: Views from Croatia*, 10–27. Zagreb: Institute for Ethnology and Folklore Research.

Poster, M. 1998. Virtual Ethnicity: Tribal Identity in an Age of Global Communications. In Jones, S. (ed.), *Cybersociety 2.0.*, 184–212. London: Sage.

Povrzanović, M. 1997. Identities in War: Embodiments of Violence and Places of Belonging. *Ethnologia Europaea* 27(2): 153–162.

Povrzanović, M. and Jambrešić Kirin, R. 1996. Negotiating Identities?: The Voices of Refugees between Experience and Representation. In Jambrešić Kirin, R. and Povrzanović, M. (eds.), *War, Exile, Everyday Life: Cultural Perspectives*, 3–19. Zagreb: Institute of Ethnology and Folklore Research.

Ramet, S. 1996. *Balkan Babel: The Disintegration of Yugoslavia from the Death of Tito to Ethnic War*. Boulder: Westview (2nd edition).

Rheingold, H. 1993. *The Virtual Community: Homesteading on the Electronic Frontier*. Reading: Addison-Wesley.

Silber, L. and Little, A. 1995. *The Death of Yugoslavia*. London: Penguin.

Skrbiš, Z. 1995. Long Distance Nationalism?: Second Generation Croatians and Slovenians in Australia. In Pavković, A. (ed.), *Nationalism and Postcommunism*, 159–173. Dartmouth: Dartmouth Press.

Skrbiš, Z. 1998. Making It Tradeable: Videotapes, Cultural Technologies and Diasporas. *Cultural Studies* 12(1): 265–274.

Stubbs, P. 1996. "Civil Society, Social Movements or Globalized New Professional Middle Class". Paper presented to the American Sociological Conference, New York, August 1996.

Stubbs, P. 1997. NGO Work with Forced Migrants in Croatia: Lineages of a Global Middle Class. *International Peacekeeping* 4(4): 50–60.

Stubbs, P. 1998. Conflict and Co-operation in the Virtual Community?: eMail and the Wars of the Yugoslav Succession. *Sociological Research Online* 3(3), (<http://www.socresonline.org.uk/socresonline/3/3/7.html>).

Verdery, K. 1996. *What Was Socialism, And What Comes Next?*. Princeton: Princeton University Press.